A SHORTER EGO

First Selection

45p

The Autobiography of

JAMES AGATE

A SHORTER

EGO

The First Selection

If you do not want to explore an egoism
you should not read autobiography
H. G. Wells

London   *1946*

Readers Union / George G. Harrap & Company

NOTE

None of the characters in this book is
imaginary, and whether any of them is real
metaphysics has not yet determined

This volume is produced in 1946 in complete conformity with the authorized economy standards. First published in 1945 by George G. Harrap & Co. Ltd., it has been set in 11 on 12-point Garamond and reprinted in Edinburgh by Morrison & Gibb Ltd. It is one of the books produced for sale to its members only by Readers Union Ltd., of 38 William IV Street, London, and of Letchworth, Hertfordshire. Particulars of Readers Union are obtainable from either address

DEDICATORY LETTER

THOMAS QUINN CURTISS
SERGEANT, U.S.A.

DEAR TOM,

I am dedicating this book to you, not in your capacity as colleague on the *New York Times*. Nor yet because you are a friend of my friend George Jean Nathan. And certainly not because, before I knew you, you had loyally and conscientiously smuggled a score of my books, including *Egos* 1–6, across the water.

Since the war I have thought often of Matthew Arnold's

The unplumb'd, salt, estranging sea.

Nobody wants to plumb the Atlantic, and nobody minds its being salt. But there is every reason why it must not any longer be estranging. I hold that the future of the world depends largely on friendship between our two nations. Now friendship cannot exist without understanding, and it is possible that this shortened version of my Diary may help to increase American insight into English ways of thinking.

The reason for reprinting? The answer is suggested by a letter from an unknown friend writing from Krugersdorp, in the Transvaal :

Two years ago I discovered *Ego* 3 in the Public Library here. I read it then and frequently since with the utmost relish and delight. Spurred on by enthusiasm, I was fortunate in obtaining for myself *Egos* 3, 5, and now 6. Apart from the autobiography, eight more of your blessed books occupy my shelves. But to my great disappointment and despite numerous efforts I have been unable to place *Ego*, *Ego* 2, and *Ego* 4 with the others. In desperation I turn to the author. . . .

Alas, the original volumes are now quite unobtainable, and I cannot hope that they will be reprinted in my time. As for

5

the future, I am with Mrs Gamp and " seek not to proticipate."
In the meantime here are the first and second volumes of *A Shorter
Ego*, my devoted publishers having faithfully promised that a third
will be added in due course. The Dedication to you is common
to them all. It is my contribution to the cementing of a friendship between our two countries as firm as that which exists
between you and me. A friendship which includes an immense
capacity for laughing with and at one another.

Good luck to you, my dear Tom. As an English poet nearly
remarked : Drunk or dry, soldier from the U.S.A., I wish you
well.

JAMES AGATE

LONDON
December 1944

1932

June 2   To-day is the day on which my review of Arnold
Thursday.   Bennett's *Journals* ought to have appeared in the
         Express. Kept out because of lists of winners in
Irish Sweep for the Derby. Had considerable difficulty in getting
consent to this review, on the theory that A. B. is no longer
news. Am told that Beverley Baxter said to his staff four days
after A. B.'s funeral: " Gentlemen, please understand that
so far as the ' D.E.' is concerned Arnold Bennett is dead." The
worst of it is that B. B. was right and in his place I should have
had to do the same. But it hurts! It is A. B.'s diaries which
have prompted this one, started by the writer in the fifty-fifth
year of his age, which sounds like something on a tombstone!
Am hoping this book will help to rid me of those *idées noires*
with which I am too much obsessed.

But debt worries are legitimate hell. Have begun retrenching.
Vacated the cottage at Beaconsfield and put up a " To Let "
board; moved to a smaller flat at £140 instead of £250, which
was the rent at Palace Court; got rid of the chauffeur and now
make Alfred Lester drive as well as valet. This is not his real
name, but fits this six foot four of melancholy fine. His previous
place was ducal, which accounts for him saying to me on his
second day: " We have been looking through our suits, sir,
and find we need two more." Upon my promising to consider
the matter he said: " They are ordered, sir. I dress my gentlemen according to their age and shape! You will approve the
patterns, sir, I feel sure."

Of course, retrenching has its difficulties. I am faced with
a big bill at Palace Court, having broken what now turns out
to be a repairing lease. Getting in to the new place has cost
£100. It is all very well selling my lovely chairs and table,
but I have had to buy something smaller to take their place.

Also, absurd business with car. Wretched back-axle dropped
out on Blubberhouses Moor, Yorks, about three weeks ago—

on Whit-Sunday, to be accurate. Had to be towed to Harrogate.
Value of car estimated at £48. Harrogate repairer told me to
sell at once, as car was shaping for a general break-up. Henley's
offered £85 if I bought a Razzle Dazzle which, on their floor,
I rather liked the look of. They wanted £240, or £155 plus
my old bus. Agreed, and took out the R.D., registered, next
day. Had not driven it a quarter of a mile before I knew it
wouldn't do. Sunshine roof beastly and no room, chauffeur's
arm and elbow jog and rub against mine every time he changes
gear. Exactly like riding in a sardine-tin. Henley's very decent
and would only charge me £10 for making the thing technically
second-hand. So bought a Riley 9, drop-head coupé, done
3000 miles, lovely condition, for £285, less £85 for old car plus
£10 for swop, making £210 plus £20 interest spread out over
20 months.

Why must I have a car ? If I don't I should never have any
golf, or week-ends, which means *no* exercise, *no* fresh air, and
no change of scene. And we know where that leads ! Besides,
I work every day and all day from ten in the morning till two
next morning, without relaxation and almost without meals.
Perhaps sitting in the theatre at dull plays is the hardest work
of all. In my agonies of boredom I could sometimes scream
aloud ! No *moral* justification for having a car, except that
I *think* I give pleasure to a good many readers one way or another,
and am entitled to have a bit myself, surely ? Alan Dent
(" Jock "), my all-but-perfect secretary, says I am the perfect
Harold Skimpole. Perhaps. Anyhow, have economised by
refusing Alfred Lester a new cap !

June 3   Question. Why am I keeping this diary ? Answer.
Friday.   Because it is part of the insane desire to perpetuate
             oneself. Because there seems to be a lot of things I
want to say that other writers put into novels and accepted
essayists into essays. Because it will be a relief to set down just
what I do actually think, and in the first words to hand, instead
of pondering what I *ought* to think and worrying about the words
in which to express the hammered-out thought. But I cannot

and never could invent a story, or be bothered to tell it, and have already published *five* books of essays, not having to do with the theatre, that have been complete and utter failures. So I am driven to this last ditch of expression.

June 7   Went to Mills's circus last night and enjoyed every
Tuesday   moment of it. Alfred Lester had never seen a circus
            before, and laughed only when somebody fell down.
Didn't believe the zebras and thought they were donkeys painted
—" they're all the same pattern."

What a relief to be able to set down here *exactly* what I think, and not to have to make an article out of it. How tired I am of being whimsical *à la* Kenneth Grahame or erudite about Toulouse-Lautrec or up-to-date with Dame Laura Knight—who sees pewter figures on zinc horses—or still more up-to-date by knowing about Thérèse Lessore, whose circus pictures were praised by Frank Rutter last Sunday.

I kept seeing resemblances everywhere. One little dwarf—some dwarfs are bigger than others—reminded me of Charles Laughton, one of the clowns wearing a flaming aureole of silly yellow hair was very like Gordon Craig, while one of the elephants was *exactly* like Eliza Aria, and wore a mantilla just like hers, only it was the size of the back of a kitchen chair. The other three elephants were all rather like Y——, the pianist. Y—— was dying a few weeks ago but, I hear, is getting better. He must weigh 24 stone, and at his worst was still eating whole chickens at a meal. One of the acrobats had a sore throat. Does Mills travel a hospital, and how do sick people who lead a rough life manage? Perhaps they aren't often ill?

There was one fellow in the show who did nothing except rope-spinning, but did it so well that we held our breaths. He was the ugliest handsome devil I have seen for years, with a squint or glide in one eye that went right round the back of his head. Watching him I wondered how we can have arrived at judging people by their morals, table manners, or other irrelevant standard.

Mills has had a career anybody might envy. Carriage-builder.
Then whip to Miss Ella Ross of Sale, Manchester. Used to
drive her famous blacks in all the show-grounds of England—
Grand Vulcan and that lot. Then the war, and Mills made a
fortune. Then the circus. Was a bit cock-a-hoop at one time,
to be expected in a man who has got on too well. Then came
a dreadful illness—eczema from head to foot, literally from the
crown of his head to the soles of his feet. Borne these two
years with extraordinary courage and patience. That a career
which began in funereal gloom should have reached these
dazzling and Olympian heights recalls the story Coquelin used
to tell of a rival of his young days who won the first prize for
comedy at the Conservatoire and ultimately made a fortune in
the *pompes funèbres*. Our Bertram has done it the other way
round.

June 8   Invited by two somebodies I don't know to attend
Wednesday.   a welcome lunch to somebody I have never heard
               of returning from Australia, a country I am not
interested in. Refused.

Took Leo Pavia to lunch at Bertorelli's, having vowed last
night to frequent Lyons in perpetuity. Minestrone, tournedos
with mushroom sauce, excellent bottle of St Julien, cigar,
13s. 11d. Tip 1s., since I must economise somewhere. Leo
is a pupil of Leschetizky and knew Brahms—*i.e.*, he once opened
the door to him. Likes to think he might have been the grand-
son of either Rossini or Meyerbeer, both of whom stayed at his
grandparents' house in Regent Square in the 'fifties, but is
afraid his grandmother was honest. Perpetually hard up, and
a wit who spends his life pouring vinegar on troubled waters.
Everybody's enemy except his own. At lunch to-day he said
it was absurd for me to keep a diary and suggested a noctuary!

June 19   At Bournemouth. Spent the morning and afternoon
Sunday.   reading four bad novels.
               Champagne, good cold supper, and bridge with my
host and hostess, George Bishop and his clever wife. During

the game had one of those idiotic nerve-troubles that seize me sometimes. All my life I have been afraid I may have some sudden, uncontrollable impulse to do the thing I most want not to do. First noticed this at Southport when I was about eighteen and used to take May, who was three, for walks on the pier. I was terrified lest I should snatch her up and throw her into the sea! Was so worried about this that I consulted a doctor.

But that is a daytime worry; the sleep-walking fear is worse. I have never walked in my sleep in my life, but for fear I should do so I cannot sleep high up or with an open window unless there is a piece of furniture against it. I dislike houses with a staircase-well for the same reason. I cannot bear to have razors or matches in my bedroom, though I am not so nervous about poisons. At one time I forced myself to keep awake in railway carriages and would not travel in an empty one. Have several times consulted doctors, and they all tell me that the people who actually do these things never have any previous fear that they may do them. The man who throws himself over Waterloo Bridge or in front of a train *for no reason* has never had any premonition of it. I suppose the whole thing comes from being overstrung. Have for years had " compulsional neuroses," like touching railings or lamp-posts, or not walking on the cracks in pavements. Have known myself turn out the gas four, eight, sixteen, or thirty-two times, always in multiples of four. Have had to have sleeveless vests to avoid pulling at the sleeves, and lots of things like that, to get out of a habit. It started when I was about sixteen. I was changing for a lawn-tennis party, and went back to tidy the clothes I had left on the bed. I remember saying to myself: " If you do that, you will do it all your life ! " I went back, and I have done it all my life. I sometimes take twenty minutes to leave a room through being obliged to do these things. It can't be drink or smoke or too much sex-indulgence, because all this started when I had no experience of these. When I was a boy I had to read the last sentence in any chapter some dozen times " to make sure," and when I am below par I find myself doing this at the theatre, even if the following dialogue is blank for five minutes. Impossible to describe the hell of all this, and to look at me nobody would believe it. My best cure is to repeat Macbeth's "Then comes my fit again," and wait till the fit passes. Except for these attacks I also am " whole as the marble, founded as the rock."

June 20   Challenged R. A. Whitcombe to play the best ball
Monday.   of self and the young pro. called Ed., or some such
           name. Whitcombe to concede 6 bisques. This is not as much as it sounds, as assistants playing with their bosses rarely play within a half of their game. Whitcombe has done 61 a dozen times or so on this course and his average round is 68. I began excellently with 4 4 3 5 4 5, the boy never coming in at all. After six holes the match was all square with all bisques intact. Then we got 1 up with 1 bisque left and 3 to play and finally 1 up with bisques gone and 2 to play. Both the boy and I did a bit of cracking hereabouts, and Whitcombe, who is like some genial, witty bear, played magnificently. He was set for a four after a huge drive at the long 17th, I skyed my tee-shot, which meant a 5 at best, and Ed. was short of the green with two good wooden shots. However, he laid his pitch stone-dead and that meant dormy one. At the 18th—206 yards from back of medal tees which Whitcombe had insisted on—I took my spoon and hit a too-good shot which tucked me up in a bank over the green. Ed. pulled his iron into some fearful rough stuff, and Whitcombe put his ball some 10 yards from the pin. Ed. got on to the green somehow and holed a good 20-yard putt for a 3. Whitcombe just missed his and we won a first-class match.

June 22   Dictated B.B.C. talk in bed, beginning 11 o'clock
Wednesday.   and finishing 2.50. How Jock stands it I don't
           know. Promised to take him out to lunch. Actually sandwiches at Bodega and draught champagne. Asked name of wine and told " Mozoo." Asked to be shown bottle and found " Grand Vin Mousseux."

French players in *Le Prince Jean*, by Charles Méré. Tedious
story of blackmail in high life. Left after third act.

Supper at Savage Club. Norman O'Neill, Stampa, Basil
Cameron, Hubert Harben, Billy Leonard, Jetsam, of Flotsam
and Jetsam, and a quite dreadful Scotch guest. Billy Leonard
supremely witty. Asked if we had heard about an actress much
in the Divorce Court going into Shakespeare. " What as ? "
said somebody. " First Gold-digger," said Billy. Following
on my saying that a critic can overlook and forget to notice a
perfect performance, Hubert Harben told me this. Asked to
what he attributed his success Tree said, " Very early in my
career I made up my mind to be always a little out of the picture !"
Bed at 3.30. Asked the people in the flat below to have a night-
cap and they wouldn't leave !

June 26   Motored down to Brighton, and noted a *Daily Herald*
Sunday.   contents bill describing the revolution in Siam as
                " Revolution in Land of Sacred Elephants." Bishop
asked me down to Bournemouth, but refused since I do not
want to spoil the recollection of a perfect week-end by one
possibly less good. My ex-chauffeur and still good friend
Ted Elliott driving, as too much Alfred Lester is melancholy.
Sometimes wish I could drive myself. Had just turned Whiteley's
corner when I ran into George Felton Mathew, editor of an
architectural review. Asked him to come along, which he
did. Asked him also whether he ever reads his paper, which
must be Greek except to estate-agents. He said, " Damn it,
I write it ! " George is a descendant of the George Felton
Mathew to whom Keats dedicated a poem, and who thought
his poems were full of a " delicate sensibility " lacking in
Keats !

Sleep as far as Crawley, and wake up in time to reflect that
On the Brighton Road, by Richard Middleton, must be very nearly
the most exquisite of all short stories.

Dined at Pec's, on balcony about nine o'clock. Anchovies,
cold lamb, an excellent Beaune and a good cigar. *L'heure bleue*,
and all that sort of thing. Felt at once cheerful and sentimental—

a rare combination. Kept repeating to myself four lines of
somebody's translation of Rimbaud :

> I want no water of Europe but the cold,
>   Dark puddle a sad-hearted child squats by
> And launches out towards the scented dusk
>   A boat as frail as a May butterfly.

I feel that this is poetry despite the words " scented dusk."

About ten o'clock the electric sign over our heads began to
function, turning our lamb into pink, newly butchered slabs.
Is there anything more romantic than a pier lit up, or more
desolating than one whose lights suddenly go out ?

June 29   A common fault with playgoers is to dislike a
Wednesday.   piece because it is not something else. Highbrow
                critics faulted that poignant anecdote, *Journey's End*,
because it was not poetic tragedy. If I republish my criticisms
I am told that they are not a history of the theatre. When I
wrote my little book on Rachel even my publishers complained
that it was a *vie scandaleuse* and not a history of the Romantic
Movement in France.

Jock has just given me a story he has been writing, which he
calls his Opus 6 and is entitled *Doubtful Joy*. It begins :

> Life is so simple in general, so complex in particular. So
> thought I at least, at the time when I first viewed Ingaret.
> She was leaning ungracefully over a four-barred gate, in
> one of the home counties, I forget which, and the day was
> a Saturday and boisterous. There was too much of her
> weight on the right foot, and the left was a shade too far
> from it. . . .
>
> Of industry by Swedish cataracts ; of the remoter leaves
> in Batavia ; of a nebula ablaze even in an opera-glass ; of
> Artemis naked. Of rare topaz pestled and mortared and
> powdered ; of the bleak cry of a lamb ; of the odour of new
> glossed paper ; of Archimedes' Principle. Such fantasies,
> recurrent irrelevant in my head, and a million else beside,
> all on account of Ingaret, and her bum and her violet eyes.

And the *nouvelle* ends :

> Then a youth from one or other of the Hams, the twain that are always meeting, a youth fearfully " Wotcher," ineradicably " Naow." This happened at an evening party at Lady Dastard's, and I must say here that I was astonished at the audacity of Ingaret, the brazenness of her. The woman was capable of reviewing troops she personally knew, of stowing away on a warship. And it was complicated by the fact that my two sons at Harrow were at that party.
>
> Then I caught her having her stockings dried by a fierce lickorish man in a cottage in Wales. It is true that a woman was more or less present as well, but a blank woman— one born to be exhumed. Then in a Cadogan house alone with the Queen of Peru, she who ultimately strangled herself through wearing too many pearls. Ingaret on this occasion gave me an icy, an appalling smile. I left immediately.
>
> Then tritely at Antibes when she was with bathers. In one of these I recognised the slim and creamy torso, the patrician postman of Burford. Beside the ungathered vice he lay, his russet hair, his russet hair. I fled in chagrin. That Ingaret should choose to appear with anyone twice seemed to me to settle the matter. She stands still as I saw her then, her arms outstretched, laughing soft and long.
>
> Yet in the end she married an old unvenerable man, one John Thirlmere. I attended the St Margaret's wedding and stood behind a pillar looking, I thought, melancholy, but merely, as I heard later, scowling.

There is a middle bit in which he asks :

> Would you eat cloth ? Would you bite, chew, swallow field-daisies ? Would you fly straight to the sun ? Or lie with a dead leper ? Or be nuzzled by drunken bears ? Or live a week on frozen Cointreau ? Would you read my nonsense ? . . .

Personally I would always read Jock's nonsense because it is great fun and is individual to him despite his resemblance to Ronald Firbank, of whom he has not read a word.

July 2   Wretched round of golf at Beaconsfield. Cheered
Saturday.   up when, at the Café Royal, somebody pointed out
              a battered creature of indeterminate sex as the
probable model for Epstein's Genesis. Leo said, "No.
Degenesis!"

July 10   Have not written in this diary for five days owing
Sunday.   to illness which started at 3.30 A.M. on Tuesday.
              Abominable attack of wind, plus panic, plus heart,
which went at 140 to the minute and wouldn't calm down.
So had to get up, dress, and prowl round for a doctor, who told
me I was not going to die that night. Would he bet? A
moderate sum, he answered. After getting rid of several balloons
full of gas went to bed and slept. Suggested to Alfred Lester,
who now sleeps "out," that he might like to sleep "in" for
one night. Glum acquiescence in the usual outraged servant
manner. Consequently refused to avail myself of his services
—which he probably foresaw—and called on Elliott to befriend
me next night, which that good soul did. Bout of wind and
panic repeated, largely through dining at Monty Shearman's off
duck and champagne, and being bored by *Love's Labour's Lost*.
    Was formally examined by the doctor on Thursday. After
an hour's poking and prodding he says he can arrange for me
to die of something other than heart. But, no drink to speak
of, a minimum of tobacco, regular meals on a diet, and above
all NO WORRY. I agree, and returning to flat find (1) letter from
Bank saying I am overdrawn £113, and will I please refrain
from drawing further cheques until, etc. etc.; (2) letter from
lawyer saying he has received letter from another lawyer threaten-
ing to issue writ against me for £500—an old loan—unless I
produce £100 in two days; (3) letter from Inland Revenue
demanding £110 in six days; (4) the milkman in person, and
(5) the manageress of the local laundry screaming on the telephone. Settle down to day's work determined not to worry!
    Indigestion came on again as I was broadcasting on Friday.
Could hardly see the paper. Came down to Southend on
Saturday. Good evening round of golf and leisurely dinner.

Arrive at bandstand at 9.45 to discover that band stops at 10. Why? Why should English seaside resorts do everything to diminish pleasure? No gambling. Good! No *divertissements sensuels*. *Soit!* No cigarettes after nine. If it must be! But why in hell's name no music after ten o'clock?

July 23   Saw the doctor yesterday, who pronounces me
Saturday.   much better and says the heart has lost that extra-
                 beat typical of over-smokers, over-drinkers, and
over-everything-elsers. Perhaps that is why I feel so run down. Have not touched bread or potatoes for a fortnight and am probably thinner, " both to feeling as to sight," as Macbeth more or less says.

Aug. 9   Leo Pavia came down for a day or two and told me that
Tuesday.   his Concert Fantasy on Johann Strauss's *Fledermaus*
                 for two pianos is to be performed this autumn by
Ethel Bartlett and Rae Robertson. The old thing is as witty as ever without losing any of his malice. Has a new story about a Jew who on the day of his wife's funeral was found kissing the cook. On being remonstrated with, said, " In my grief should I know what I do? " Admits to being a good enemy but a dangerous friend. It is wonderful how he responds to the slightest kindness or attention, particularly if it includes a good bottle of Burgundy. He reminded me at dinner to-night that his grandmother was sister to Sarah Bernhardt's mother. As Leo is a Dutch-Italian Jew of Spanish extraction, the child of parents born in Venice and Amsterdam, and educated in Vienna, I am inclined to believe he speaks the truth, at any rate about this relationship with Sarah.

Aug. 12   My article on Southend appeared in *D.E.* Terrific
Friday.   commotion. Pier-master rang up before breakfast,
                 i.e., my breakfast, conferring upon me the freedom of
the pier for the rest of my stay. I suppose I pitched the note a bit high, for unless I had golf I should not stay here half a day. It is young Winsor who keeps me here; he is immensely keen

and I enjoy our matches enormously. He senses my infatuation
with the game and we spend hours discussing the balance and
rhythm of clubs. Apart from golf Southend is exactly like its
reputation, and every evening the trippers leave behind them
a faint odour of stale perspiration and decaying food. Yet
essentially the sentiment in my article is sincere—about the poor
enjoying themselves with the implication of their right to enjoy-
ment. Anyhow, the thing is a very artful piece of journalism,
and the hotel staff now regard me as a god. Very pleasant.

Terrific golf match this evening. Young Winsor and myself
v. Denny and a man called Notley. Card for the best-ball score :

$$
\begin{array}{cccccccccc}
4 & 3 & 2 & 4 & 3 & 3 & 3 & 4 & 3 & 29 \\
2 & 4 & 3 & 3 & 3 & 3 & 3 & 3 & 2 & 26 \\
  &   &   &   &   &   &   &   &   & \overline{55}
\end{array}
$$

My own score was 72, my best anywhere ever, and the two 2's
in the second half were mine ! I know the course is short. But
the fact remains that the professional competition record is 68.

Aug. 19   Broadcast extremely badly and was seized with the
Friday.   notion that I had delivered the talk before. I wonder
             whether the article from which it was made was
originally a broadcast talk ? And even that, said Ernest Fenton,
was probably *née Sunday Times.* Fenton is Leo Pavia's bosom
pal ; *i.e.*, they have been each other's hair-shirt for forty years.
You never know whether they are on David and Jonathan's
terms, or Cain and Abel's.

Aug. 20   Slept at 74 Kensington Gardens Square, which
Saturday. continues to feel like somebody else's flat. The
             floor of the entrance hall thick with bills, writs,
etc., so that I could hardly open the door. Nearly destroyed an
offensive-looking missive from the Post Office, but eventually
opening it found it to contain £3, refund of deposit at Beaconsfield. Letter from the Bank, " more in sorrow than in anger."
Fortunately the telephone had been cut off owing to account
not being paid, so no creditor could dun me that way !

Aug. 27   Letter from Jock saying he was taken last night
Saturday.   to King Edward VII Hospital, Windsor, and is to
                   be operated on before morning for appendicitis.
Confesses to feeling " a little scared." Characteristic that I can
be more philosophic about other people's major troubles than
about my own minor ones. I feel quite confident that Jock
will be all right. Very tedious of Mrs Micawber to want a
Cæsarian operation just when Mr M. is about to get busy. Shall
have to continue with present amanuensis—very agreeable,
skittish, and eager to be helpful.

Gladys Cooper at her best last night. Tremendously competent as ever. The piece—*Firebird*, by some unrememberable
Hungarian, Lajos Zilahy—was adapted by Jeffrey Dell, the
adapter of *Payment Deferred*. As I was entering the theatre Dell
rushed up to say that they had sold *Payment Deferred* to Metro-
Goldwyn for Charles Laughton. Price 20,000 dollars. If this is
true I make either £250 or £500 according to the terms of my
contract—I forget which. I also read this in to-night's *Evening
News*. But in view of absence of news from my agent, A. D.
Peters, am sceptical. These strokes of luck do not happen to
me, and I shall not build on this one. I shall not ask Peters,
being a firm addict of the ostrich policy in good news as well
as bad. Nevertheless, I *did* find a black cat on my bed last night.
A *small* black cat.

'Phone news about Jock excellent.

Sept. 3   All right about *Payment Deferred*. Jock gave me a
Saturday.   shock the day before by saying Peters had told him
                   there would be " about £100 " for me, but that in
view of my extravagance I was not to be told. However, I
opened the subject. It now seems that the amount is as follows :
Sale of film 20,000 dollars, roughly £5000. Of this Gilbert
Miller bags nearly half, leaving £2800 to be divided between
Forester and Dell, and as I get 20 per cent. of Dell's share that
means £280 to me, say a round £250 after paying Peters' com-
mission. Perhaps, lest I be suspected of venality, I had better
put down why I should get anything at all. It happened like this.

Going to Paris with Monty some four years ago I read Forester's novel *Payment Deferred* in the train, boat, and again train, and stayed in my bedroom at the hotel without dinner until I had finished it. I *immediately* saw Laughton in the part, and proposed the adaptation to at least half a dozen playwrights and play-wright-hacks including (I think) Knoblock, Beverley Nichols, and Van Druten and (I am sure) Monckton Hoffe. Nobody in the least interested. Then I worried Peters so much that he ultimately found Dell and persuaded him to tackle the job. The play being made and me satisfied—though I had to insist on some alterations and the point of the whole thing being rammed more firmly home—then came the bother of persuading first Laughton and then the managers. Charles was very good about it and did not give me more than a year's trouble. Managers just weren't interested. One night in December, of I forget what year, I thought it was all fixed. Charles, Elsa Lanchester, and I all got together at the Vernons'. Frank Vernon wanted to make a highbrow thing of it with significant lighting and all that. I wanted Brixton realism for this tale of a common-place if murderous bank-clerk, and Virginia Vernon, who is a woman of sense as well as vivacity and charm, agreed with me. Anyhow, they promised to do it the following May. Next morning they wouldn't do it till November, so I called the whole thing off. I had taken the piece so much under my wing that everybody regarded it as my play. Alec Rea was afraid of it, Basil Dean kept saying he wanted to look at it, but I was shy of his magnoperative preoccupation elsewhere, and at last I tried Edgar Wallace. Edgar said he would do the play if I would put everybody into evening dress. Finally Gilbert Miller took the thing and produced it with moderate success. The critics almost without exception behaved like idiots. What is it Max says about dramatic critics ? Something to the effect that they are a very fine body of men, " like the Metropolitan Police Force." And with about as many brains ! The highbrow kind said the play wasn't poetic tragedy, or something of the sort, and the others thought it was sordid. Of course it was sordid ; that was the entire point. Sordid, and not sentimental. God,

what fools ! I took care not to criticise the play at all, and Rees
sent his assistant, a brilliant young woman who wrote a ladylike,
sniffy notice.   Anyhow the thing is now sold, and should, I
think, make a good film.

Sept. 16   Every time somebody's Autobiography comes out
Friday.   I turn to the Index to see if my name occurs, and
               of course it never does.   I suppose everybody does
this.   What is less pardonable is that when somebody sends me
for review an anthology with some such title as *Niceish Bits of
Current Prose* I look to see if by any chance they have got a bit of
mine.   Never a hope !   The most extraordinary people are
there.   Every bullet finds its billet, but Gerald Bullett has never
bagged any of his *billets-doux* out of my stuff.   Honestly I think
that the soldier's letter out of *Responsibility* should be included
in any Anthology of Letters.   Some day I shall suggest to
E. V. L. that he should make a final selection and call it *The
Last Post.*   This is the letter:

> DEAR MUM, AND DAD, AND LOVING SISTERS ROSE, MABEL, AND
>   OUR GLADYS,
>   I am very pleased to write you another welcome letter
> as this leaves me at present.   Dear Mum and Dad and loving
> sisters, keep the home-fires burning.   Not arf !   The boys
> are in the pink.   Not arf !   Dear loving sisters Rose, Mabel,
> and our Gladys, keep merry and bright.   Not arf !

No anthologist or even reviewer has ever tumbled to this.
Blast their silly souls, do they think I wrote it ?   If they do,
then they must think me a major novelist.   If they don't, then
the thing should obviously be in any Anthology of the World's
Best Letters.   Damn it, they can't have it both ways !

Sept. 18   Took Jock to Burnham-on-Crouch, me sitting in
Sunday.   the dickey.   Discussed in a high wind and at fifty
               miles an hour the merits of " When daffodils begin to
peer "—never mind what decision we arrived at—Jock pointing
out the perfection of the word " peer " and the bird-persistence
of the repeated " With heigh ! with heigh ! "

Sept. 19   Went to a film, arrived back at 6.30 and started
Monday.   dipping into *The Tempest*. Read all the lovely poetry
of the masque at the end, and delighted to find in the
beginning this description of Southend :

The approaching tide
Will shortly fill the reasonable shore
That now lies foul and muddy.

Sept. 20   Peter Page bad with gout in both ankles, which makes
Tuesday.   him stoop till he seems about four feet high. Had a
drink in the interval of some play with him and Bertie
Van Thal, of Peter Davies, the publishers. A pleasant young
man. Left Globe Theatre at 10.45 and arrived here at 12.15,
where I had Allan Walton, his friend Henderson, and Elliott to
cold partridges and an excellent sparkling hock. The talk was
goodish. They wanted to know about the play and I was too
bored with it to tell them. Finally I said it was the kind of play
which has witty intervals.

Sept. 23   My brother Gustave arrives at 11.27 P.M., and we
Friday.   sit up till two in the morning playing iron shots on
the carpet and fondly imagining the bedroom next
door to be unoccupied. Are disillusioned about this in the
morning. Played two rounds of golf with G., who is fuller of
theory than ever, but lags behind it in fact. He does everything
except hit the ball. I gave him five bisques, halved in the morning
and lost on the last green in the afternoon going round in eighty
and seventy-eight with two sixes and a seven in each round !
A Mrs Pawley, a young Englishwoman held to ransom by
brigands in China and in imminent danger of death by torture,
writes the most casual letters asking for the ransom to be paid
quickly, and adds, "Please send me some lipstick." G. tells
me of an ingenious Chinese torture. They make tiny cuts in
the skin not deep enough to draw blood and then with a fine
camel-hair brush paint the exposed nerve-ends with a solution
of cayenne pepper.

Sept. 30   A very busy week, largely devoted to playing golf
Friday.   with Gustave and getting the 'flu. On Sunday we
             lunched with Peter Page at Colville Hall, meeting
Monty at Chelmsford and taking him down with us. Found
Mark Hambourg there with his witty wife, who told us about
a big party given by Nigel Playfair followed by an entertainment.
" You can't think what a bad entertainment it was ! " Mark,
in his quietest mood, played to us after lunch.

Walked on front yesterday and listened to band. Nobody
round bandstand except a few people huddled in chairs and
looking exactly like the characters in *The Cherry Orchard*. They
were all there : Madame Ranevsky, Gaev, Dunyasha, and even
the German governess holding an umbrella against the wind
and sitting next to an empty chair. All in black with a rampart
of piled-up chairs behind them. Incautiously I asked Jock
if he knew anything more desolate than a seaside place out of
the season. He replied : " Whence comes this sudden ebullition
of unmitigated sanity ? " He *loathes* Southend, and I was about
to raise the subject of Osbert Sitwell's *Before the Bombardment*,
in which the deserted seaside resort is beautifully done, leading
to the old discussion of Art *v.* Nature, when the band struck up
something rather jolly.

Read in evening paper how Mrs Pawley, still in power of
Chinese bandits, writes :

> The messenger came to-day and this is a chit in reply.
> The bandit chief says that he must [underlined] have the
> cash soon, as he is getting fed up with keeping us. He is
> writing to you demanding the ransom and won't tell us
> how much he wants.
>
> If the messenger does not come back in five days' time
> we are to be put through appalling [underlined] tortures ! !
> In ten days we are napoo.
>
> Seriously, get us out, please, as we are filthy [underlined]
> and bored stiff. Love to all from Charles and me, Tinko.
>
> P.S. Soap required urgent [underlined twice].

" Bored " is the operative word, as Belloc would say.
In the evening sat in the lounge nursing my cold and listening

to the hard-working hotel trio. All women. Meditations
and Meanderings in Monastery Gardens. Nobody in lounge
except Elliott and me. A perfect Bateman drawing. Went
to bed early and read new story by Hergesheimer in Benn's
ninepenny series. Why are not all novels published at nine-
pence? Must advocate this in *D.E.* The story is *Love in the
United States*, and H. seems to have *exactly* Arnold Bennett's
quality. Why has nobody pointed this out?

Oct. 1   Shanks's new novel *Queer Street* published. He gave
Saturday.   me the worst possible review of *Gemel*, merely a
              three-line slating for irrelevances. Have accordingly
written him :

> *Palace Hotel*
> *Southend-on-Sea*
> *October* 1, 1932

DEAR DICK,
   Do you NOW regret your review of *Gemel in London*? I
have sent to the local coal-merchant for some coals of fire,
but he has run out of stock !

> Yours affectionately,
> JAMES

Had ten minutes to spare to-day while Jock was typing, and
picked up James Joyce's *A Portrait of the Artist as a Young Man.*
I hope I don't miss anything of this quality while I am reviewing. Jock has learnt a bit of shorthand while in hospital and
is now much quicker. Nice of him. To-day is the sixth anniversary of his starting work with me. I mean he has completed
six years. We had a good lunch on the strength of it. The
decorators are out of " Cranley " and it looks very pretty. Now
for the carpets and curtains.

Oct. 13   The past fortnight has been completely taken up
Thursday.   with correcting proofs of my anthology entitled *The
              English Dramatic Critics.* Had to wire in, though
Jock did most of the wiring. That is to say that he read the
proofs and I made the corrections, which is more or less the
way the Anthology has been compiled. Jock says I am one of

those rare writers who do not write their books " until day of publication," as reviewers say. But he put it better than that : " You don't review books till day of publication, and damn it, you don't write 'em either ! " My 'flu or cold lasted all this fortnight. Ill, nervy, and very irritable. Decorators have now finished at " Cranley," but too seedy to take any pleasure in it. Must start the Sanatogen cure again. Have bought the picture of the view from this hotel window which Allan Walton did when he was down here. He has done another one, the view of Queen Victoria pointing to the pier with the garages behind. I don't like this because he has given it the colour of Martigues, all crude and staring blues and yellows— but loveliness in the wrong place. The note of Southend is *pearl*. There was a magnificent sea and skyscape here yesterday. A storm was brewing and all the estuary was the colour of sulphur deepening to burnt treacle, while, ten or more miles away, the mouth of the Medway lay in golden sunlight.

My day yesterday. Had stayed the night at Ernest's, who at the moment is not quarrelling with Leo. Woke about ten, when Jock arrived. Dictated *Tatler* article. Luncheon at Café Royal with Joe Ackerley of the B.B.C. and discussed my talk about *Children in Uniform*. Owing to 'flu I had not seen this play, and so my talk was general and based on the criticisms I had read. This did not satisfy me and Joe agreed. So I rushed off to the matinée which finished at 5.10. Back to Ernest's and re-wrote one thousand words which I broadcast at 6.50. Quick work. Then half an hour at B.B.C. photographer's. Took a pick-me-up at Heppel's, but no time to dress or dine, so swallowed a sandwich and off to *Service*, a foolish play about a bankrupt stores which amused everybody very much except me. But then I once kept a bankrupt stores, and know how much more interesting it is than this sentimentalised, fairy-godmother version of it. So I yawned and nodded till eleven o'clock, when I could get some food. But food, when you have had none for hours, means a lot of drink and a dish you only look at. Then home by car to Southend and had to keep awake because Stan insisted upon falling asleep,

which he did twice, and we should have gone into the ditch
if I hadn't nudged him in time. Why do chauffeurs insist on
spending their time sleeping with their wives like Alfred Lester
or at the wheel like Stan ? Why can't I get a chauffeur who
can and will chauffe ? Is it to be wondered if I feel a wreck
this morning ?

Nov. 16   The publication of the second volume of A. B.'s
Wednesday.   *Journal* reminds me that I had better resume this,
                      interrupted owing to unprecedented work and
worry. The principal events during the past month have been
as follows, in order of importance :

(1) Mrs Pawley ransomed.

(2) Letter from B.B.C. saying they are thinking of changing
their dramatic critic and will I become their film critic? This
would never suit me as I should have to see at least ten films
a week instead of three or four. Could not afford the time,
and the *Tatler* might not like it. Besides, I've been something
of a success as the B.B.C. dramatic critic and think better to
rest on those laurels.

(3) Turn down B.B.C. proposal.

(4) Sacked by B.B.C., but pleasantly. After all they are in
the right. It is only fair to the theatre that they should change
the critic from time to time. The next fellow will be either a
fool or a highbrow-prig, probably both.

(5) *Immediately* sell Arthur Barker a book of broadcast talks.

(6) Terrific onslaught by·all creditors at once.

(7) Order some new clothes, having been very shabby lately,
and

(8) Change the Riley for a 17/75 Talbot, in excellent condition,
having done only 8000 miles. Have, alas, to fork out £54,
which comes out of my secret savings fund—odd articles, etc.
etc.—now standing at £75.

(9) Advertised for new chauffeur-valet, Stan having fallen
asleep at the wheel three times in a fortnight. Put advert. in
Daily Telegraph and received 211 replies. I interviewed the
odd eleven, of whom *only one could drive*, and he handles the car

like a virtuoso. Is a pleasant, civil-spoken youth, who looks like being good company without being cheeky. Engaged him, and both satisfied.

(10) Finally moved in to " Cranley " and spent all day yester-day hanging pictures. Dined with chauffeur at 10.30 off cold pork and beer. There was half a bottle of Bollinger in the larder, but I had an economic fit and only gazed at it. The house looks very pretty, and Allan Walton has decorated it charmingly and with complete success. Front room in French grey, dining-room in beer-coloured varnish, walls and ceiling, work-room in fawn with plain oak furniture and trestle-table, unstained like an orderly-room, bedroom in white. Curtains by various good artists.

No really good plays during the last four weeks, except perhaps Maugham's *For Services Rendered*. The one evening I enjoyed was supper with Clifford Bax and Gwladys Wheeler. I think Bax is very nearly the most delightful man in all London. He almost reconciles me to beards.

" Those admirable critics, James Agate," said Jock to-day. In the outside world Baldwin has been telling everybody what will happen in the next war. There seems no doubt that we shall all perish, miserably. But this, fortunately, includes the French !

Dec. 29   A very busy month, about which I will try to recol-
Thursday.   lect something as soon as I have recorded that
              the *Spectator* calls the Anthology " slovenly." This
adjective to ME, who have a complex about being thorough. I left the Anthology to speak for itself on purpose. However, the *Times Lit. Supp.* weighs in this morning with two respectable and respectful columns.

Of the month's events I remember little except work. Dinner to J. T. Grein. This was a fiasco. The thing was given by the Critics' Circle to mark J. T.'s seventieth birthday and fiftieth year as a dramatic critic.

Presumably, then, the speeches should have been about J. T., whereas Morgan, who was in the chair, spoke for twenty minutes about Shaw. It seems he was originally down to propose

Shaw's health and declined to scrap the speech which he had prepared. It was an *oration* in *The Fountain*'s best prose. I sometimes wonder whether Morgan's studied stuff may not go the same way as that of Walter Pater, George Meredith, Henry James, and George Moore, who is his idol. Samuel Butler said : " I never knew a writer yet who took the smallest pains with his style and was at the same time readable." Li at a party somebody asked me to state offhand who in my opinion were the six best prose-writers, I should say, Job, Shakespeare, Bunyan, Defoe, Dickens, Shaw. If pressed for the reason I should say it was because they never thought about style and so achieved a rhythm like that of the golf-caddie who does not know how to swing a club but just swings it.

Dinner to J. C. Squire. A worse fiasco. Not far from me was a rude, much be-Tatlered society madam. She was about a quarter tipsy, and throughout the entire meal I wished I was anywhere else. Opposite was Vyvyan Holland, looking the oddest mixture of Oscar Wilde, J. B. Priestley, and Lilian Baylis. Chesterton, who was in the chair, made a fine speech including one sentence about English tradition, " of which our more patriotic newspapers naturally know nothing." Duff-Cooper followed with fifteen minutes of Tory nit-wittery, after which Rothenstein spread himself in the Jewish manner for another ten minutes. Then Squire spoke and talked about nothing except the difficulty of seating five hundred guests.

Made my broadcasting farewell on the 21st. Tried hard not to force the note, and am rather disappointed at the small number of subsequent protests ! I seem to have made my acquiescence with the B.B.C. policy in sacking me too convincing. It was gratifying when Hibberd came to the mike after my talk and publicly thanked me and wished me " au revoir," *officially*. I dined with Siepman and Fielden at Boulestin's afterwards. They told me to " keep in touch " and " not go away." They also want me to prepare a series of talks about great plays of the past, *i.e.*, *The Second Mrs Tanqueray*, with a gramophone record by Mrs Pat giving the big scene. To be called " Stars in their Courses."

1933

Alan Parsons died on Sunday morning of pneu-
monia after 'flu. I met him at dinner at the Garrick
on the first night of *Dinner at Eight* some ten days
ago. Looking at the bill of fare, he said, " Oysters, caviare,
roast pheasant, foie gras, really the food in this club is the lousiest
in London." He was a remarkable figure with his great height,
fine head of grey hair, and majestic collars. The rest of him was
a scale of descending magnificence, often ending in coloured
socks with dress-clothes. He suffered from claustrophobia,
and watched nearly all plays standing up at the back of the dress-
circle. Wrote most of his notices half at the Garrick before
the play and half after the first act, since " my two million readers
have got to know about this play whether I do or not." He
hated the outlying theatres and called all the rubbish " my
favourite play." Not a first-class judge of pieces, but a capital
judge of acting. I remember Viola Tree bringing him to my
flat in Doughty Street some ten years ago to ask whether he
should give up the Home Office for journalism. I advised No
unless he had a private income, but Alan said he would sooner
starve than continue auditing the accounts of the Runcorn Fire
Brigade. Soon after, he joined the *Daily Sketch* as Mr Gossip
in succession to Peter Page. *The Times* says wrongly that he
chose dramatic criticism. He didn't, for the good reason that
if a man had the qualifications of Shaw, Montague, and Ivor
Brown all put together he would not be allowed to exercise
choice. You are pitchforked into dramatic criticism or not
at all. Alan was a violent anti-snob, on which subject he could
be vitriolic. Otherwise the kindest of men, and a crony of
Monty and St John Hutchinson. After two years of Mr Gossip
he became dramatic critic to the *Daily Mail*, and will not be
replaced easily even if he thought Shakespearian production
ended with Tree. I shall miss him greatly, as we 'all shall. Not
an enemy in the world.

The past three weeks have been entirely taken up by my finances. In the meantime I wander about the flat like an impecunious squirrel in its cage. I suppose in the future my creditors who see me lunching will want to know why I drink beer instead of water. Alan Parsons told me that when he had a trustee the fellow used to badger Viola because she bought *best* end of mutton !

The point I tried to make about *The Fountain* is that its frantic reception by the hicks and hayseeds of America was a joke. I can't read the esoteric stuff, and just don't believe that anybody except Darlington, who is Charles's shadow, and Charles's lovely wife can read it either ! Am afraid my article mortally offended both of them. I wound it up in verse, Charles having been a prisoner of war in Holland :

> He dwelled among the untrodden ways,
>   And wrote, where Zuyder Zee'd,
> A book which all reviewers praise
>   And nobody can read.

Naughtier still was my notice of a novel by " Hilda Vaughan," the aforementioned lovely Mrs Charles Morgan. This contained an Imaginary Breakfast-table Conversation at More's Gardens, beginning : " MRS M. (*opening letters*) : ' Good morning, Charles. I see they've given me the Hawthornden. What have you got ? ' " Seriously, when it comes to the sublimated stuff, say a play by Turgenev, there's nobody to touch our Charles, or get within a mile of him. His fault as a dramatic critic is that he insists upon looking for sublimation everywhere and being very cross if he can't find it. A character has only to mention the soul, and Charles will think nobly of it for the rest of the column.

Feb. 20   Lunched with Lionel Fielden and Cecil Madden,
Monday.   both of the B.B.C. Fielden told me of a lively
            bit of dialogue at a dinner-party an evening
or two ago.

A Brigadier. There must always be righteous wars.

Fielden. What in your opinion, sir, would be a righteous war?

Brigadier. Damn it, a war to prevent naked savages raping one's womenfolk!

Fielden. The first time a naked savage lays a finger on your lady, I give you my word, General, I'll enlist!

True story: The Mayor of some Lancashire town being presented with a pair of statues for the Town Hall remarked after inspecting the nude figures, "Art is art, and nothing can be done to prevent it. But there is the Mayoress's decency to be considered!"

March 6 Spent the morning with Dame Madge Kendal, who
Monday. will be eighty-four in a week's time. The old lady
was in tremendous fettle and looking as imposing as ever. With the exception of Queen Victoria she must be the greatest English public monument since Boadicea. Her voice was ringing and full, her gestures magnificent, and her sense of humour quite unimpaired. I took with me a little silver basket of camellias and forget-me-nots, like one of her old bonnets. The object of the visit was to arrange for her appearance in my new series of broadcast talks: " Stars in their Courses." I wanted her to do *The Likeness of the Night*, to which she objected that there are no good speeches for her. The same with the old comedies, and as for the *Lady of Lyons*, it appears the effect is visual and depends on her play of shoulder. The real reason is that the old lady insists upon playing Rosalind, in which I am told she was always not *bad* but something different, *not Rosalind*. A young man called to tune the piano, and Dame Madge didn't object. I did, and strongly, saying I didn't hear her voice often enough to have so great a pleasure spoiled. We got on like two houses on fire. Apropos of the Queen she said, " That's a good woman. I used to read to her grandmother, the old Duchess of Cambridge."

March 8   Went to bed late last night after a *very* nervy day—
Wednesday. all to pieces. Read in Mathews's *Life* for an hour
             and considerably comforted by this passage written
by Mathews the Younger :

> My father was of a remarkably sensitive temperament,
> quick in his speech and manner, and his nerves seemed hung
> on elastic wires, which the slightest touch agitated. The
> falling of a spoon on the sideboard, or the jingling of glasses,
> would shake him to his foundation. His irritability was
> excited by the veriest trifles, while he would bear real mis-
> fortune with perfect philosophy. And yet, in the midst of
> a frenzy of passion, such was his keen sense of humour, that
> one touch of the ridiculous, like a drop of oil on troubled
> water, would restore his equanimity in a moment.

As Mathews *père* speaks of his " invincible hypochrondria "
I think he must have been very like me.

Lunched with Charles Laughton, who asks my advice as
to whether he shall join the Old Vic with Flora Robson. Won't
play Falstaff, whom he hates. " I had to throw too many of
his kind out of our hotel when I was sixteen." Is making a
Henry VIII picture and intends to show him not as a phallus
with a crown but as the morbid, introspective fellow he actually
was.

March 10 Shaw's plays are the price we pay for Shaw's pre-
Friday.   faces.

March 14 I saw in some paper last week the statement that the
Tuesday. chief delight in doing a job is having it behind one,
           and knowing it won't have to be done again.   I
disagree. I believe that the old charwoman who desired for
her epitaph :

> Don't pity me now,
>   Don't pity me never ;
> I'm going to do nothing
>   For ever and ever

was a self-deceiver. At least I will lay odds that anybody meeting her in Heaven will find her scrubbing marble and dusting porphyry with a new-born gleam in her old eye. I do not believe that the Creator's feeling about the Universe is relief in having finished the job, and knowing it will not have to be done again. I believe that creation is unceasing, and that, if it were not, day and night would cease to be. My experience is that we are all of us grumbling about not being happy while continuing in an orgy of indifference and inefficiency. Last week my new-cut latch-key would not go into the lock. Last month I had my study measured for a carpet which on arrival swarmed up the walls. I have just ordered some summer vests and I feel it in my bones that pants will arrive. The world's worker of to-day works no harder than is necessary to enable him to shuffle off to the pictures, not realising that if he put more heart into his work he would have more zest stored up for play. Never mind something attempted; something done is worth a night out. People may say that I am a writer, and presumably enjoy working, and ask me to suppose that I sold gloves, or kept other people's accounts, or laid tables, or scraped boilers? My answer would still be the same. Is it supposed that the dramatic critic putting on a boiled shirt on Saturday night when he was hoping for a week-end is any better pleased than the mechanic slipping into his dungarees on Monday morning after a week-end no employer dare destroy? Were I engaged in those other trades I should try every day to be more obliging, accurate, deft, and expeditious than ever before. This is my personal experience : There is only one way whereby I can endure the dog-labour and hell's torment of writing, and that is by working at every article as though it were the first I have ever written. Analogies are treacherous things, but there is one I can't resist. The captain of an ocean-going ship may owe his tailor and possess too many wives in too many ports. But in getting his vessel from one side of the ocean to the other that captain has achieved something. Every man, in my view, has a ship, and that is his job. Let him bring that ship safely to port and it matters less that the waters through which he has brought it may have been muddy. We cannot be perfect beings, but we can all do our job perfectly, or with such perfection as lies within our personal competence. Noble natures may descant after their fashion about the nobility of this ; as a practical philosopher my point is that the only enduring happiness comes through work. It may be true that " there is no work, nor device, nor knowledge, nor wisdom, in the grave, whither thou goest." But that is only half the verse, for the other half runs : " Whatsoever thy hand findeth to do, do it with thy might." With our might, therefore, though we have not " any more a portion for ever in anything that is done under the sun."

In the meantime it is a chastening thought that, despite the foregoing, and because I was too lazy to look it up, I recently attributed " Look like the innocent flower, but be the serpent under't " to Macbeth instead of to his lady.

March 26   Lunched at the Savage : cold beef, asparagus, and
Sunday.   a pint of Pol Roger. Very good. Took Elliott to a
                concert of Russian music at the Palladium. Really
went to hear a piano concerto by Dohnányi, but it turned out to be Rachmaninov No. 2. So I slept. Then Irene Scharrer played that *bloody* Chopin Ballade in A flat, of which I am tired though I liked it when I played it myself. She was in poorish form and, I thought, vulgarised it, with some wrong notes. Best thing in the performance was Moussorgsky's *Pictures from an Exhibition*. Glazounov's *Carneval* is dull after Berlioz and Dvorák, and so is Dvorák. Wood conducted, looking more than ever like a taller brother of Willie Clarkson and wearing what, except for undertakers, must be the last frock-coat in London. Thin house. Elliott sniffed and snuffed throughout, which I thought very Russian of him.

March 30   Settling down quietly at Westcliff, which of course
Thursday.   makes me feel ill. One is all right as long as one
                goes on racketing. Shall just have to wait till
the nerves quieten down. Doctor says minimum of drink,

but not to make a martyr of myself. In the last five days total consumption five glasses of mild ale and one pint of fizz.

Decided to paint outside of house bright apple-green for the woodwork and make the stucco cream. Saw decorator and asked for estimate. Wrote goodish article for *S.T.*, not top-notcher, but will do. Subjects : a play about Walter Scott and a musical comedy based on *Ambrose Applejohn's Adventure*.

Landlord called and I think I persuaded him to pay half the cost of decorating. Good concert on wireless. Strauss's *Don Quixote* from Birmingham. Never heard it before. Pure haschich, or hashish, however you spell it. First-class shoulder of mutton at ten o'clock and a pudding that smelled of the washing and tasted like hair-oil but otherwise excellent. Had the good luck to pick up Beethoven No. 5 *after* the slow movement. Read enough of a travel book by one de Valda to give it a middling notice and of a volume of sketches by E. M. Delafield to give it an ecstatic one. Turned in at 12.30 exactly. Surely fresh air, golf, hardly any drink, less tobacco than usual, and early hours with an interest in simple things should make a difference if persisted in. If I could only stop this bloody thinking about myself !

April 13   Have spent most of the past fortnight quarrelling
Thursday.   with the B.B.C. A minor point raised by me was
                that I attempted to deliver to the B.B.C., at its own
request, the original script of *The Only Way*. Arriving at seven o'clock and the Talks Department having closed, I handed the parcel to the commissionaire at the reception desk and declared its value, sentimental and in cash, saying I didn't suppose Sir John Martin-Harvey would lose it for a thousand pounds. Whereupon the stout fellow declined the responsibility and I had to wait until somebody could be found to take it home for safe-keeping. Whereupon I wrote to the B.B.C. suggesting that Eric Gill should design them a cupboard to match Prospero and Ariel. " A navel would make an admirable keyhole ! "

Also wrote to *The Times*, which had announced the death of somebody at his London address *and* his country seat. Asked if it was not adding to Death's terrors to make a man die twice over.

April 14 *Friday.*   Bergel drove me down to Southend. Lunched at the Palace and afterwards played golf at Orsett.

         Bergel was seldom on the course, but as I never played better in my life we beat the pro., who gave us three bisques. I told B. he must come down again and have a round *on* the course. He told me two good stories. A friend of his meeting Manet in his last years asked him if he remembered George Moore. Manet said he did, adding, " Ce pauvre George Moore ! Il était si embêtant ! "

The other story was the plea put forward at the Southend police-court by a drunk : " The boys insisted on going to Canvey Island and it was the thought of leaving me native land as started it."

Apart from golf—B. is in the long-hitting stage of the game —he was thoroughly amusing. So I told him my idea for a play on the Stanley Baldwins, taking Drinkwater's *Abraham Lincoln* as model. In the last scene Baldwin, having lost the election and his job, can't keep up the instalments on his furniture, which is on the H.P. system. The play ends with Mrs B. fingering the sideboard and saying, " Now it belongs to Drage's ! "

April 15 *Saturday.*   Humourless reply from *The Times*.

May 11 *Thursday.*   Events of past month. Have engaged a York- shire cook, deaf and with a glass eye, but a worker.

    B.B.C. capitulated.

    Bought an exquisite black mare from Albert Throup, and named her Black Tulip. My interest in her now exceeds every- thing. *Totally* indifferent to golf, plays, films, books, music. Don't think of anything else and go every week-end to see her at Birmingham. " How other passions fleet to air ! "

June 17   Have not given a thought to this diary for a whole
Saturday.   month, having been wholly preoccupied with Black
                 Tulip, who has won 2nd at Oxford, 1st at Bath and
West, two 3rds at National Hackney Show at Bournemouth,
and 1st at Leicester.   Satisfied.

Went up to Alderley Edge to adjudicate at a Dramatic Festival.
Left London about noon, dined with some nice people, dutifully
absorbed a lecture by Brother Mycroft on the first principles of
adjudication, adjudicated, supped, and started back for town
at one in the morning, arriving about six—all this to get to
Wimbledon show by midday.   Tulip won her class here.

June 20   Motored to King's Lynn for Royal Norfolk Show.
Tuesday.   Dined at Duke's Head.   No bedrooms anywhere in
                 the town.   Proposed to go on to Hunstanton.   Land-
lord said Sandringham Hotel *full up*, but would 'phone Lestrange
Arms.   Did so and reported they had reserved rooms.   Jolly
evening with Geoffrey Bennett and Albert Throup, who bet me
10*s*. we should beat Wensleydale Madge.   At 12 P.M. Lestrange
Arms 'phoned that they kept no night-porter and would shut
me out if I didn't come at once.   Left and knocked up night-
porter at Sandringham to inquire where Lestrange Arms might
be.   Received directions.   Spent one hour trying to find it.
No luck.   Saw large reflection advertising Glebe Hotel, A.A.,
and all the rest of it.   Rang and knocked.   No answer.   3 A.M.
Back to Sandringham.   Could we have two sofas ?   Why sofas ?
Plenty of bedrooms !   We occupied rooms 7 and 8 on the first
floor.   Charming country to travel in !

June 21   Tulip made a grand show and was 2nd to Fleet-
Wednesday.   wood Nanette, beating Wensleydale Madge (cost-
                 ing me my bet of 10*s*.) and three others.   In
championship class stood 3rd to Morton's Vitality and Nanette.
As both these had previously won a Hackney Society Harness
medal Tulip won this.   She hardly broke at all, and showed the
most classic action seen out for ten years.   A champion in the
making and all she wants is time.

June 29   Conversation last night over dinner with Monty
Thursday.   Shearman.

M. I was very much astonished, James, when K——, who
is a real intellectual, said he admired your work very much
and would like to meet you.

J. A. (*seizing chance*). But, of course, Monty, the real
highbrows do like me. It's only the semis, the people who
only go to *Othello* if a nigger's in it, the Gate Theatre crowd,
who dislike my work because I see through their pretence.

M. K—— was one of your supporters about *Cavalcade*.

J. A. *Cavalcade* was an entertainment. I never said it
was a work of art, and everybody who isn't a complete fool
agrees with me that it was a rattling good entertainment.
I wish you'd get the point that what matters about a critic
is what he praises and what he fails to praise. Nothing else
counts. In ten years I have never said a play was a work
of art when it wasn't, and I haven't missed one that was.
Noé, L'Ame en Peine, Journey's End, Musical Chairs, Martine—
I was first in the field with all of them.

M. K—— says you write well.

J. A. There he's wrong. By hopping about from one
bit of gusto to another like a kangaroo I give the illusion
of good writing. But that's only because it doesn't bore
you. Of what really makes writing—the bone and the muscles
under the skin of the prose—I know nothing whatever, no
more than I did twenty years ago.

After getting that lot off my chest I felt better!

Aug. 28   Ivor Brown, having been terrifically good for weeks,
Monday.   was not quite in best form yesterday. Hopefully
                   asked Jock whether he agreed that Ivor's writing was
falling off. Jock said, " No. It's falling on. Get on with your
work ! " Looked in at Ivy, which was crowded. Asked Abel
if anybody was there, meaning theatre-folk. Abel said, " No,
sir. Only trash ! "

Thought of a middle-page article for the *Daily Express* entitled
" My Ideal Day." In my case it would be as follows : I should
want to get up so fit that I did not think about myself at all
(it is a staggering thought that millions of people probably

do this every morning). After bacon, in whose gravy two halves of a very small kidney have nicely browned, I tackle the first draft of my *Sunday Times* article, happy in the blessed thought that the week's playgoing is behind me and I have three or four clear days before I need put my nose into a theatre. After cold beef and one glass of beer I snooze for half an hour over coffee and a cigar, while Jock gives a post-prandial recital on the gramophone. (When I asked one day for a particular record, Jock said, " Can ye no listen to a conseedered programme ? ") I then re-write the *S.T.* article, taking great pains about semicolons and such-like. (Millais once confessed that the only thing he enjoyed about portrait-painting was putting the high-lights on the boots of his subjects ; the only thing I really enjoy about writing is the punctuation.) After tea depends upon whether, like a golf course, I am inland or seaside. If I am inland I motor to a course forty miles away, play a match with the local assistant which ends on the last green, dine somewhere, and am then driven forty miles back to town, rather slowly, in the cool of what has been a very hot day. Then bed. If I am at the sea the same programme holds, except that after a keen match and dinner I listen on pier or promenade to a band playing Strauss waltzes through which the sea can be faintly heard. The bandstand looks as much as possible like a wedding cake, it is brilliantly lit up, moths flutter, and the smoke of one's cigar goes straight up and is very blue. After the crowd has dispersed one goes to sleep on a bench near the hotel, until it is one o'clock and it begins to grow cold. Where do the ponies come in? One mustn't be greedy, and in this ideal day they do not !

Sept. 5   Dined with Sydney Carroll, who is quite cross because
Tuesday.   I will not touch his open-air Shakespeare. He told
                    me that a woman producer is the best for temperamental actresses. Heard at rehearsal recently :

TEMPERAMENTAL ACTRESS (*with winning smile*). I don't feel I'm *quite* right here.

WOMAN PRODUCER (*promptly*). You're bloody, darling !

Sept. 17   Lunched at Café Royal with Cedric Hardwicke, who
Sunday.   has a theory that when Shaw is dead and actors can
             cut as they like Shaw will turn out to be great theatre !
George Bishop's wife told me she thought of re-writing the
plays as Shaw would have written them if he had been a meat-
eater and a wine-bibber. "Like duplicate bridge," this delightful
creature explained. Hardwicke also explained how in *Yellow
Sands* he made all the lines of his body, including his coat-collar
and moustache, droop, whereas in *Show Boat* they all turned up,
and in *The Barretts* they were rectangular, including his walk
across the stage, which was either parallel to the footlights or
at right angles to them.

CEDRIC. My theory of acting is that it is so minor an art
that the only self-respect attaching to it is to be able to reproduce one's performance with mathematical accuracy.

J. A. Quite ! A professional is a man who can do his job
when he doesn't feel like it ; an amateur is one who can't when
he does feel like it.

CEDRIC. It shouldn't make a hair's breadth of difference to
an actor if he has a dead baby at home and a wife dying.

J. A. But if one is dying oneself, or has the toothache ?

CEDRIC (*smiling*). Have a cigar !

We then discussed what was wrong with Maugham's *Sheppey*.
I said that an author who gets into a pet when Christ's
commandments are not kept can only make the pet convincing if we feel that the whole body of his work is
an argument for Christ. Cedric asked if I meant that it
was Shaw's subject and not Maugham's, and I replied :
"Of course ! "

Took Leo to supper at the Trocadero and was very glad
when he only wanted to drink beer. This enabled me to have
my usual pint of champagne. I am dead without it. But I
cannot afford to buy champagne for other people. If, therefore, I invite anybody to a meal—which owing to the impecuni-
osity of all my friends I must always do—either I must behave

like a cad or remain dead. I prefer the former. Leo said that to get the best out of a love-affair one should never ask for more passion than the beloved one is competent to provide. It is impossible to convey the amount of erotic disillusion in Leo's voice as he said this. Wordsworth would have called it disappointment recollected in tranquillity. Apropos of Gibbon, Macaulay, and Carlyle, Leo defined History as "the way things get about."

Oct. 11   Spent nearly all day at the lawyer's making my
Wednesday. will. Left him at 5 and went to see a picture at
              the Empire. Got to my doctor's at 7, got away
from him at half-past, and in the Little Theatre at 8 for a cheerful play about a neurasthenic who was sent to a mental nursing home and turned into a lunatic. Arranged with Jock to bring a cold fowl and bottle of wine to Ernest's. I had had no food all day, and the arrangement was that we should gobble and swig these down, write twelve hundred words about the film for the *Tatler*, then motor back to Westcliff about 2 A.M. Carried out my part of the programme, but no Jock, so ate a very worried supper all by myself. Much too tired to write the article by hand, so motored back to Westcliff, relying on local typist to get me out of my difficulty early in the morning, which she did. Had an early telephone call from Jock saying he had fallen asleep at home, which I must and do believe because I know he has been suffering from insomnia. But whatever the cause the effect is the same on me, and I get into Lear-like rages which approximate to nerve-storms and from which I do not recover for two days.

Oct. 24   Lunched at the Savage Club. Nearly lost my temper
Tuesday.   with Herman Finck, because he would have it that
              Glazounov was a better composer than Berlioz.
However, I didn't quarrel, and forgave him because of his saying that Basil Cameron, when he conducts Sibelius, looks more like a tobacco-pouch than ever!

Nov. 18   *Idées noires, très noires,* all the time at Brighton, and
Saturday.   I hope it's liver. Much better on my return and
in fair form in the *S.T.* I rather like my description
of Constance Collier in the revival of *Hay Fever* : " Magnificent,
now like the wife of Herod, now like Bernhardt in the rôle of a
Byzantine Empress stung by a horse-fly and neighing with
fury, now like somebody in *Hypatia* wearing a Græco-Roman
bun." Didn't feel up to dressing, so found myself conspicuous
in a terrifically smart house.

Supped at Rule's with Monty and arrived home, or rather
at Ernest's, to find two communications. The first was from
somebody signing him- or herself " Elfin," and wondering why
Lady Blessington should not on some evenings have danced
naked on the dinner-table for the entertainment of Captain
Jenkins's guests, and on other evenings relentlessly pursued
discussions of Raphael's cartoons. Then follows this passage,
in which " double-jointed " is, I think, the operative word.
" I know an Irish girl, born double-jointed, to whom dancing
is an instinct and a joy. To see her dancing with my children,
especially the baby aged four, is something marvellous ! She
always flings off practically all her clothing. So does the baby
and the bigger boys. Yet she is the purest girl I have ever
met—it shows in her face."

This business of turning the house at Westcliff and the flat
at Kensington Gardens Square into the cottage at Hadley
Green while living at Ernest's up those four flights of stairs
is going to prove tedious. Have decided to redecorate only
my bedroom, which was the former occupants' nursery and
is painted a bright, unforgivable pink. The other decorations,
in eau-de-nil and apple-green, are delightful.

Nov. 25   When does a man begin to die ? Up to now I have
Saturday.   always been able to get back to the meridian of
health by taking exercise and just not drinking
or smoking. But the time must come when all these will
not avail, and one will have struck the moment when there
is no more life on tap, as it were, and one begins to

dwindle. I am fifty-six. Have I four more years of good recuperation?

Foreseeing the time when I may not be able to work, I shall want something to look back on, and therefore I am gingering up my work *now* to read good *then*. Or will even that satisfaction be denied? Won't one just not want anything at all? That, of course, would be the real death. It has been occurring to me lately that if death is real death and not the prelude to something else we shall never know the how and why of things. Owing to sentimentalities of the " beyond the grave " order— though St Paul gives them a grand coating of words—I have always thought, or even supposed, deep down in my mind, even taken for granted, that one would one day *know*. But if we don't? Suppose it all really is a secret. What a sell! Even the parsons and the priests won't realise they were wrong all the time. The other day in a monumental sculptor's Tom Tiddler's Ground I saw a stone with an angel clinging to it. On the stone was scrawled in blue chalk SOLD. I hate the idea of Evolution. You cannot evolve without discarding, and to be discarded contains a horrid hint of impermanence. Besides, Omnipotence, if it be Omnipotence—I am afraid to use the word God—can have no need of Evolution. I am inclined to think that there *is* Evolution, but that Somebody already knows all about Evolution and where it will end. My best hope is in a rearrangement of the Time dimension, on the lines that Has-Been Is, no past and no future but a permanent Now. That would be a good working Eternity. Given health I want nothing better than this world, which has beauty and effort sufficient to content me. To stop now and re-live my life for ever and ever wouldn't be bad. Lots of hell, but plenty of heaven, thank God! At the same time I realise that all this has puzzled better brains than mine, and that I should be more usefully occupied in changing my spectacles, which are beginning to give me headaches.

Lunched at the Savage with José Levy, Isidore de Lara, and Jean Joseph-Renaud. Renaud is the ex-amateur world-champion fencer and a *littérateur* of sorts. Told some amusing stories and how everything that Pierre Loti wrote is pure fantasy. The Icelandic fisherman lives so much among decaying fish that he stinks to knock you down even at five hundred yards. All the perfumes of Arabia will not, I suppose, sweeten that walloping hand. Renaud talked also of Sardou and said, " Ce n'était pas de l'art mais de l'adresse."

Called at *S.T.* office and corrected my proof. Asked Hadley, who was looking ill after an abscess, why he did not take a holiday. " Physician, heal thyself ! " he replied. Motored to Barnet and stopped at a telephone kiosk. I had written : " The one thing an Aspasia forfeits is the right to snub ; Miss Cooper was as genteel as an icicle and as heartening ! " It occurred to me that the first half of the sentence convicts me of thinking Victorianly about a Greek matter, so I arranged to have it deleted. The house is getting on very well and is going to be charming. On the way back went to another kiosk and arranged for the phrase " ferocity of predestination " in connection with Alcibiades to be altered to " fury of predestination."

Nov. 28   Lunched with James Douglas, who said, " What is
Tuesday.   wrong with the modern newspaper is that it is never
             two days alike. After all, the man who subscribes to
a paper on Monday likes to recognise it again on Tuesday."

Went in the evening to the Garrick Theatre, where they are trying to revive the old music-hall. There was a chairman's table with Charles Austin as chairman, but owing to the L.C.C. only ginger-beer allowed. Growlers stationed outside the theatre and old-fashioned notices stuck up inside. Audience consisted almost entirely of young Yids and their women-folk. Round the chairman's table were Harry Preston, Bertram Mills, A. P. F. Chapman, Malcolm Campbell, Jimmy Wilde, Kid Lewis, Rev. C. B. Mortlock, not wearing his dog-collar, George Bishop, Noel Curtis-Bennett, and myself. Harry Preston looked as though he thrives on operations. As much the old beau as ever, and as always seeming to take Jimmy Wilde under his wing. I still foolishly and fatuously regard Jimmy as the greatest genius I have ever set eyes on. You can match Shaw with Voltaire,

Bernhardt with Rachel, Hobbs with Grace. But no other boxer has ever given two stone away and been uniquely superior to all others in his own class. He is like Shakespeare. Other boxers abide our question. Not Jimmy. When I first knew him Wilde looked to be a wistful human scarecrow, with a yonderly expression that suggested the chorister in a decline. Belcher, who, some twenty years ago, drew him at the National Sporting Club having the tape bound round his hands, did not see him so but gave him the face of a wizened old man. This seemed supremely untrue then, and the contemporary photographs do not bear Belcher out ; the odd thing is that Jimmy has now grown to look exactly like Belcher's cartoon. I sat next to Kid Lewis, another grand fighter. We were all introduced, and Chapman got the most applause.

Ernest told me this true story of two soldiers from Walsall who, during the war, were accosted by an arm-waving Frenchman anxious to obtain some information. One of them went on ahead, leaving his mate to deal with the stranger. Presently the mate caught his friend up, and No. 1 said, " Well, wot did 'e want ? " No. 2 replied, " Aw dunno. 'E started jabberin' some bloody lingo, so I 'its 'im in the bloody ear-'ole ! " Walsall, says Ernest, who was born there, would see nothing remarkable in this tale.

An interesting talk with the little barber over the way, a Dublin Jew of my own age. He had a bad nervous breakdown some four years ago, could not cross the street, and would go off into floods of tears. Doctors no good, so he set about curing himself by sheer will-power. For six months he took four pints of milk a day and a weekly $2\frac{1}{2}$ lbs. of cod-liver oil. No smoke and no drink. Walked in the park for two hours every day, and every Wednesday went to Clacton by boat. Went to bed by himself every night at eight o'clock and rose at 8. Was cured in six months and kept most of the treatment up for another twelve. Defied the doctors and came out of hospital to treat himself. There's courage for you !

A delightful *casus belli* has arisen. There was an account in yesterday's *Times* of the exhumation last summer of the bodies of the little Princes in the Tower. The bones found in 1674 under a staircase in the White Tower were assumed to be those of the young Princes and were buried as such by Charles II's order in Henry VII's Chapel, Westminster Abbey. After examination last summer they were re-inurned, and the Dean of Westminster read part of the Burial Service over them. A fuss is now being made because the Princes were members of the Roman Catholic Church of the England of the pre-Reformation days, and therefore the rites should have been Roman Catholic and conducted by the Cardinal Archbishop of Westminster. Against this is urged the legal continuity of the present Anglican Church with the pre-Reformation Church of this country. Charming!

Supped at the Café Royal with Donald Calthrop. There were some other people present, and the talk turned on the poverty of modern acting. A young woman objected that I was comparing Laughton, Hardwicke, Evans, and the others "who are young, with Irving, Ellen Terry, Mrs Kendal, and all your great ones after they had attained maturity." She said, "What was Irving like when he was young?" And Calthrop very finely answered, "Irving was never young!"

1934

Jan. 22
Sunday.

Excellent concert at the Savage Club on Saturday night. George Bishop in the chair. Giovanni, the conjurer, did some marvellous card-tricks and took a man's braces off! Mark and Benno played the Liszt Concerto for two Pianos, a work never performed. But why must they play loud enough for two Albert Halls?

Have hit upon a device for saving money. Shall put £2 into my pocket every morning and £3 each on Saturday and Sunday. At night I shall put all I have left into a petty cash drawer, and empty this weekly into the Post Office Savings Bank. Shall put into same account all odd sums from extra bits of work, sale of books, etc.

Heard from Albert that Tulip is wintering well. Had the Pascal-like thought to-day that an inch added to Tulip's front would alter my entire world. Meanwhile I am without a novice for the coming season.

My knee has gone wrong. This is the one I hurt during the war, meaning that I fell off a horse in England. Jock says that the leg, and probably the other one too, will stiffen permanently so that when I sit down I shall have both stuck out in front of me. Presumably when I go to bed they will be pointing ceilingward. Age, I do abhor thee! And Jock likewise.

Opened Post Office Savings Account with £12.

March 2
Thursday.

Lunched with Hamish Hamilton and Graham Robertson at the Jardin des Gourmets. Talk so good that I have no idea what we ate and drank. G. R. is like a spar of the 'nineties washed up on the beach of to-day, and a very charming and responsive spar, full of sly fun.

He told us of a dreadful piece of symbolic painting by Spencer Stanhope, in which Patience seated on a commodious

47

tombstone smiled at Grief in the person of a widow sitting on the ground surrounded by her weeds. He suggested to some of Stanhope's entourage, though not to the painter himself, a companion allegory entitled " Amazement on thy Mother Sits."

J. A.   Is Stanhope dead?

G. R.   Not more than usually.

H. H.   But is he actually dead?

G. R.   Yes, of course. We all are!

Robertson asked us to go round to see his pictures, and in the car talked about the films and how he hated them. The most illustrious of our younger comédiennes had sent him to see her new film with a request for a report thereon.

G. R.   I said the close-ups made her face look like a billiard-table and the amplifiers gave her the voice of an elephant gargling. She just smiled, and any lady who can smile when you unload all that on her must be a real lady!

The house is a museum with Graham Robertson for curator. Having duly admired the Rossettis, Burne-Joneses, Sargents, a not very good Whistler, and a magnificent Albert Moore, we were asked if we could stand the Blakes, which are tremendous. The finest, over the mantelpiece, is a picture of God creating Adam. G. R. maintains that this is better than Michael Angelo, who forgot to make God *tired*, whereas Blake's Almighty is exhausted after the work of Creation.

The room was littered with photographs of Sarah, and on the staircase was a drawing of G. R. by her with a scrawled date which looks like " 18881 "!

G. R.   She just put down a lot of 8's and then went on to something else!

Also on the staircase a diabolically clever drawing by James Pryde of Irving as Dubosc in *The Lyons Mail*, and G. R.'s own pastel portrait of Ellen Terry " done while she was drying her hair." G. R. said he had given up talking to young people about Irving because they just can't understand what you mean : "I should think he'd frighten them out of their wits."

March 3   On Saturday last dined at Oxford with the Mermaid
Friday.   Society, the purpose of which is to drink rum punch
              to the " souls of poets dead and gone." Answered
for the guests and was, I think, in fair form. Took as my theme
Butler's reflection in the *Note-books* that it was a good job we
proceed from the cradle to the grave and not the other way
about. Elaborated this with illustration of the human body
as railway-train heading for tunnel obviously too small for it.
Argued further that while being snuffed out like a candle is
tragic, to attend the original kindling must be ignominious.
Referred to some female's novel about the soul-state of a Spanish
matador, and asked what we should think of a book by a Spanish
Miss recounting the soul-history of a Tottenham Hotspur
centre-forward.

Usual business of menu-card signing followed, and was told
of a financier who never signed one of these without crossing
it ! Dinner was at Christ Church, a beautiful college but too
short of w.c.'s. Had to walk nearly a quarter of a mile and
then found a lot of people queueing up. This prompted me
to say to the President of Magdalen : " If it had been a question
of *making* water, do you think, sir, that Philip Sidney would have
said what he did ? "

Leo and Ernest in good form these days. Ernest complaining
of the difficulty of keeping a roof over his head, Leo said that
for forty years he had found it a struggle to keep himself under
other people's roofs !

I have come to the conclusion that there are some minds
with which it must always be impossible to establish contact.
In a wireless talk the other day I had this passage : " A friend
of mine has a beautiful Matisse in which a young woman sitting
on a not very low chair has an arm so long that its wrist doubles
itself on the ground. Yet if this arm were the right length
the picture would be ruined. Now when a second-rate artist like
Lawrence paints Kemble as Hamlet with his head half the size it
ought to be, all the world cries out. This can only mean that the
liberties with truth taken by second-class artists matter enormously,
whereas in the case of the first-class they don't matter at all ! "

A listener replied to this as follows : " I do not think art is untrue. In the picture which you said showed a lady's arm much too long, I believe a photograph would have come out the same. I have taken photographs which resulted in legs being two or three times too long."

Again, I had mentioned the picture by Ambrogio de Predis in the National Gallery entitled " Angel Playing on Musical Instrument." The " Instrument, which is more or less fiddle-shaped, is held near the chin, but insufficiently cuddled ; and it is obvious that the angel could have no control over it. The bow is at least two inches out of place. If the angel held the fiddle in the manner used by every fiddler that ever was, the picture would be ruined." About this my correspondent said : " I believe the angel you mentioned, playing a violin, was deliberately made to do it in a way not real, because if it were not unreal, no one would believe it to be an angel ! "

March 8   Letter from George Mathew :
Wednesday.

                                   12 *Tavistock Place*
                                          *W.C.*2

MY DEAR JIMMIE,

I know now what we ought to have said to the idiot at your club last night who repeated the old parrot-cry that " perpetual peace would not be good for humanity " and that " an occasional war is necessary to keep our souls alive." We should have asked him to be explicit about how often wars are advisable, how long they should last, and what might be regarded as a satisfactory number of persons killed, wounded, and crippled for life ; whether the decade after the Great War could truthfully be said to have revealed any notable resurgence of idealism and nobility, or the converse (*vide* contemporary novels, plays, and newspapers) ; whether the conflict should be conducted with gentlemanly restraint or with the maximum scientific devilishness, in order to do our souls the maximum amount of good ; whether a cause should be found for the war, or that formality be dispensed with wholly ; whether the bold and physically fit persons who are the first to be killed in a war might not have produced, had they survived, a better progeny than the cautious

and neurasthenic persons who manage to be left alive to
become the parents of the race; and finally, whether it might
not be logical to amend our prayer and cry, " Give us War
in Our Time, O Lord ! "

Yours always,
GEORGE MATHEW

P.S. The League of Nations would come in handy. Once
the salutary qualities of warfare were generally made known
the whole thing could be organised from Geneva, which
would see that the dangers and hardships (and therefore the
spiritual benefits) were equably distributed throughout the
continent. Why should Belgium or any other cockpit mono-
polise all the blessings ?

March 9   Played bridge with Douglas Furber, who claimed
Thursday.   that he had been having tea with a woman calling
              herself Printemps Rosenschweig ! !

March 10   Repeating some ribald story of a young actor who
Friday.   died recently, I said I hoped he wouldn't have been
              annoyed.

JOCK. *Be* annoyed, you mean. He's very angry you've
not talked more about him since he died.

J. A. Can ghosts be angry ?

JOCK. What else is there to do in the shades except take
umbrage ?

May 2   On Sunday afternoon George Bishop said suddenly,
Wednesday. " Come with me to Tangier on Friday." I accepted,
              and since Monday morning—it is now Wednesday
evening—have written one book article, two articles under a
pseudonym, one film article, one *Sunday Times* article, and have
seen a play. Also made final arrangements for the purchase of
a Bentley, 6½ litres, 1928 model. When new cost £2800 and have
got it for £275, getting the Vauxhall taken off my hands at what
it now stands me in. Nett result £50 down and 18 instalments
cf £14. Also received a visit from my delightful bailiff, who
advised me in the matter of some dozen or sixteen writs, the

same number as the lines Hamlet wrote into *The Murder of Gonzago*. They are all small, thank Heaven, and the aftermath of Westcliff. And I thought they were all paid!

May 9   This cruise is, I must suppose, exactly like every
Wednesday. other cruise. No reason why it should be different.
             By the way, I ought to have remembered my man-
overboard complex. A ship's side is to me what a tube station platform is to other people, so that I spend the entire voyage blotting myself against the cabins away from the sea. I settle down to do some reviewing, and on the first page of the first book I find the words, " Of course, he may have jumped overboard. Many people do."

Have won every night at bridge—over £5 at sixpence a hundred! Principal opponents are a young woman who looks like Madge Titheradge, Norma Shearer, and Cicely Courtneidge, and her yachting husband.

Not much good talk. Except that George, on sighting Tangier, said, " Not my idea of Africa ! " Also that the Atlantic Ocean is the only really convenient way of disposing of old razor blades.

According to George we nearly had a mishap in the Thames, owing to a boat in front turning round too quickly.

" Who told you ? " I asked.

" *One of the management !* " said George.

Four hours at Gibraltar which, of course, I must spend in getting melancholy over the tombs in the Trafalgar Cemetery.

Promised myself that I would not be done by the natives, and in less than two minutes of landing had bought a *Daily Mail*, Paris edition, 14 days old! Drove round the rock and asked the chauffeur if he knew England. He replied, " Yessir. Verr grand country ! " I asked him what part of England he had found very grand. He said, " Barrow-in-Furness."

May 10   Summoned to the bridge by the Captain, who
Thursday.   explained everything, including a device for rescuing
              men overboard. Somebody presses a button,
which releases a life-belt, etc. But I know that if I do it, it will

be at dead of night, with nobody about. Note that I have not
dared to write this sentence until after my last night on this
blasted boat.

May 19   Must really keep this Diary more up to date. On
Saturday.   the way to Arles stopped at Salon, where I think I
              saw my mother-in-law. If I was not mistaken and
it was indeed she, she has grown very old and grey and bent. But
I am sure that I could not mistake that excessively delicate walk.

They told me at the café that my father-in-law shot himself
a year or two ago because of money troubles. Also told me
that Edmée was at home, but of course I did not call. If I am
ever to see her again I think I ought to write and ask permission,
and not look in upon her in passing. There is a decency to be
observed in these matters.

I saw M. Fabre, the mayor, who married us. He looked a
little older but was still stroking his beard in the way I remember.
I was conscious of no emotion whatever except a vague curiosity.
1918, the War, Salon, my marriage—all this seems utterly and
unbelievably dead, and I don't want to revive it.

Perhaps this is the secret of immortality, that when you get
into the next state you don't want to revive the old one, and
if there isn't any next state you won't be there to want! Or
am I content that all connected with Salon should be dead
to me because I never really liked it? One must not colour
truth with preferences. If I had really loved Salon and all
that I might want to revive it, which would knock on the
head my new notions about immortality.

At Arles met Anthony West, the son of Rebecca. He is a
pleasant and extremely intelligent boy, and I liked him ten
times more when I heard that after three days in Arles he was
" fed to the teeth."

George Bishop is a delightful travelling-companion except
that his metaphysics are entirely sentimental, and he will drag
Browning into life at the Old Port at Marseilles and wonder
why the niggers and prostitutes and Mediterranean riff-raff
can't be brought to brace themselves up and march breast

forward never doubting clouds will break. Henceforth I am
going to call him " Blougram Bishop "—and hope never again
to hear that thing about " a chorus-ending from Euripides." I
should not so much mind " a Hackney-showing at Olympia."
To me " a fancy from a flower-bell " is no more proof of the
existence of God than a sting from a nettle. It is *as much* proof,
but no more. Whereas George only sees proof in things which
are pleasant to him. I can just conceive that God, while equally
manifest in the evil as in the good, is still more quintessentially
existent in the battle between them, because peace would mean
inertia.

We travelled from Marseilles to Paris on the 10.30 train on
Sunday. There were five first-class passengers ! Arrived at
the Gare du Nord at 11 o'clock, and were so tired-out that
we spent what was left of the evening sitting in a café opposite
the station. If anybody had told me thirty years ago that I
should spend a night in Paris gazing at a station-clock !

Almost the first person I saw when I got back was Dicky
Clowes. A witty and charming man, and a great friend of
Jock's. He said, " Hello, Jimmy. How did you enjoy being
away with Bishop ? I suppose you've now got *Sordello* by
heart ! "

July 3   Account with respect to James Agate's book entitled
Tuesday.   *First Nights*—From his Secretary, Alan Dent.

10th JANUARY, 1934—For having morosely looked through the *Sunday Times* articles, tastefully choosing such as should appear in permanent book form	4½ hours	9s.
20th FEBRUARY—For having sulkily specified and ordered the agreed copies of the paper	1 hour	2s.
21st MARCH — For having interestedly (promise of emolument having been made) flourished scissors and brandished gum-brush to neat and tidy effect	15 hours	30s.

25th JUNE–3rd JULY—For having diligently corrected and re-corrected proofs, correcting some of the corrections, verifying a thousand allusions, laboriously examining and comparing corrections with Author, and general erasing and polishing .   .   .   17 hours   34*s.*

28th JUNE–14th JULY—For having keenly compiled an Index to said Book, comprehensive, accurate, and not without fun .   .   .   .   33 hours   66*s.*

13th JULY—For having enthusiastically revised proofs of Index and verified that all corrections have been correctly made .   .   .   .   .   3 hours   6*s.*

                                                                            147*s.*

Aug. 21   Autobiography accepted by Hamish Hamilton, and
Tuesday.   I get £200 on account of royalties.
          Went South and set off for short jaunt with Leo Pavia. The old thing is more unprintably witty than ever. Proposed to lie at Bexhill-on-Sea. (The turn of this sentence reminds me of a Shakespearian postcard Bruce Winston once wrote to Sybil Thorndike: " Lay last night with your husband at Tewkesbury.") Filthy hole, dull and, I gather, purse-proud. After dinner sat on the front in a green alcove rather like an outdoor setting for *Much Ado*, and watched a worn moon preside over a green sea and a silver taffrail. Nobody passed. Complained of this to girl at hotel cash-desk, who said icily, " How many people would you require ? " Straightway collected luggage and left Bexhill for smaller and filthier hole.

Aug. 23   The Lyric venture owed its success to a fluke.
Thursday.   *Abraham Lincoln* was playing to empty houses until one night W. J. Rea fell ill and Drinkwater played his part. The evening papers got hold of it, and the house was full. Then Rea returned and the house continued full until the end of the run.

Sept. 11   Absurd play at the Westminster entitled *Rose and*
Tuesday.   *Glove* by the Editor of *The Bookman*. This is Marlowe's
               Edward II re-written to prove that there was, in
Stalky's phrase, " no beastly Ericking " about the King and
Piers Gaveston. The *Times* critic said that the author was
entitled to telescope history and re-interpret it. I think I must
now write a play to prove that Nero went behind the scenes at
circuses for intellectual conversation, and another to show that
fire descended upon Sodom because the inhabitants refused to
pay poll-tax. Some years ago, being at Warwick, I went to
see the monument to Piers Gaveston put up by, of all people,
Mr Siddons ! It is in a wood and I couldn't find it. Coming
into the town I passed a villa residence with a charming lawn
and two gateposts to the drive. On the lawn was a double-
perambulator fully tenanted, and on one gatepost was " Piers,"
on the other, " Gaveston."

Sept. 17   At Brighton. Lunched at the Albion yesterday and
Monday.   insisted upon being allowed to pay. Among the
               lunchers was Seymour Hicks, complaining that they
had given him a too large and therefore property lobster from
Drury Lane. Also A. W. Baskcomb, who has recovered from his
stroke to the extent of being able to walk with a stick. But he
cannot make himself understood though he tries hard. It is
pitiful that this superb portrayer of melancholy should come
to this plight and, I fear, end.

A grand game in the afternoon with young Riseborough.
R. gave me four bisques. I won the first three holes and lost
the next three. Then the match went ding-dong to the fifteenth,
by which time I stood one up with all bisques gone. At the
sixteenth I missed a two-foot putt to become dormy, the ball
sidling away as if it was bewitched. At the seventeenth I holed
a twelve-yard putt and so became dormy one. This unnerved
the boy, who hit a poor drive while I got mine away superbly.
R. then hit a brassie within six yards of the pin. This unnerved
me, and I cut my mashie shot slightly so that the ball, pitching
on the green, ran all round the right-hand bunker before toppling

in. I got out too well and so the match was halved. An exciting game, a good, modest young pro., and a lovely day.

Sept. 19   I hear that Lilian Braithwaite came off the stage
Wednesday.   the other night after *Family Affairs* clutching her
               throat and with an expression of Phædra-like
anguish. Asked what was wrong, she said tremulously, "The humour of this play is choking me!"

Sept. 27   Called on Dame Madge Kendal. She talked of
Thursday.   her father, "who, if he had lived, would now be
               nearly a hundred," obviously forgetting that she
herself is eighty-five. A bundle of majesty still. Some of the things she said to me. Apropos of to-day's players: "My dear Mr Agate, you must not ask me to be impressed by any modern young actress. I saw Ristori! When the executioner bound Marie Antoinette's hands behind her and cut off her curls the tears used to roll down Ristori's face as she said, 'Louis loved my curls.' To do this in full view of the public, Mr Agate, is acting."

"Ristori was a greater actress than Sarah because she had no sex-appeal."

"I once heard Sarah recite *Les Deux Pigeons* in a drawing-room. I watched not Sarah but the audience, and whatever it was she made the pigeons say and do, the effect on the audience was improper."

"The greatest of all was Rachel, whose life I dare say you have read." (I did not point out that I had written it!) "My father used to say that Rachel hardly ever made a gesture and would recite fifty lines of Racine or Corneille without one. But that on the rare occasions when she did make a gesture it swept everybody out of the theatre."

Apropos of *Joséphine*: "There is nobody living to-day who could play Napoleon except, possibly, Cedric Hardwicke. He would be able to play him in a little way."

"S—— [I have forgotten the name Dame Madge said] was an actor of the old school. When, as Virginia, I embraced him as Virginius I used to take his temples in my two hands. Once this caused his toupet to rise and leave a gap. But he covered his head with his toga, and the audience perceived nothing. At the end he used to take my hair, which was long enough for me to sit on, and wrap it round the handle of his dagger before plunging the blade into my back."

She then recited some Wordsworth, and insisted on escorting me to the door herself.

Nov. 2   News to hand that Laughton has retired from the
Friday.   rôle of Micawber in the film of *David Copperfield*
              in which Hugh Walpole is to play a clergyman. Does
not Hugh see that to bring a well-known character from real life into an imaginary sequence of events is to destroy the reality of that imaginary sequence ? It is no use Hugh modestly pleading that he is unknown. His features have been made public over and over again in connection with this Hospital and that Benevolent Institution. They are as well known as St Paul's Cathedral and better known than its Dean. People on beholding Hugh's features in this film will not be able to help nudging and whispering to their neighbours, or simply saying to themselves, "Look, that's Hugh Walpole, the author of that nice long book about Susan Saddleback !" If they are Americans they will say to each other, "Gee ! Didn't he lecture last fall at Utah ? Do you remember, dear, how nice he was about the younger novelists ? " By which time, of course, the thread of the film-narrative will be thoroughly broken. If Hugh must play I would sooner have seen him as Micawber, since the shock of his appearing at all would be got over early on, after which we could go back to uninterrupted Dickens. Besides, where is it to end ? Why not Priestley for Traddles, Beverley Nichols for Steerforth, Virginia Woolf for Mrs Gummidge, Rose Macaulay for Rosa Dartle, Ursula Bloom for Dora, Vera Brittain for Agnes, Dorothy Sayers for Miss Murdstone, Clemence Dane for Betsey Trotwood, G. B. Stern for Miss Mowcher, Ethel Mannin for little Em'ly, and me for Mr Dick ?

Nov. 23   Supped at the Savoy Grill with Rayner, Driberg of
Friday.   the *Express*, and a most amusing cove who does
             their cookery articles.   He seemed asleep most of the
time, but hearing Galsworthy mentioned opened his eyes to
say, " A dreary dog ! " and at once fell asleep again.   Exactly
like a character in *Alice*.   This reminds me of an old story about
Mostyn Pigott.   Roused from his after-lunch nap to give his
opinion of Columbus, Mostyn said, " A damned interfering
snoot ! " and went to sleep again.

Dec. 22   To-day I took out to lunch Fred Leigh, a great
Saturday.   help in putting the new flats to rights.   Fred, who
             with his height, tummy, and yellow hair looks like
a German tenor's Siegfried, has been many things—currier,
railway-painter, actor, singer, boxer, and the youngest publican
that ever held a licence in the Midlands.   As a young man he
painted the girders at New Street station, Birmingham, and was
sacked for falling asleep on a plank in the roof a foot wide !
Among his feats of strength were to press a 150-pound dumb-
bell six times from the left shoulder, to lie on the floor and raise
5 cwt. of sand to the standing position, to carry six jars of whiskey
containing four gallons each up two flights of stairs (one under
each arm and two in each hand), to throw an eighteen-gallon
cask of beer from between his legs over his head in one lift,
and to take two sacks of flour weighing 2 cwt. each off two
grocery counters and walk off with them.   During the war when
in France with the R.G.A. he used to carry six hundred-pound
shells, three in each arm, down the duckboards to the gun.   In
November 1917, when strafing Fritz at Metz, in one morning
he lifted two thousand hundred-pound shells on to ten men's
backs, to put beside a four-gun battery.   Only four hundred were
fired and then the battery pulled out and retired thirty-five
kilometres to Beaumetz.   The 51st Division took ten thousand
prisoners, but Fred would rather have fired off the balance of the
shells.

1935

Jan. 11 Apropos of a play called *Father of Lies* at the Royalty I
Friday. asked my godson, Paul Dehn, what he knew of
diabolism. He said, "If you throw holy water over an
evil spirit one of two things happens. If he's merely a satellite
it makes him sizzle. If he's a practising diabolist or the Devil
himself he rises twenty-five feet into the air and spins. *And
that's true !* "

Jan. 23 Luncheon at the Mayfair to Joseph Thorp, who
Wednesday. is leaving *Punch* after being its dramatic critic
for nineteen years. Present : Our host, whose
name I did not catch, Ivor Brown, Herbert Farjeon, W. A.
Darlington, Charles Morgan, Thorp, a man from *Punch* whom
I didn't know, Horace Horsnell, Tibby Griffith, and self. We
ate pâté de foie gras, hot lobster, and a perfect tournedos, and
drank sherry, Pouilly, Corton, Château Yquem, and old brandy.
Talk *very* good, except that I monopolised too much of it. Told
Thorp his lunch reminded me of Sydney Smith's idea of Heaven—
" eating pâté de foie gras to the sound of trumpets." T. said
instantly, " There are no trumpets here except yours, James."
This conversation happened :

HIGHLY DISTINGUISHED CRITIC. Three or four times
I have refused to write anything at all about a play. It seems
to me that editors ought to leave it to their critics to decide
whether a play is worth writing about.
OUR HOST. But even the worst play takes one out of
oneself.
ANOTHER CRITIC. A brothel would do that.
H. D. CRITIC (*staggeringly*). I wish my august paper would
let me write notices about brothels !

Othello at the Old Vic, with a very good Desdemona by a
new actress called Vivienne Bennett. Extremely moving, in

spite of the fact that she has a dimpling-dumpling face unsuited to the tragic. Supped at the Savoy Grill with Monty and Tim Dawes. Monty told me that his colleagues in Whitehall—I know the sort, spineless, glassy-eyed nincompoops with hands like slices of cold turbot—regard my last letter in *The Times* as Being in Poor Taste. Got home about two and sat up writing. *Ego* was just being born, and I looked out into Doughty Street saying, " And all the air a solemn stillness holds."

Jan. 24   *Ego* born.
Thursday.   Gray's line was still in my mind when Arthur
              (Arthur Wright, my valet, chauffeur, and factotum)
brought me my tea. I said, " Good morning, Arthur. I don't know what sort of a day it is, but *all the air a solemn stillness holds.*" Arthur replied, " Not half, sir. Even the coalmen are crying their wares in hushed voices ! " A lot of Arthur is pure Beaumarchais.

The *Times Lit. Supp.* magnificent about *Ego.* A column and a quarter of stuff I should have blushed to write myself, and I have no idea who the author is. " A philistine with the conscience and equipment of an intellectual is enough to upset anybody." *News Chronicle* first-class. Lunch in honour of the book given by Hamish Hamilton. At the Ivy. Guests were Eiluned Lewis, Harold Dearden (most amusing), Jock, and me. E. M. Delafield joined us and was witty. Marie Tempest came over and said that Willie had a great idea for the matinée. Mary to sit on a throne, with a masque of all the arts and sciences. The whole of London's, the country's, the world's genius to take part. Somebody said, " Would you like God to do anything ? "

The *Standard* came in while we were having lunch. Howard Spring's notice is nonsense. He talks of the book being " chiefly external shell, not the kernel of the man, not the ego." How damned silly ! Why not say straight out that the book *is* the man and that he hates and despises him and finds him a bore ? I needn't say that I am concerned with what H. S. says only in so far as it affects sales.

Dined with the Antiquarian Booksellers' Association. Poor do, and made bad speech. Humbert Wolfe very moving on the function of poetry. " Just as the art of architecture is to get the most room into the least space, so the function of poetry is to compress the most of eternity into the smallest time."

Looked in at *The Manchester Guardian* to see whether *Ego* had been carved or butchered. Review written by Harold Brighouse and very noble. I am " moving and just about George Mair and Basil Hastings."

Jan. 30   Lunch yesterday with Norman Collins at the
Wednesday.   Reform Club ; I didn't know there were so many
                respectable people in London. For a publisher,
N. C. is extremely jolly. He is writing a tragedy in the Websterian mode, to end with the line : " Her winding sheet shall be my handkercher." Told me several good stories, and I told him one about a party at which there was discussion of X, a well-known dramatic critic who has been booming away for donkey's years.

FIRST GUEST. It's time X was dead.
SECOND GUEST. But he *is* dead.
J. B. PRIESTLEY. By God, I wish he'd stiffen !

Jan. 31   Invitation to appear on the stage at Balham Hippo-
Thursday.   drome. Whether twice nightly not stated. Have
                instructed Jock to send courteous refusal.

As I write, the wireless is in full blast, or rather whimper, at Sibelius's 4th Symphony, Royal Philharmonic Society Concert, Beecham conducting. Very lovely and not at all what I should call a symphony. Why should it be ? One of the Savage Club's many conductors told me recently that there was a time when the Society was so hard up that it couldn't afford to engage a virtuoso, and the solo part in the concertos was played by anybody who happened to be passing. On one occasion, said Herman Finck, there was no audience except the bust of Beethoven. I expect this is an old joke. To-night's concert began with Mendelssohn's Italian Symphony. Fenton, who is sitting with me, says that to turn Christian was the most Jewish thing Mendelssohn ever did !

Wire from Brother Mycroft : " Regret delayed congratulations on *Ego* writing fully having read twice." I call my brother Gustave " Mycroft " because he is to me what Mycroft Holmes was to Sherlock.

An amusing mail has just arrived. It contains :

(*a*) Invitation to judge at the Royal Norfolk Show.

(*b*) Letter from Buckie Taylor, who as a kid lived in the Lower Seedley Road, Manchester. This makes four of us born within half a mile of each other—Buckie, Sidebotham, me, and Walter Greenwood, author of *Love on the Dole*. Buckie writes : " I elected to be a Unitarian because I had always thought one God enough for anybody. . . . Once I went in school hours to a slaughter-house. There came a terrific storm with lightning and thunder and torrents of rain. I was very scared because I thought I was being punished by my one God. I was terribly good for weeks afterwards."

(*c*) Letter from Lionel Fielden asking if he should go to India for five years as controller of Broadcasting. *Pros.* 350 millions without wireless, the fact that he enjoys teasing pukka sahibs, and the heat, which suits him. *Cons.* Television at home likely to give him new scope. Loss of friends. Acquisition of liver. I shall tell Lionel that he really must make minor decisions like this for himself.

(*d*) From my brother Edward this superb letter :

30/1/35   *Clapham Common, S.W.*4

DEAR JIM,

I saw a copy of *Ego* at May's on Sunday. I think it a very handsome volume. I have seen half a dozen of the best papers' criticisms. To my mind, the most satisfactory is the *Times Lit. Supp.* I am waiting till it gets into the library here to read it quietly. It is sure of a sale. There are one or two points that I shall mention—an extensive exposition of the æsthetics of Autobiography you are sure to get from Brother Mycroft.

> " We do not like to see French words introduced into English composition . . . but it is better to use a French word than to misuse an English word." (Lord Macaulay.)

Mycroft would have said this off his own bat ; I can only do it by quotation. I could not have failed to find the passage, but he could never have discovered it—there's the difference between us ! Oh, how second-hand is my little mind !

> " The rage for horses has become a positive epidemic ; many persons are infected with it whom one would have credited with more sense." (Lucian.)

That is naughty of me and, moreover, third-hand, as I don't know a word of Greek !

> " The ancients oftentimes thought a life well spent in polishing one single book ; we moderns on the contrary can no sooner propose anything, but we are daily importuned to know when it is to come out." (Simon Ockley— Introd. *History of the Saracens*, 1708.)

> " Certains auteurs, parlant de leurs ouvrages, disent : ' Mon livre, mon commentaire, mon histoire, etc.' Ils feraient mieux de dire : ' Notre livre, notre commentaire, notre histoire, etc.' Vu que d'ordinaire il y a plus en cela du bien d'autrui que du leur." (Pascal's *Pensées*.)

This, however, is not applicable to *Ego* ; only it is such a jolly quotation, I thought you'd like it !

The photo of you and Gus on the sands is very quaint. Gus even at that age is alert, confident, authoritative, with spade erect. But I am sure you did not look like that ! A doped walrus ! I admire your Concerto ! Typical is the love of grace notes and the marking of *cresc.* even before the music starts ! If it were played in Chelsea studios as the latest thing in Poulenc or Satie, how those sandy beards would quiver in ecstasy !

Yours ever,
EDWARD

Feb. 3   Brighton.   At breakfast Leo said, " I can't see why
Sunday.   you don't preface your new Diary with another
            account of your life.   It could be quite different and
you could call the book *Alter Ego*."

We had a drink at the Metropole before lunch, and Leo said, " The worst of this place is that they let in too many Christians." At lunch, and apropos of a well-known homosexual, he said, " I hear he is writing an autobiographical novel called *Lui et Lui*." As Jock said the other day, " Old Pavia is a rancid and venomous toad, but his wit is unending ! "

I feel I ought to say what Leo looks like. He is sixty, middle-sized, with a bullet-shaped head cropped close, and extremely short-sighted. This makes him screw up his eyes, thus increasing the resemblance to an india-rubber doll whose expression changes at will. He invariably says the wrong thing, but deliberately and at the top of his voice. A gormandiser without a palate. Extremely untidy, and I remember that one day after he had tried to cook for me I found stumps of asparagus sticking to the bottoms of the chairs. Yet this apparently warped and twisted creature is possessed of greater kindness of heart, if he likes you, than almost anybody I know, though affection with him generally takes the form of bickering. A great reader with a wonderful, unprecise memory. A brilliant musician *manqué*—largely because he has always gone out of his way to annoy people who have tried to help him. If I had to put him in three words I should say—a Jewish Dr Johnson.

It is a unique sight to see this odd creature ambling along a London street with his head on one side and pouring out invective to which Ernest Fenton impassively listens. Fenton is over six feet and looks like a vicious Renaissance cardinal out of a play by John Ford. Both are a bit of the 'nineties which has unaccountably survived.

My fresh air allowance at Brighton has been limited to twenty minutes on the front at Worthing yesterday, and the walk to lunch and back to-day. The rest of the time taken up with another article on *Love on the Dole*, about which I already have one-and-three-quarter columns in the *S.T.* Sometimes I find it easy to do two or even three articles on the same play ; at other times it is like—as Rebecca West said of reviewing a novel twice—being sick off an empty stomach. The worst of over-work is that I have to do the stuff I really want to do in

odd moments when other people would be playing or resting.
It is now a quarter to five, and am leaving for London, with
six books, including a novel of five hundred pages, to read
between now and midday to-morrow. The *S.T.* cut out my
notice of the new play at the Criterion. Here it is : " I do
not propose to bother about this one. I sat it through, and
have nothing to say."

Dined at the Royal Albion. In the smoke-room before dinner
Leo had a talk with, but did not introduce me to, a youngish,
very well-groomed man-about-town. After he had gone Leo
said, " When I first knew him he was third footman to Lord
B——. I stood in the dock with him in 1902 on the charge of
resisting the police outside the old Spaten Buffet in Piccadilly
Circus."

From Brother Edward :

Clapham Common
Feb. 1/35　　　　　　　　　　　　　　　　　　　　*S.W.*4

MY DEAR JIM,

I have, by now, had opportunity of reading *Ego* properly,
and hope my total impression may not be unacceptable to
you. I know you don't think much of my literary critical
faculty—neither do I—but a few stray remarks may not prove
foolish and might even be useful.

The general effect on me, then, is one of *honesty*. Not as
if a man said, " I know I'm a rapscallion, but I can't help
it," but as if he said, " I know I'm a rascal, and I *could* help
it—if I chose." And in that " if I chose " lies the comedy
and the tragedy of the book. You really make yourself blacker
than you need be painted ; and if this sophism of yours
may attract some, be sure it will repel others.

Yet, in this specious and twisted outlook, the book is *honest*.

Another great point in your favour is the book's originality
of form. I suppose there are many autobiographies these
days : statesmen ; clowns ; actresses, fallen out ; financiers,
found out ; Oxford dons, down and out. I do not read
them, but I am told they are *all alike*, each according to its
class. But I would swear that yours, in *its* own class, is
something different. I would not compare it with the

Autobiography of Edward Gibbon, or the Journal of John Wesley (about whom Johnson said, " He can talk well on any subject"); but it reminds me most strongly of Horace Walpole's Memoirs, and Letters. A great critic said of these two works : " He keeps the mind of the reader constantly attentive and constantly entertained. His superiority is seen not in industry, not in learning, not in accuracy, not in logical power, but in the art of writing what people will like to read."

And that hits your talent off to a nicety.

But beware of one or two things ! Over-emphasis defeats its own object. One adjective properly chosen is often more efficacious than five. For, " qui ne sait se borner, ne sut jamais écrire."

Ever yours,
EDWARD

Feb. 24   Fulfilled my promise to speak at the O.U.D.S. Jubilee
Sunday.   Dinner. In a fit of economy hired a car for the week-end costing only £2 10*s.*, with the result that an example of a much-advertised small make turned up ; it looked like a louse and crawled like a beetle. George Mathew very rude about it, said he thought the make ought to be called the Festina Lente.

It took the piddling little car three and a half hours to get from Birmingham to Oxford, with the result that we arrived in time for the second part of *Hamlet*. The theatre, which is rebuilt, and is now very large, commodious, and in every way up to date, is not in my opinion nearly so well suited to these shows as was the old theatre, a huddled pig-sty entirely constructed out of inconveniences. The huddling had the effect of bringing the young men on the stage and the young men in the audience into close communion, so that the whole University seemed to be seconding the actors, who often badly needed it. Now everything is spacious and aloof, the community of thought and feeling is lost, and, what is important, the young voices have not enough strength to fill the huge auditorium. I thought the costumes and music delightful and the acting weaker than in any O.U.D.S. production I have seen, except that the King, Mr John Wentzel, spoke the soliloquy beginning, " O, my offence is rank " with an appreciation of the meaning seldom encountered on the professional stage, most exponents of that part not exhibiting the vaguest notion of what Claudius is talking about. Peter Glenville has one radiant smile and two beautiful legs, all three being obviously inherited from his mother, Dorothy Ward, his acting being very nearly as boyish but not quite so principal.

It was after one o'clock before we sat down to supper at the Clarendon. I very quickly became involved in an argument with the producer, an Oxford don, about the character of Gertrude, who, he said, was a placid cow and nothing more. It has always seemed to me that Gertrude is one of the *optional* characters in Shakespeare. Sometimes she makes one think there is a good deal going on beneath the surface ; at others she is just a fool. " More matter, with less art," and " The lady doth protest too much, methinks," have never struck me as coming from a fool. On the other hand, " Nay, then, I'll set those to you that can speak " is not the utterance of a smouldering volcano. " As kill a king ! " is open to lots of interpretations. The *illusion* Shakespeare gives me of Gertrude's character insists that she was not privy to her husband's murder. If she had been, Claudius would have gone to her in his trouble, evinced in his abortive prayer, as Macbeth went to Lady Macbeth for comfort. But I feel that Gertrude had a very shrewd sus-picion that something was up, and would not have been surprised at any moment to learn what that something was. On the other hand, there are passages in which Gertrude just talks common Shakespearian form. For example, there's the famous passage about the " long purples." If Gertrude was a deceitful woman with her wits about her she would have kept off this subject ; on the other hand, she would have had to be a fool indeed to go maundering off into ribaldry at such a moment. Isn't it likely, however, that it is not Gertrude talking, but just Shakespeare following the good Elizabethan fashion of relishing a dirty joke at any time and in any context ? This brings us back to the point on which Walkley was so very sound, the point that there is no character in Shakespeare apart from the words in which that character is defined: " If we want to understand the play of *Hamlet* we shall not do so by assuming that it is a piece of real life, lived by people who have independent lives outside it." This independent life of a character or " precedent *état d'âme*," as Walkley calls it, is a mere illusion created by the dramatist from which flow all kinds of interpretative nonsense. Commentators who find Hamlet mad in one place and sane in another invariably attribute the inconsistency to Hamlet himself instead of to Shakespeare, who may have found it convenient to have Hamlet alternately mad and sane. I do not think it can be safely argued that Gertrude was both cow-like and volcanic because some of her lines are placid and some eruptive.

But I couldn't get my Professor to see this, and in any case I should have had to convince him across the fair body of Miss Oriel Ross, who is much too beautiful to be interested in this kind of debate. Nor could I get him to see that even if Gertrude is the character he thought she was, he must not allow the actress who plays the part to suggest that placidity is her entire range, because then the audience has no more interest in the closet scene than if Hamlet were arguing with his mother's bolster. Darlington, in the *Daily Telegraph*, described the Queen as " rather inadequate." Ivor Brown, in the *Observer*, said that Gertrude " was pitched on a shrill monotone and never suggested a lady likely to stir fratricide for her possession." The *Sunday Times'* Own Correspondent said that " the actress's monotonous plaintiveness was apt to exaggerate the goose-like qualities of the Queen of Denmark." Such a consensus of opinion seems to me to be something which no amateur producer has the right to ignore ; but the gentleman in question stuck to his guns, for which I respected him, and insisted that what he had sought for was a poetical rather than a theatrical interpretation of the play, for which I respected him less. *Hamlet* in the study may be no more than a poem; on the stage it must not be less than a play. I got so angry that when I was making my speech I was still thinking about this and was therefore, I think, a little below par. I told them about Fred Leigh seeing me off :

FRED. I've put in two shirts, two collars, two white ties, both dirty, and two waistcoats, one of which looks all right. And you'll find the notes for your speech in your breast-pocket along 'o your 'ankercher.
ME. But I haven't written any !
FRED. I found some old ones in a drawer, and they'll do.

I also pretended that the entire Gielgud coterie had rung me up after the show, hoping the new " Hamlet " had not done too well. On the whole quite a good evening, with two really witty speeches by John Sutro and a man called Felton. The latter told two lovely stories. An esoteric producer was heard to say to another, " The trouble with the girl is that she will get the line brown and I want it green." The same producer said to another young woman, " No, my dear, throw the weight on the left leg, not on the right. It's quite simple. Just a matter of foot-architectonics." Peter Glenville recalled how last year the O.U.D.S. went up to London and gave two performances— at the B.B.C., where the actors were heard and not seen, and at the Open Air Theatre in Regent's Park, where they were seen and not heard.

Feb. 25   Received this delicious letter from a very, very old
Monday.   friend :

Feb. 24*th* 35

DEAR JIMMIE,
    Thank you again and again for *Ego*, which I could hardly put down for meals and sleeps.
    Your body, I suppose, is bound to wear out, but surely you should continue on the mental plane for ever. You are just as necessary to rid the world of cant, hypocrisy, and small meannesses as any Bishop is to show the way to Heaven by other means. In fact if you can't go on for ever I would have you borne up to Heaven thus : drawn by all your ponies turned Pegasuses—Talke Princess, First Edition, Black Tulip (who appears half off the ground already) and the rest—

in a glass chariot, composed entirely of champagne bottles, you reclining in perfect ease in harmony with your digestion, your nerves and your creditors.

Good luck, dear Jimmie, to everything you put your hand or brains to.

Yours sincerely,
ETHEL

Letter from Brother Edward:

Feb. 24/35

Clapham Common, S.W.4

DEAR JIMMY,

Ego. May I advise one or two alterations in any reprint? I should like to see some of the numerous bills of fare deleted. (They are perhaps the only bills you will ever have any chance of getting rid of!) The constant description of what you eat and drink together with the cost becomes boring. In any case it is uninteresting; and the phrase "a pint of Bollinger" so often repeated becomes unbearable. The mixture of Daisy Ashfordian naïvety and Anita Loosian sophistication is unpleasant in a full-grown writer. And let me implore you to cut out your bowels, your heart attacks, and your stomach. Did Molière live for nothing? Besides, even if true, such inventories read like advertisement-columns in the less stately Sunday papers. These are, after all, only little things and perhaps purely personal prejudices (how many more p's?) about a book which is certainly alive and original. I'm not a younger Pliny or a Voltaire at letter-writing, but I'm going on, so——

Incompetence. Your favourite topic: *allons-y!* This I find to be the most virulent disease attacking all manifestations of human activity with which I am acquainted. The translation of musical texts is simply appalling. Beecham used to come to me in despair with operatic versions and say, "Mr Agate, will you *please* make these singable!" And these works had been published; and these works had been performed; and these translators had got the jobs! One priceless bit I must quote. One of them in an old French song translates "Quand parrain vient sur son âne blanc"—"When god-pa calls in his motor-car!" Incompatibility of musical and verbal accent: distortion or destruction of original vocal phrasing; the shirking of a scheme of rhyme laid down in

the original language of the libretto ; total disregard of what
is vocal ; snippets of phrases in choral parts without subject,
object or verb ; etc., etc. Rank incompetence !

Translation of Books. I find in a German novel that the
hero goes to the sacrifice (*Opfer*) where the author says he
went to the opera (*Oper*). This was published by a first-class
English firm. What happens to a druggist who puts arsenic
into a prescription " by mistake " ? Two or three years
ago an announcer at the B.B.C. said that Mme Gerhardt
would finish her recital by singing Brahms's " Blinde Kuh "
—" Blind Cow." Quite correct literally, but unfortunately
" blinde Kuh (spielen) " in German means " to play blind-
man's buff," and the delightful song is all about that charming
game.

Publishers. (With special reference to translated and un-
translated works.) Here you will probably entirely disagree
with me and tell me that publishers know their business
better than I do and that I shouldn't presume to meddle.
However, I will bravely say what I think. First, they will
publish the Memoirs of any kitchen slut who had the good
luck to whore it with Louis XIV. But ask them to publish
the Memoirs of La Rochefoucauld and they will laugh you
out of their office. As regards their musical books they
will publish lives of musicians by critics of very little if any
real ability, yet entirely neglect works which Grove's *Dictionary
of Music* tells them are " epoch-making," " the chief modern
authority," or " the best critical biography." (Even Grove
himself, the best musical dictionary we have in English,
will devote an article to a song-writer on the level of Maude
Valerie White or Frank Lambert, but ignore a French or
German critic of the standing of Ernest Newman.) They
will also publish a translation of the life of a brilliant French
writer—a life which has been quite ordinary—but not the
brilliant writings of the author himself.

As regards personal dealings with publishers, after laborious
research in the British Museum (which, though it has taken
many months and is by no means yet finished, I have enjoyed
immensely and which has widened my knowledge consider-
ably), I have been able to send to various London publishing-
houses written lists of the finest books in French and German
of the past ten or twenty years which have not yet been translated into English. The subjects are History, Memoirs,

Biography, Philosophy, Religion, Music, Theatre, Novels (Art and Travel I have not yet explored). The publishers have been eighteen in number, and each firm has had lists of books sent them of the kind in which they are in the habit of dealing. My authorities have been the *Encyclopædia Britannica*, the Cambridge Histories, Larousse, Brockhaus, and various Histories of Literature, etc. Each book has been looked up in the Catalogues of the B.M. to see whether translated or not, and I have examined about three-quarters of the books themselves, to verify their excellence, etc. I don't think I could have been more thorough, although I may have been entirely on the wrong tack. Still, I thought the sending of such lists would be a better introduction and some reason for writing rather than simply asking for translation work. I have introduced myself, with qualifications, to each firm. Perhaps you can tell me if and where I have gone wrong, for *all* the lists have been returned unwanted. Some publishers were curt and snappy ; others cold and supercilious ; others just polite. The only one who took any real interest and discussed the works I mentioned was Hamish Hamilton. He promised by letter to read a very good biography of Catharine de' Medici by Mariéjol, which I recommended him, and promised me the job if he decided to take it on. Alas ! I heard no more from him. Spanish I have not tackled properly yet, although there is a whole literature in that quarter unknown to England. I have never dropped my Spanish, and my master told me when he saw me off by train from Barcelona—and wept, poor old dear !—that although I could not *speak* it fluently, I *knew* the language better than many Spaniards. Financially, my knowledge of Spanish has yielded me exactly ten-and-sixpence—for the translation of a stupid aria ! But I have never given it up, and I find that running over Spanish irregular verbs is an infallible cure for insomnia ! But it is all very discouraging. In 1934 I made exactly £49 1*s.* 10*d.*, less than the wage of an office boy. And 1934 won't come again and one doesn't grow younger.

Present Discontents. These are few, but acute. I am worried and terribly depressed because I have no work or signs of work. At the present hour, six P.M., and as it grows dark, I sit in my room in my overcoat, two pairs of socks and one pair of gloves, and pretend I am warm, as there is no money for a fire. As there are no pennies for the gas-meter either,

I make shift to read by a candle a German work on the Religions of the World! (How like me!) I have not decided whether the chapter on Mediæval Monasticism or on Buddhist Speculation more nearly befits my condition. I shall probably decide to-night, as I think it is going to snow. Wherefore, laying aside all malice, and all guile, and hypocrisie, and envie, and all evil speakings—I shall be much pleased if you will stir your old stumps and find me some work. At fifty-five one wants the ordinary creature comforts, which borough councillors, haulage contractors, undertakers, and other of the world's scavengers seem to enjoy without let or hindrance.

Ever yours,

EDWARD

P.S. I came across a sentence the other day that will please you. It is the last in *Les Caractères* of La Bruyère and runs : " Si l'on ne goûte point ces ' Caractères,' je m'en étonne ; et si on les goûte, je m'en étonne de même." What a good work! Jock shall decide for us whether it is as good as the " Characters " of Theophrastus written one thousand years earlier, and which La Bruyère translated.

March 4   After a week-end of solemn thought, a decision and
Monday.   a re-decision, an orgy of boat-burning, and a frenzy
             of re-building boats, I now come to the conclusion
of the whole matter *in re* Robey's daring to play Falstaff in
Henry IV : Part One. Regretfully but finally, I must believe
that Sydney Carroll's casting must be, in the nature of things
and arguing from first principles, impermissible. It is all very
well to say that the clowns in Shakespearian plays were played
by buffoons like Tarleton who spent half their time dancing
round performing bears, and that therefore they should be
played by to-day's music-hall comedians. There is muddled
thinking of two kinds here. First, Falstaff is not a clown in
the sense that Dogberry is. Second, the parallel would only
hold if it were the custom to give the comic parts in a modern
tragedy to music-hall artists. What exactly happened at His
Majesty's Theatre ? Robey came on to the stage rightly determined to be as much Falstaff as possible, and as little the familiar
George. But he is only human like the rest of us ; he just could

not resist evoking old laughter in such a line as : " What doth
gravity out of his bed at midnight ? " in the third word of which
he broadened the vowel as, on his wonted stage, he broadens
it in his stories of Nottingha-am and of the Man who Ba-anks
at Co-ox's. This, of course, proved irresistible, and the audience
did not resist it. But it was also purely naughty. Again, there
were occasions when the harking back to the vaudeville mood
was involuntary, in the sense that Robey had recourse to it
to cover up the gaps when he was waiting for his words. Actually
he knew his lines ; they were in his mind, but slow in tumbling
out of it. Illusion in the theatre is like a wall of nursery bricks
which, built up block by block, can be demolished at a blow.
Even if George's lapse in each kind, voluntary and enforced,
was only 5 per cent. of the whole performance—and on the
first night it was perhaps rather more—the resulting 10 per
cent. was enough to ruin it as a performance of Shakespeare's
Falstaff.

Yet without lapses of any sort I cannot believe that the thing
was feasible. Ivor Brown has said that, however skilfully Charlie
Chaplin were to play Hamlet, we should still be conscious of
the moustache, the cane, and the boots. If Nellie Wallace were
as good an actress as, say, Kitty Clive, she could not, at this
time of day and because of her other glory, be accepted as Maria
in *Twelfth Night* ; one would all the time be conscious of that
stringy boa and wilting hat. What is sauce for the goose is
sauce for the gander, and though Robey does heroically I can
no more believe in his Falstaff than I would believe in Dean
Inge's Yorick. He is without the depth of philosophy to cope,
for example, with the reflection upon the ragged army, and is
unable to speak the lines : " Tut, tut, good enough to toss,
food for powder, food for powder, they'll fill a pit as well as
better : tush, man, mortal men, mortal men." There is doom
here, and a sense of the sadness of things, and he who speaks
of it is the Falstaff who would not have Doll Tearsheet remind
him of his end. Take again the scene in which Falstaff, pretending
to change places with the Prince, asks if he remembers a virtuous
man of noble carriage—both a's lengthened, if you please !—and

then has the words : " And now I remember me, his name is
Falstaff. If that man should be lewdly given, he deceiveth me."
When this is Shakespeare the lewdness is merely Elizabethan ;
in Robey's mouth the words suffer a sea, or rather music-hall,
change into something rich and strange ; wondrously rich, it
goes without saying, but strangely alien to Shakespeare.

People will doubtless flock to see the experiment, and many
will like it. Sydney is not to be blamed for his freakish casting
of the principal part ; I don't see how otherwise this play should
be expected to attract. Apart from Falstaff it has always seemed
to me on the dull side. Does anybody really care about those
Plantagenet wars which contrived to be pettifogging, civil,
internecine, and guerilla at the same time ? Part One always
seems to me enormously inferior to Part Two. Hotspur is
always singled out for admiration though to me his tirades are
something tedious, and I very much prefer his counterpart in
the sequel, which is Pistol. Has any commentator ever pointed
out that Shakespeare probably invented Pistol to keep the noise
going, and because he could not allow that sail which had bellied
so eloquently in Part One to flap against the mast in Part Two ?
And then again perhaps I prefer Pistol to Hotspur because he is
" louder and funnier."

March 5   Luncheon at the Savoy of the Grand Committee
Tuesday.   for the Marie Tempest matinée. Everybody there,
               including J. M. Barrie, who in accents drugged with
mawkishness made reference to Mary's toes. An unhappy
variant of the *Kiss for Cinderella* mood. Mary cried, and somebody wondering whether the tears were real, I said, " Of course
they're real ; everybody knows she can cry off the stage." And
I told them the story of how Willie Browne came down to
breakfast one Sunday morning to find Mary in floods of tears
and screaming, " James Agate says I can't cry, and damn it,
he's right ! " She looked lovely to-day in a hat of white kid,
chic as that worn by Donatello's David. Sat next to Athene
Seyler, who reported Lilian Braithwaite as saying about some
actress who has had too many failures recently : " Of course

she's a good actress. [Pause.] But somehow she seems to have lost the knack ! " Athene says that Lilian is the most literally minded woman living. She says exactly what she thinks, and this in an insincere world passes for, and is, wit.

March 11   Once again I find myself alone in my opinion, and
Monday.   it doesn't worry me in the slightest.   Every film
             critic in London has given enormous praise to W. C.
Fields's impersonation of Mr Micawber in the Metro-Goldwyn-Mayer film of *David Copperfield*. It is my unshakable opinion that this is the only blot on a film which is very fine so far as it goes. (" Are tears the dewdrops of the heart ? " Can that be even a reasonable presentation of this book which omits not only Miss Mills but the waiter who was content to lose on the ink, the breeder of Suffolk punches, Mr Creakle, Mr Mell, Mrs Crupp, Miss Mowcher, Mr Spenlow, Mr Henry Spiker, Hamlet's Aunt, Mrs Steerforth, Rosa Dartle, Traddles, and the elder Miss Larkins ?)

I have long had a great admiration for Fields as a buffoon, but I do not feel that he is or ever can be Mr Micawber. Chesterton has said : " There is a peculiar quality as of celestial pre-existence about the Dickens characters. Not only did they exist before we heard of them, they existed also before Dickens heard of them."   Now one of the things which were ordained before ever Time or Chaos was is the gentility of Mr Micawber. Not so much gentility itself as gentility's aura. He is silent about his family, whereas Mrs Micawber is eloquent about hers, and from this deductions may possibly be drawn. But this does not alter the fact that Mr Micawber's fundamental and initial trait is his air of breeding. Consider the facts. He wore an imposing shirt-collar in which he was in the habit of settling his chin ; Fields wears a collar which no more imposes than does Grock's, he never settles his chin in it, it is an incongruous piece of furniture, and we feel that it would not be there but that the character may not be portrayed without it. " Mr Micawber," said Mr Quinion, " is known to Mr Murdstone " ; Fields's Micawber would not be allowed within a mile of that

august personage. Mr Micawber was a monument of conde-
scension ; Fields would not patronise a fly, though he would
breathe on it in a beery way. Mr Micawber's house in Windsor
Terrace " was shabby like himself but also, like himself, made all
the show it could " ; Fields makes no show, for he has no atom
of personal vanity and we wonder what the absurd clothes
are all about. Young David received the impression that Mr
Micawber had been an officer in the Marines ; Fields suggests
a retired bo'sun. David washed his hands and face " to do the
greater honour to his (Mr Micawber's) gentility." Fields's
Micawber would have washed his hands and face to do honour
to Master Copperfield's gentility. Mr Micawber carried his
gentility with him to the debtors' prison : " There was a club
in the prison, in which Mr Micawber, as a gentleman, was a
great authority." When next he turned up it was " with his
eyeglass, and his walking-stick, and his shirt-collar, and his
genteel air, and the condescending roll in his voice, all complete ! " In the middle of his denunciation of Heep we read
of his " genteelly adjusting his chin in his cravat." And when
we finally take leave of him as he sets out for Australia in " a
complete suit of oilskin, and a straw-hat with a very low crown,
pitched or caulked on the outside," he still maintains " the old
genteel air," folds his arms in a resolute manner, and " stands
as if he were then stationed on the figure-head."

I do not mind so much that Fields is short whereas Mr
Micawber was tall. Or that Fields has a mop of hair whereas
Mr Micawber was so completely bald as to have the notion
that Nature had fitted him to be a Judge and even, stimulated
by the partiality of Mrs Micawber, " saw himself, in his judicial
mind's eye, on the Woolsack." What I mind very much is
the lack of education in the actor's voice, and in place of that
condescending roll the rich encrusted accents of the music-hall.
Mr Micawber had a little Latin and a little less Greek ; Fields
has nothing but gags. Mr Micawber was both voluble and
volatile ; Fields has to grope for his words, and has, possibly
in consequence, a continuous air of being slightly at a loss, like
Robey with his Shakespeare. In a famous passage Mrs Micawber

expressed the conviction that Mr Micawber's manners peculiarly qualified him for the Banking business. My still firmer conviction is that Fields's manners peculiarly disqualify him from the Micawber business. In this film he gives a magnificent impersonation not of Dickens's character but of Ally Sloper, whose bulbous nose and watery eye he reproduces to perfection.

March 17 Bought a bright bay pony with four white feet who
Sunday. looks like making a fine mover. Shall call him
           " Ego."

April 2 Bought a new car—Humber 12. Very pretty colour,
Tuesday. almond with green wings. Chose this shade so as
           to be able to spot it in car parks and after theatre.
Arthur and I have parted company. One has no right to stand in a man's way however much one likes him. Have taken on a new man. Very small, but so is the car.

April 13 An absurd and irritating day, the absurdity con-
Saturday. sisting in my allowing myself to be irritated. A
            hundred and one things to do before I can get
away on what I insist on calling my Easter holiday. This means that between now and next Saturday I have to write 1 *Express* article, 1 leader page article for the *D.E.*, 1 preface for a book of Cape's, 1 *Tatler* article, and 1 *S.T.* article about any general subject, there being no new plays, and to attend and speak at a dinner in Birmingham. Just as I was getting ready to start Eiluned Lewis got through on the 'phone. She was nervous about this week's stuff, in which I say that you couldn't cast Henry Arthur Jones's *The Liars* to-day because the nearest the modern actress can get to a lady is the mannequin. Eiluned was quite justified in getting hot and bothered; the article *is* a bit of a snorter. No time for breakfast, and round about two at the Savage bolted some tough boiled mutton and raw turnips while one of our chattier members recounted at greater length and complexity than any Variations Brahms ever wrote how he met Marie Dressler on William Hearst's ranch in California. Called

at *S.T.* and got my article through *as I wrote it !* 4.45 and light not too good. Joggled down to Thorpe Bay, where Winsor was waiting on the tee. Held back by couple in front, an annoying matron with, and proud of, a son who, Winsor tells me, has only been playing a fortnight. If they would let us through we could get past the four-ball match in front, charming old walruses who naturally don't see the fun of giving way to Female and Offspring. We take an hour to play six holes, by which time I am 4 down. Finally Female waves us on, but by this time the game is ruined and we take $2\frac{1}{2}$ hours to complete a round we normally do in $1\frac{3}{4}$ hours. Winsor becomes dormy 5, but I take him to the seventeenth green. Am ridiculously disturbed at being unable to hold my own at a half. Time was when I would back myself at these odds against any pro. in England, on any course. And to think that now I cannot hold my own with the assistant on a potty little mud-heap like Thorpe Bay. As Marie Lloyd used to sing : " I can't forget the days when I was young ! " Carminati, the head-waiter here, brought balm to me at dinner, and Irvine, the wine-waiter and second in command, solace. They are the most understanding, considerate, and kindly pair I have ever met. That brute, Fred Leigh, just laughed at me, and said I ought to be thankful that golf matches are decided on points. Like most Colossuses, he is the gentlest of souls, and at any hint of illness or low spirits comes lumbering up with the solicitude of a mother-elephant.

April 14   Went to bed last night at 10.30, utterly whacked,
Sunday.   and very nearly slept the clock round. Composed
              costume suitable for gent on fine Sunday at Southend
in April. Light blue shirt and collar, same colour stockings, violet and maroon tie, sporting small check jacket and waistcoat, Harris tweed plus fours large check, soft light-brown felt hat, old brown shoes, nondescript handkerchief, and monocle. Opening exchanges at breakfast :

ME.   Morning, Fred. How do you like the *tout ensemble* ?

F. L.   Too much toot, James, and not enough of the other thing !

April 15   Motored to Birmingham, where I was the guest of
Monday.   honour at the Shakespeare dinner of the Central
             Literary Society. The Lord Mayor intimated at the
beginning of the proceedings that he couldn't stay late. But
did that shorten the early speeches ? No ! The loquacious fellow
who proposed the toast of The Immortal Memory took thirty-
seven minutes over it ! Just when my turn came the Lord Mayor
said he was sorry it was past his bedtime and left, taking the
Lady Mayoress with him. I was so angry that I made a magnificent speech out of pure pique. There had been a boxing jam-
boree in the town, and the hotel was full of notabilities of the
ring, including Jimmy Wilde, now a tiny, stoutish, baldish, figure
to whom the aura of greatness still clings. When young, Jimmy
looked old beyond his years ; now he is old he has reverted to
babyhood. To me he is a figure of glory never to be dimmed.
We had some pleasant talk, for his modesty is boundless as his
fame. He has accepted back-numberhood with philosophy.

April 26   A mixed evening, yesterday, which began with
Friday.   confusing two phials which have stood on my
             dressing-table for months. One is a Heppel con-
coction for waking the dead, and the other a sleeping draught
left over from some illness. Desiring to be in good form for
the theatre followed by Dorothy Ward's party, I made a dive
for the Heppel and realised afterwards that I had grabbed the
wrong bottle. By midnight I was fully awake again and thoroughly ready for the party, which consisted of Dorothy herself,
radiant in sky-blue satin and tangerine hair, Delysia with four
rows of pearls against shoulders gleaming like Cornish cream,
Vi Loraine with a nose which is the Supreme Architect's masterpiece in putty, that combination of ship's figure-head and old
war-horse which is Bertha Belmore, and Vera Pearce, deliciously
explaining how in inoculating her some surgeon had broken
his entire stock of needles against an impregnable thigh. And a
lot more people, so that I had the sensation of really Seeing Life.
    Spent from half-past three till four in the morning trying
to dissuade young Peter Glenville from playing lead in a play

on Rossetti which Nancy Price has in hand. Reminded him how Gyles Isham would have done better on the London stage if he had not made such a handsome beginning at Oxford. I hear, by the way, that Gyles, whom the Garbo has chosen for leading man in her next picture, writes from Hollywood to say that he has been there six weeks and that the most he has so far seen of the goddess is the tail of her skirt disappearing through a distant doorway.

May 7
Tuesday.
That there has been no mention of nerves and golf lately does not mean that I have not been indulging in both. Am ignoring the nerves. After not touching a club for weeks have taken the game up again with as much zest as ever. But less skill. To-day I played the worst round of my life, hitting *every* drive off the neck of the club and sending the ball ten yards to square leg.

Have been reading Dame Ethel Smyth's good little book on Beecham. Years ago I was lunching at the Waldorf, having vaguely noticed that at the table behind me was a party of ill-kempt, unwashable as distinct from unwashed, tramps whom I took to be the members of an orchestra. Suddenly I heard a silky, purring voice say, " Gentlemen, you may take it from me that Brahms never wrote anything that mattered." Without looking round I said loudly, " Nonsense, Sir Thomas ! " Instantly the voice resumed, " Gentlemen, you may take it from me that with the exception of four symphonies, four concertos, two hundred songs, and a vast quantity of chamber music, Brahms never wrote anything that mattered ! " It was in my father's dining-room that my brother Edward persuaded Beecham to give his first concert in Manchester. Delius's *Sea Drift* was in the programme. The attendance in the Free Trade Hall was under two hundred.

Dame Ethel devotes the second half of her book to her adventures in Egypt, including the laying-out of a nine-hole golf course in the Nubian desert and her investigation into the nature of a hermaphrodite. But she does not say whether the hermaphrodite played golf, or what was its handicap !

May 10   Motored from Southend to B'ham, avoiding London
Friday.   and going round by Bishop's Stortford and Bedford.
              Wired Albert to say I was coming and telling him to
get the animals shod. Jock, checking the telephone operator,
was just in time to overhear and stop her sending a telegram
ordering the animals to be *shot* !

May 12   Brother Mycroft was in excellent form yesterday.
Sunday.   He told the chauffeur that he drove too fast on
              crowded roads, and also told Albert that he drove
the horses too fast on the hard ground. Instructed all of us in
the topography of the place though he had never been there
before, and wound up by finding fault with the local railway
time-table. After much telephoning with stationmasters they
were forced to agree that *Mycroft was right* and that a fast train
from Birmingham to Manchester, which was not in the local
guide, did in fact run on Sundays !

May 29   The *Daily Express* asked me to do an impression
Wednesday.   of the Rattenbury trial at the Old Bailey. The
              facts were very simple and hardly disputed. Mrs
Rattenbury, aged thirty-eight, wife of an architect aged sixty-
seven, had been the mistress of her eighteen-year-old chauffeur
named Stoner. Somebody had hit the husband over the head
with a mallet, both of them having at one time or another taken
the blame on themselves.
    It was all very like the three French major novelists. The
way in which the woman debauched the boy so that he slept
with her every night with her six-year-old son in the room,
and the husband, who had his own bedroom, remaining cynically
indifferent—all this was pure Balzac. In the box Mrs Rattenbury
looked and talked exactly as I have always imagined Emma
Bovary looked and talked. Pure Flaubert. And last there
was that part of her evidence in which she described how, trying
to bring her husband round, she first accidentally trod on his
false teeth and then tried to put them back into his mouth so
that he could speak to her. This was pure Zola. The sordidness

of the whole thing was relieved by one thing and one only. This was when Counsel asked Mrs Rattenbury what her first thought had been when her lover got into bed that night and told her what he had done. She replied, "My first thought was to protect him." This is the kind of thing which Balzac would have called sublime, and it is odd that, so far as I saw, not a single newspaper reported it.

All the time I was sitting there, there was something at the back of my mind which gave a picture of the woman in the dock better than the parallel with Emma. I couldn't think what it was, but on getting home told Jock, who found what I was looking for in my old *Manchester Guardian* cutting-book. The passage is part of a notice by Montague :

> The Lady Ellingham of the play is animated by Mrs Campbell into one of the women whom she acts as a class rather than individually—so that her acting almost seems like an argument, a theory of femininity, like Matthew Arnold's about "things that live and move Mined by the fever of the soul." Her Lady Ellingham seems, behind all that she directly says, to be asserting the title of a certain temperament to more of the good things of the emotional world than it commonly gets ; the appealing lassitude, the troubled and plaintive tenderness all seem like changing modes following some one quest.

The general opinion appears to be that the woman will get off.

May 31   Mrs Rattenbury acquitted and Stoner condemned
Friday.   to death. The second must not happen. If I had
             been on the jury I would have stuck out for a verdict
of manslaughter, bad though that would have been in law, because there is no certainty that the recommendation to mercy, made in this case, will be given effect to. Such a recommendation should automatically mean that the man will not hang. In its account of the last scene *The Daily Sketch* has this cryptic sentence : " A mere boy, but it may be that he behaved as a man behaves." What a rum thing is the mind ! This trial has moved me immensely, probably because I saw part of it, while the dreadful

affair at Quetta makes no impression. The 20,000 said to have
perished in that earthquake might be flies. I see no remedy
for this ; one can't order one's feelings, and to pretend something
different is merely hypocrisy. I suppose one could just shut up
and perhaps ought to. Meanwhile the Rattenbury verdict,
happening in the afternoon, has given an immense fillip to
Emlyn Williams's *Night Must Fall*, a good, highly imaginative
play about a murder in an Essex bungalow.

June 5   To-morrow is the National Hackney Show, and
Wednesday.   the fever of waiting, which has endured since
                  Altrincham last September, is ended at last. Eight
months of getting ready. It is an immense strain, and the result
of disobeying the maxim : " Le plaisir est comme la glace.
Glissez, mortels, n'appuyez pas ! " I can never remember the
exact form of this, or who said it.

As we were setting off in the car the newspapers came out
with the placard : " Mrs Rattenbury Stabbed and Drowned."
Reggie Arkell said this was the most dramatic thing he had
seen in the streets since " Titanic Sinking." The two things of
this kind which have shocked me most have been the arrest of
Crippen, about which I read on the pier at Llandudno—I can
still point out the exact plank on which I stood—and the newspaper
placard announcing the death of Marie Lloyd. I remember
how this rooted me to the pavement in Tottenham Court Road.

June 8   Appalling weather throughout yesterday and the
Saturday.   day before. Torrential rain and an icy gale blow-
                  ing. The show-yard a sea of mud which pulled the
goloshes off my shoes. The horses floundered about with mud
up to their knees and hocks and cloaking their white fetlocks,
and the waggons churning up the ground and sending out
sprays of porridge. Everybody miserable, and some question
of cancelling the show. However, they went on with it, and at
night the horses had to stand in six inches of water and could
not lie down, while the grooms had to do the best they could.
The boxes were like the bed of a river. In the circumstances

we did pretty well, Black Tulip getting second. Ego stood second for a long time, but the mud proved too much for his strength and in the end he was placed fourth. But I am convinced that he is my best animal, and he created a great impression. The classes were the strongest for many years.

June 10
Monday.
King's Heath Horse Show. Tulip terribly fresh and excited and for a long time refused to settle. I think it was the cries of the hundreds of children round the ring which upset her. When she did at last settle she gave a magnificent display, and having been pulled in last went right to the top and won first prize and champion twenty-guinea cup.

A little worried during the day by signs of nervous exhaustion in the right hand. At one minute I could not lift a teacup, at the next I could and did pick up a sledge-hammer. Worried because in the evening I had to write my *Express* article by hand and didn't know whether I should be able to manage it. Put the thought out of my mind with an effort and ultimately managed all right.

June 11
Tuesday.
Smethwick Horse Show. Same horses, different result. Tulip went so high off her hocks that she couldn't go in front, which made her break continually. Brilliant snatches of forty yards or so, but never once round the ring, or even half of it. Tulip is a temperamental madam and played hell in the train both going to and coming from Weymouth and again in the motor horse-box to-day. Ego has lost so much condition through the Weymouth experience that we have decided not to take him to Richmond and to keep him for Olympia.

June 13
Thursday.
Decidedly not our lucky week. Tulip gave a beautiful show at Richmond, going particularly well up and down the stand. Never broke once. Nanette headed the class and then came Nork Spotlight, Nigel Colman's new stallion. I don't care for his legs and feet, and,

being a stallion, he is too cresty and too thick in the jaw. But he is a tremendously gay little horse with lashings of front action and more presence than I have ever seen in an animal under 15 hands. He was rightly placed. In the opinion of ringsiders Tulip was an easy third, but the judge preferred Wensleydale Madge, which was below us at Altrincham last time out. Showing is a rum business. Second at the National, first and cup at King's Heath, an abominable show and third at Smethwick, and now fourth at Richmond! Like golf, showing is " Aye fechtin' agin ye." But I never liked Tulip better than to-day, and so I told Albert. After which we drowned our sorrows in cold salmon, strawberries and cream, and hock.

June 23   Motored to Brighton and at the Royal Albion un-
Sunday.   fortunately fell in with Monty and St John Hutchinson.
                 Unfortunately because they had been festivating at Glyndebourne, about which I have " views "—all the stronger because I have never been there ! Something tells me that there is as much intellectual snobbery here as there is social snobbery at Ascot. This is not invalidated by the fact that the operas are exquisitely done ; there is often very good racing at Ascot. The bee in my bonnet is that people go to Glyndebourne because it is the musico-intellectual thing to do. But I do not believe that they would go if it could not afterwards be known that they had gone, if they had to see and hear the operas through a leper's squint and not show themselves or talk about it afterwards. They make much play with the fact that Mozart is produced at Glyndebourne as nowhere else, that such singing and playing cannot be heard elsewhere. This again doesn't wash with me. People who are real theatre-lovers are always going to the theatre and not waiting for the transcendent visiting star. It's the old highbrow business of pretending that the wireless is not worth hearing because the real thing is better. And I honestly doubt whether the people who make so much fuss about Glyndebourne are sufficiently fond of Mozart to tune in to him at home and spend an evening silently listening to an opera with none of their co-intellectuals to see how enthralled

they are. Do they, as Jock and I do, go to the fag of changing
gramophone records to hear a Mozart symphony? I suppose
in the last two years we must have played the E flat and the
little C Major fifty times. It is true to say that neither of us can
live without music, because whenever we have a spare minute
and can find nothing good on the wireless we rush to the
gramophone. Whereas I feel that your musico-intellectual
cannot live without other people knowing that he cannot live
without music! I absolve Monty and Hutchy from these
charges because I know that both are genuinely fond of Mozart.
But I can't help using them as whipping-boys for my *bêtes noires*,
which of course is wildly tactless on my part and shocking
manners. I forget exactly what insults I hurled at them over
Harry Preston's lobsters, but remember Hutchy saying that
it was a pity I didn't know any intellectuals, and my very nearly
retorting that if he was a specimen I didn't want to! In fact,
the row was as undignified as if we were three third-form boys.
At least my side of it was, for I began it and lost my temper,
whereas Hutchy and Monty kept theirs admirably.

June 25   I am in the condition known as licking one's wounds.
Tuesday.   This as the result of the horse show at Olympia. On
             the first day of the show in the morning try-out of
the class for novice ponies under 14 hands Ego was placed
absolutely last! This was quite right. We have known all
along that he is not a pony, and we ought to have waited to
show him until he has grown over 14 hands, which we think
he will do before August as he is exactly 14 hands now and
has grown more than an inch in the last three months. In a
class full of real ponies he looked like a small giraffe, and in
addition was horribly narrow and tucked-up as the result of
Weymouth. Also he went very sluggishly and was so obviously
not himself that we took his temperature and found it to be 103.
We got leave not to show him in the afternoon and packed the
poor little chap off home.

    Then yesterday a dreadful thing happened. The general
opinion seemed to be that in the open class under 15 hands

Tulip would be second to Nanette. The judges, however, thought otherwise. In the morning try-out they first of all pulled her in fifth and after she had given a grand show up and down the stand sent her down to sixth. They seemed so determined not to like Tulip that Albert and I debated whether or not to send her in for the show proper in the afternoon. But we decided, wrongly as it turned out, to do the sporting thing. Jock suggests that as Tulip cannot do better than last but one I should change her name to Penultima Thulip!

June 26   Stoner reprieved.   340,000 people signed the
Wednesday.   petition.

The other day I said in the *Express* that Henry James " would not last ten minutes on this paper, not because James wrote too well but because he did not write well enough." I was making the point that a man must suit his style to his medium, and that in a journalist the first essential is to say what he intends without any possibility of misunderstanding. I thought at the time that the passage was dangerous, but decided to risk it. This has brought the family down on me in the person of Brother Edward:

June 22nd, 1935

Twit! Twit! Henry James wouldn't be on the *Daily Express ten* minutes! For one thing he'd never have had his article ready; for another, he'd have been too frightened. But put the converse: is there anyone who could stay on the front page of the *Times Literary Supplement* for *two* minutes, let alone five years, among the celebrities of the *Daily Express*? You ought to be fair!

How Henry James would have beautifully laughed!

I am sorry if you must do this sort of thing to eke out your living!

EDWARD

June 29   Tulip made a great show at Sutton Coldfield,
Saturday.   winning first and champion cup and beating an
                  animal put three above her at Olympia.

July 1   My brother Edward is in great form these days :
Monday.

28th June 1935.

Why do people laugh when I tell them I am reading *The Laws of Peace and War* by Grotius (published in 1625) ? They do not laugh if I say I am reading Lord Birkenhead's recent book on International War. ("Very interesting," they say; "sure to become a classic; what a brain!") Yet on nearly every page of Birkenhead's book he sends you back to refer to Grotius as his authority; his own work being an amalgam of the two older masters, merely brought up to date to include the Great War!

Why do people snigger when I tell them I am reading de Tillemont's *Histoire des Empereurs* or his *History of the Church during the first six centuries*? They only half snigger if I say I am reading *The Decline and Fall*. And yet Gibbon got most of his information from the old Frenchman who died in 1698—and acknowledges the fact !

Why do people guffaw when I tell them I am reading the *Voyage to the Moon*, by Godwin, the model of *Cyrano de Bergerac* and Swift ? I will throw in Lucian and Voltaire as make-weight. But no one smiles if you say you are reading Jules Verne's wizardry, or the fantastics of Wells !

Why do people shun you on hearing that you read Fontenelle's *Dialogues of the Dead* (1685), the leading idea borrowed avowedly from our old friend Lucian ? And Fénelon copied the scheme, and Landor followed suit. But if one reads Landor, one is learned, certainly, but still just within the pale, not as yet a pariah !

Ever yours,

EDWARD

July 4   A filthy two days. Started on Tuesday morning
Thursday.   with food poisoning, but insisted on going to
              Lord's for the S. African Test Match. Chose a seat
near the gents' place, where I could be sick *ad lib.*, and freely availed myself. Unfortunately Lord's very draughty, and spent yesterday in an agony of rheumatism in neck and shoulder in addition to the unabated other thing. Sent for doctor last night, who prescribed castor oil. Better this morning, having

spent two days wondering if I should ever be able to work again, etc. etc.

I think this ought to be set down. The management of the Regal Cinema announced the other day the personal appearance of a Miss Marcia Marsh, described as "Dillinger's girl friend." Dillinger, it had better be recorded, was America's most notorious gangster last year. Ushered in by the usual hugaboo proper to these occasions, Miss Marsh presented herself as a pleasing vision in flamingo red, silver shoon, and the flossiest possible platinum mop. All that she could be prevailed upon to say, however, after the usual expressions of gratification at being in our midst, was the following, which Jock wrote down verbatim: "I was *not* Dillinger's girl friend—I just went around with him!"

Logically I cannot justify being uppish about this sort of thing as I spent lunch-time at the Holborn Restaurant to-day poring over the Mahon Case in the *Evening Standard*'s series of Avory's Trials. If I must have my drug, why shouldn't people of less education have theirs? By the way, Jock tells me that an intimate enemy of mine said the other day, "Of course James likes Southend. It's the one place where he can be sure of finding people commoner than himself!"

July 8   The post this morning brought me the following
Monday.   skit on Walt Whitman. It is in Brother Edward's
             best vein and in my view exactly hits off the
old ruffian:

Walt Whitman to his Friend

I

O Popanax! My beloved!
Tell me how to greet thee!
Arms a'stretch or a'kimbo,
Ear taut to the ground for the echo of footsteps,
    Squirrel-like, panting, awaiting;
Or more manly and reserved,
In accordance with common decency?
    (I can do it either way.)
        O Popanax, tell me how to greet thee!

II

O Popanax! My beloved!
Tell me how to woo thee!
Shall I caress thee as the porpoises churn the water
    Till they grow tired?
Wilt thou strip and race with me on the wave-beleaguered
        sands,
Or must I tarry, till the whippoorwill cries
    Orchestrally in Alabama,
Before I cling to thee—we two alone—
    Acrobatically performing?
    (You must wait—you see I am not ready!)
    O Popanax! Shall I put it in writing?

III

O Popanax! My beloved!
Tell me how to love thee!
I have heard the march of Mohawks;
    (In Longfellow—the old curmudgeon—
    Or was it before the French Revolution?)
I have drummed taps upon Americanos' bums;
(Goethe boasted he did something of the sort on his Italian
        Journey—
You can never be sure of these Germans!)
I have seen Walden's woods hatchet-bent
    To the muscular form;
I have heard sea-gulls crying when the moon was low;
I have sat as nurse by side of bed-racked soldiers,
    Comforting them with a kiss (purely maternal, I would not
        hurt them),
    And taken their last Envoi
    To their grandmothers;
But never have I met the absolute
            "Yes."
    Shall I divine it
    Among your moustachios?

                                                    E. A.

July 22   Sumptuous day of wind, nerves, asthma, etc., ending
Monday.   with the doctor coming at two in the morning to
               give an adrenalin injection.

July 23
Tuesday.   Absurdly weak, and have to sacrifice the Royal Welsh Show at Haverfordwest, to which I have been immensely looking forward. Instead motor to Southend and try a few shots with the new driver, brassie, and spoon Winsor has been making for me. One shot with brassie 220 yards uphill against wind: pretty good for man *in extremis.* After which nothing satisfies me but must seek out local doctor to ask if really am *in extremis.* Find delightful boy, a locum, with a bright, stove-like smile like Moray McLaren.

DOCTOR. What's wrong?

J. A. Funk.

DOCTOR. Let's just run you over. (*Does so and begins to laugh.*)

J. A. What's funny?

DOCTOR. You haven't half got an aortic lesion. I could hear it a mile off!

J. A. It's compensating, isn't it?

DOCTOR. It's compensating all right. But it's a hell of a lesion! I'm not much of a doctor. Only two years in practice, as a matter of fact, but I should have recognised your trouble on my first day at the hospital.

J. A. But it's not my heart that's worrying me. I know all about that.

DOCTOR (*contrite*). Sorry. What *is* wrong?

J. A. Sheer funk. Think I'm going to drop down in my tracks.

DOCTOR. When?

J. A. Now. Any time.

DOCTOR. Not with that heart you won't. You'll have lots of warning. Swelled ankles, easily tired, out of puff, all sorts of things. In the meantime don't play golf in the sun.

J. A. I don't. I play it damn' well in the shade.

DOCTOR. Ah, Rugby's my game. (*Discussion about merits of both games considered as rivals.*)

J. A. (*resuming*).   What about my stomach ?

DOCTOR.   Oh, just jiggered up generally.   Can't help it with that heart.   I'll give you a sleeping draught and a nerve tonic, and if they don't put you right I've been taught wrong !

July 24   J. A. doesn't take either, sleeps like a log, and
Wednesday.   wakes to go round Thorpe Bay (16 holes) in 66
                    gross.   Sixteen holes only because J. A. cuts out two in the middle through fear of over-tiring himself.   What bilge Cicero and Charles Morgan write about the compensations of old age !

See charming bungalow at Thorpe Bay and decide to make offer.   This means cancelling offer for house in Hampstead.   Do so.   The agent who shows me round the bungalow is pure Dickens.   Calls me " friend," and when I ask whether Thorpe Bay isn't a bit damp in winter—when I shall lock up the house— replies, " Damp ? Not a bit of it.   My father, who had arterio- sclerosis, was nine years in bed in the same avenue ! "   He ends by referring me to a colleague " who has the monotony of bungalows in Thorpe Bay " !

July 29   Have let the flat in Kensington Gardens Square
Monday.   and the house at Barnet, given notice to leave Doughty
                    Street, and taken a flat at Belsize Park and a bungalow at Thorpe Bay.

Worsley Show on Saturday.   Tulip third and should have been second, but Ego romped home in the novice class, every- body liking him immensely and telling me he is the best horse I ever owned.   I don't know how much altitude there was in Hamlet's chopine, but Ego now only wants the thickness of a slipper's sole to take him out of the pony class and put him among the big horses.

Spent the week-end with Brother Mycroft, who was at his most amiable.

Plucked up sufficient courage this morning to get Jock to

sack the chauffeur! The young man may be *sans reproche* as a driver, but for some weeks I have not been *sans peur* as a passenger. I am always having to nod apology to other road-users. Jock reports that this professed bachelor took his dismissal very well, saying that he didn't mind for himself but he was sorry *on account of his wife and two kids*. Peters, always at his cheeriest in time of trouble, told me at lunch that all chauffeurs calling themselves single are married, whereas the "married couples" who go as butler and cook have never seen each other till they meet at the registry office.

Aug. 2   Rang up the Kentish Town Labour Bureau, and
Friday.   informed no chauffeurs on books. I have advertised
           in the *Daily Telegraph* and received twenty wildly unsuitable replies, including one from a fellow whose unique recommendation was that he is a first-class rifle-shot! I think I shall have to imitate a friend of mine who once advertised his house: "This highly undesirable residence with all its hideous appurtenances miles from anywhere and without view, airless and draughty, poky and rambling, with every old-world inconvenience and no sanitation, has THIS to recommend it—it is DIRT-CHEAP." The result was that inquiries poured in, and a really delightful house that nobody would have looked at if it had been advertised in glowing colours was sold in forty-eight hours. Shall therefore insert:

> Wanted: Incompetent, careless chauffeur, unable valet or wait at table, no references, licence handsomely endorsed, educated Borstal, last position Wormwood Scrubs, surly and disobliging, heavy smoker and total imbiber, eleven children, married when suited. Genteel crook preferred, robber without violence not entertained.

The annoying thing about this Southend hotel, where I propose to be in residence for a month, is that from breakfast-table or writing-desk to nearest lavatory is 100 yards or thereabouts. (Arnold Bennett would have chronicled this.) In all other respects the hotel is ideal, and it has a view which Canaletto would have painted.

My failure with that old harridan, *Time and Tide*, is complete. Have courted, and done my best to make conquest of, Sylvia Lynd, Vera Brittain, and Viola Garvin, but alas, all to no purpose! Individually they are dears, together they are the Medusa. And I, in print at any rate, appear to be Anathema. Says Medusa this week :

> Without malice, I think I may say that there are many who dislike Mr Agate as a critic and who cannot stomach his manner of false heartiness or the mess of, so to speak, literary boiled beef and carrots which he places on the bill of fare every Sunday.

This makes me want to imitate Jonathan Wild's young woman who visited him in prison to ask, " Why bitch, Mr Wild ? Why bitch ? " Why " *false* heartiness " ? Is this the result of subduing my lion's roar to Bottom's sucking-dove quality ? By the way, Phyllis Neilson-Terry is still peacocking it as Oberon. I remember last season how Oberon had to make exit round the bend of one of those discreet little paths which, in public parks, disappear into shrubberies. First the King of the Fairies vanished and then, like a serpent, his long and trailing cloak started to negotiate the bend. The man with me, a motor-fan, said in a stage whisper, " He won't do it unless he goes into reverse ! "

Aug. 3   Bout of wind and panic started at midday and
Saturday.   lasted till ten at night. Tried every known remedy,
                physical and spiritual, without effect. Motored to
Creeksea and actually found this very desolate spot on the Essex coast which might be part of an early Conrad story. Watched a barge with brown sails tack against the tide, come to anchor, and make fast almost within hailing distance. But even that didn't lift the depression, which, however, just about bed-time unaccountably cleared. The only measure I can give of these attacks is to say that the wretchedness would not be increased

by a wire saying Tulip had dropped down dead, or lightened by the news that somebody had left me a fortune. Obviously I cannot sit in a theatre in that state, and as it is unlikely I shall ever come out of that state, what is to become of me? Answer: Matches and the street-corner. Unless, of course, I die the same night. And so on and so forth. No other complaint or illness affects me in this way of paralysing the will.

In the meantime sent round to the Labour Exchange for a chauffeur-handyman. Only three turned up, all the others having gone away for the August Bank Holiday! One was patronising, another was your obvious rolling-stone, married but not living with his wife. The third was an orphan, a waif and stray from Durham, father killed in the war, had always lived with his granny. No other relatives except " lots of aunties." Wages? Would take anything, and in addition put up with any conditions of living, hours, work, etc. This, of course, always gets more out of me than the cleverest bargaining, and the Orfling starts on Tuesday.

Aug. 4   Much better to-day, largely owing to the inspiration
Sunday.   of Turkey rhubarb, the friend of my youth. Motored
              to Clacton, my stand-by when I was ill in 1928.
This is the best air in the world. See by the papers that John Tilley is dead. I genuinely feel this. Tilley's buffoonery sprang from his naïve and fumbling mind. It was that timidity of which every man in his heart of hearts knows something making itself vocal, and we all knew kinship with it. An old Scotch caddie, when I asked him what he thought of the relative merits of young Tom Morris and Bobby Jones, answered sternly and reprovingly : " Baith o' them played pairfect gowf." Similarly I never worried about the relative merits of John Tilley and Gillie Potter. Both have tickled me infinitely, and there is no more to be said. Even the staidest of the Sunday papers records that at one period Tilley was a traveller in moth-proof paper-bags! It was exactly this sort of thing with which he would convulse a house.

Aug. 5   In eighteen hundred and heaven knows what Villiers
Monday.   de l'Isle-Adam wrote a Cruel Story entitled *L'Affichage
            Céleste.* This was about " le grand vulgarisateur,"
to wit, the plan to utilise the sky for advertising :

> Il suffit de réfléchir, un tant soit peu, pour concevoir les
> résultats de cette ingénieuse invention. Ne serait-ce pas
> de quoi étonner la Grande Ourse elle-même, si, soudaine-
> ment, surgissait, entre ses pattes sublimes, cette annonce
> inquiétante : *Faut-il des corsets, oui, ou non?*

To-night, on the golf-links and against the setting sun, I
saw an aeroplane with the streamer : " Eat Sharp's Mickey
Mouse Toffee ! "

Aug. 8   Orfling departs. Nice child, but no notion of
Thursday. driving. Temporary chauffeur, an ex-Petty Officer,
            makes a remark which, on one of my bad days, I
should find discouraging. Seeing me cock an eye at a lugubrious
Daimler, he says, " They use 'em for black work. It's an
'earse ! "

Aug. 9   " Change and decay in all around I see," runs the
Friday.   old hymn. This does not apply to first-nighters, in
            whom there is only decay.

Aug. 14   On tour. Enormously impressed with Haworth
Wednesday. Parsonage—the only place of its kind which has not
             disappointed me. The day was dressed to suit,
sombre and cheerless, and the brow on which the house stands
was wind-swept and forbidding. The house is large enough
to have permitted all that secrecy of composition. I was struck,
as always on such occasions, by the deadness of it all. This
actual table, that very chair—these accentuate the physical
aspect of death. The Brontës were far, far deader after I had
seen their relics than they seemed before. With an effort I put
this thought away and took to noting the good taste of everything they handled, the elegance of their china, dresses, shawls,

trinkets, and small possessions. Furious to find that modern carelessness has penetrated even here : somebody's book called *Bride of Quietness* has a typewritten label calling it *Bride of Quiteness*. Peering at and poring over some of Branwell's letters, I got the impression that he might easily have been the master-spirit. Of all the quartet he seemed to be the least dead ; I had the feeling that something of him might still stir in that house. The church, too, was impressive. Emily and Charlotte are buried by the chancel—Anne lies on the hillside at Scarborough —and as one bent down to read the brass tablet the silence of the grave seemed to make itself heard. It is right that these two should be here, at Keighley where they belong, and not in any busier part of the world. I think I should have moped at this point if I had not recalled the sternly exhilarating lines of another Emily :

> Ample make this bed.
> Make this bed with awe ;
> In it wait till judgment break
> Excellent and fair.
>
> Be its mattress straight,
> Be its pillow round ;
> Let no sunrise' yellow noise
> Interrupt this ground.

I have never seen any reference to the odd circumstance of the Brontë parents' double denial of their offspring, the mother's forced because she died when Charlotte was five, and the father's wilful because to the end he believed himself to be the Brontë who counted. The chauffeur had never heard of the sisters, and I told George Mathew we must make allowances : " Neither Charlotte nor Emily would have made head or tail of the internal combustion engine." George said, " Rubbish ! They *were* internal combustion engines ! "

Aug. 15   Ego carried all, or very nearly all, before him at
Thursday.   Bingley yesterday, winning the novice class and
               reserve for champion cup.

Aug. 22   Letter from Jock saying :
Thursday.

It is excellent that I am empowered to be so helpful : an arrangement known to the vegetable world—I seem to remember—as symbiosis. Any slight frigidity in this prose may be put down to the facts (*a*) that London is panting under a heat-wave, and (*b*) that your letter to me this morning was about as impersonal as if it had been directly addressed to your typewriter. But then I suppose I have come greatly to resemble that jaded machine.

Good show at Marton, near Blackpool, yesterday. Ego won two firsts and novice champion cup. Everybody, including all judges, likes this noble horse. I hear on all sides that if he will grow another two inches he is a world-beater. Tulip second in her class. Gave Albert dinner at the Metropole and afterwards to *White Horse Inn*, whose tunes are as captivating as ever. The most remarkable thing in Blackpool is not the view *from*, but the view *in* the Tower—to wit the Ball Room. Seven or eight hundred couples under the coloured lights make a wonderful parterre. A mastery of rhythm such as you don't see in London. Influence of cinema apparent, since every girl is a Garbo, Shearer, Loretta Young, but oddly enough, no examples of Gracie Fields.

Aug. 23   Not so successful at Penistone yesterday. In the
Friday.   open pony class, against all ages, Ego was second,
                   just beaten by Barcroft Belle, champion everywhere.
Tulip, who in the big class was obviously an easy second to Vitality, was put down to fourth, at which the stand gasped. She went gloriously, and the crowd applauded her all round the ground, while she was being shown and after. George Lancaster, who generally carries all before him for Mrs Henriques and was a little disgruntled at only getting two 3rd prizes, said to me when he came out of the ring, " I think, sir, you and I had better be getting back to England ! " An odd thing happened in Ego's class. Some ass had chalked a broad white line at right-angles to the grandstand. Now Ego had never seen anything like this, and every time he had to cross it he shied,

stopped, and then jumped. In so doing his crupper came off twice, and it was a sheer miracle that with a horse so highly strung there was no accident. From his seat in the trap Albert could not see the line, and watching the class was very nervous work. Without this nonsense I am persuaded Ego would have won.

Aug. 26   This burlesque of my Diary manner has just come
Monday.   from Brother Edward :

THE MISSING FORTNIGHT

Monday.   Wire from Albert Throup : " Nogo has tooth-ache." What shall I do ? Publisher writes : " Nogo giving readers headache." What have I done ?

Wednesday.   Sold my tricycle to Hedges and Butler and bought a Rolls-Royce from Mudie's. Shall be able to feed at Scott's and the Carlton simultaneously. Have taken bungalow at Penzance, and Jock has given notice. Haggled for private removal van. Cheaper in the long run. Also the short.

Tuesday.   Great conclave of wits at the Savage. Was mooted : If to be deprived of one toe, which would you prefer ? Am broadcasting about this to-morrow.

Saturday.   Telephone ringing all day *re* toe. Lilley and Skinner, Whipsnade and *Everybody's Weekly* unanimous. Massine less sure.

Tuesday.   Read four novels, five of them rubbish. Albert wires Nogo's tooth extracted at Giggleswick, my dear old school.

Wednesday.   Late lunch at " The Nettle." One cheese-straw and a pint of finger-bowl. Stung for £3 14s. 4d. without tip. Slept till six.

Thursday.   Started hiking for Conway. Am told my sandals go well with cricket blazer. Got as far as Peak Forest. Dreadful bout of wind after bottle of non-vintage Dillinger in Severn Tunnel.

Friday.   Wrote five thousand trains for Continental Brad-shaw. Shrimped at Bognor, then back to Perth.

Saturday.   Insane letter from Edward. Starving. " Les Parents Pauvres " ? *Oui, certes !* Sent him three pounds, and forgot to post it.

Sunday.   Wrote eighty-one thousand words for the new paper *Mice*. And a further eighty-two thousand for my Diary. What a *corvée* life is !

E. A.

Aug. 27   To-day was wet, and Blackpool on a wet day is as
Tuesday.   good a place as any. I spent the morning between
               the sea and the shops, resisting with difficulty the
temptation to buy something flashy in wrist-watches. How
potent cheap jewellery is, as Noel would say.

A wet night at Blackpool is another proposition. It *sogged*
down, and everybody was driven indoors—greatly benefiting
the places of amusement. We chose *Shout for Joy* at the Opera
House. A good turn was one in which four of Louis Quatorze's
courtiers threw two girls from one to another—an essay in
the art of being at once Herculean and mincing. A band of
Mexicans, or some foreign breed, rattled off on piano-accordions
a medley of " Soldiers of the Queen," " Dolly Gray," " Everybody's Doing It," " Alexander's Rag-time Band," " Tipperary,"
" The British Grenadiers," " There's a Long, Long Trail,"
and " Land of Hope and Glory." This was announced as a
selection from Noel Coward's *Cavalcade* ! For an encore the
conductor gave a rousing performance of " The Lost Chord "
on an instrument combining the virtues of cornet, coach-horn,
and tooth-comb. These being acclaimed, the set revolved showing St Cecilia in full blast with a triptych of Opera House angels,
the whole impregnated with Blackpool chic. The audience
was immensely impressed, and I thought it quite pretty. Afterwards a Mr Randolph Sutton asked in three verses how a widower
can thrash an eight-year-old son who, besides being half his
father's weight, has his dead mother's eyes !

Sept. 18   Altrincham. This last of the season's shows
Wednesday.   bears to Richmond and Olympia the same relation
               that the St Leger bears to the Derby. Of all
one-day shows distinction is most coveted here. It was a great
day for Ego, who looked absolutely lovely and went gloriously.
The arrangements were shocking, all the Hackney classes except
Ego's taking place at the same time as the big public luncheon.
This lasted for hours owing to the local Member spilling himself
about milk and Abyssinia. The result was that while the popular
side of the ring was crowded the grandstand was empty except

for half a dozen enthusiasts. Ego's exit after he had won gave me a greater thrill than any I have ever known outside the theatre ; his quality of sheer grace took everybody's breath away.

Sept. 19   Poem from brother Edward :
Thursday.

Browningesque

The bee's at the sting,
The fuchsia's forlorn,
Bill is at Selsey,
The curry's in comb.

The pong's on the ping,
The quail is unborn,
Carlyle's in Chelsea,
The Barretts are home.

                                        E. A.

Sept. 29   To-day's euphuism encountered in a modern novel—
Sunday.   the description of a hand as " that quintet of alabaster peninsulas."

Sept. 30   Winifred Holtby died yesterday at the age of thirty-
Monday.   seven. When I first met her three years ago she was ill, and in spite of her cheerfulness I felt it was serious. The occasion was a debate at some women's club, in which we fell upon one another with great determination. She and Vera Brittain had given me dinner at the Café Royal, at which neither of them ate or drank anything while insisting on lots of everything for me. The next time we met was when she took the chair for me at one of the *Sunday Times* Book Exhibition lectures. Third and last time was one of the Foyle luncheons. Harry Preston was in the chair, and she hung on this symbol a dazzling speech on the function of gaiety. Anybody who has ever done any public speaking must have realised that the fireworks had a logical framework to support them. It was a wonderful and,

I believe, impromptu effort, with an argument exactly marshalled in three parts gathered together at the finish, every word in place and no loose ends. I was sitting next to her and I told her just what I thought about the speech, and I believe she was happy that afternoon. I did not know Winifred Holtby well in the sense of meeting her often. But one did not need long-standing friendship to recognise a forceful character, a forthright mind, and a gracious personality abounding in that unquenchable gaiety of which she had spoken. She had a beautiful voice, and her speech had a conscious loveliness while remaining free from affectation. She antagonised nobody. To have a soul of steel, to be incapable of delivering hurt, to find all possible fun in life, and to walk crowded streets with the gait of one striding empty moors—these are the things I admired in Winifred Holtby.

Oct. 5   Alexander Korda having asked my advice about
Saturday.   two versions of *Cyrano*, one of which cuts down
                    the famous Nose cadenza to almost nothing and
the other funking it entirely, I asked Brother Edward to have a shot at it. I had reckoned without his contempt for the cinema. By return of post I got a flea-in-ear refusal out of respect for (*a*) the original Cyrano, (*b*) Rostand, (*c*) himself. He wound up with Cyrano's " Que je pactise ? Jamais, jamais ! " I have never known Edward when he would not sooner starve than compromise or truckle.

Oct. 8   An idle day, which means that I have overlooked
Tuesday.   an article. Shall occupy it in setting down something
                    about actors and acting, since after all that is probably
what most people read me for. As I have written elsewhere all I have to say of the players of my youth and in view of my vow to say no more about Sarah—which I made some three years ago and have kept—I shall jot down some recollections of my father's table-talk. When I was a boy we had a Sunday dinner-table to absent oneself from which was an unheard-of thing. At dessert my father would hold forth about all the

great actors and actresses he had seen. The list began with
Macready, of whom he had no very great opinion ; he was too
cold. Phelps was a great name, together with the Younger
Mathews. Fechter, too, he thought a brilliant actor, and I, who
had already read George Henry Lewes to Fechter's detriment,
had some difficulty in restraining my tongue. Then there was
a great deal of talk about Fanny Kemble, and Helen Faucit, and
especially about Modjeska, an exquisite Polish actress who was
a beautiful Juliet. In 1881 Modjeska appeared in Manchester in
Frou-frou, and W. T. Arnold wrote in the *M.G.* as follows :
" The opening of the fourth act was touchingly played with a
kind of sad dignity which suited the part. The scene with
Sartorys was moving and powerful and the death scene in the
fifth act touching. Its great merit was the continued thought
for the child at the dying woman's feet. Sarah Bernhardt forgot
him too soon." I was only four years old when this appeared,
and not a noticeably better dramatic critic than some of my
young colleagues to-day. Also I did not see Modjeska, though
when years later I saw Sarah play Frou-frou, Arnold seemed to
me to have committed rank *lèse-majesté*.

Three names were continually on my father's lips—those
of Alfred Wigan, Barry Sullivan, and " Little " Robson. The
critics of the past treated Wigan rather shabbily, and the best
thing I have ever been able to find about him is Henry Morley's :
" Mr Wigan has been for many years quietly and steadily
advancing in the public esteem as a careful and conscientious
actor, who understands the art to be an intellectual one, and so
pursues it." But that, considering that it was written in 1853,
says a great deal more than it appears to do on the surface.
About Barry Sullivan my father always said that he was the
last of the great actors, and could and did tear a passion to
tatters without being ridiculous—which cannot be said of to-day's
actor, who is much more likely to be ridiculous without tearing a
passion to anything approaching tatters. But the best intimation
of Barry Sullivan's quality came to me not from my father but
from Courtenay Thorpe, that fine intellectual player of the
'nineties. Thorpe, as a young man, was walking with Barry

Sullivan in Westminster. The great actor was explaining to him a point in his Hamlet, and neither of them noticed that they had arrived at a scene of congestion, cordons of police, and all that goes with the opening of Parliament. They began to cross the road and were stopped by a bobby. Whereupon Barry with a magnificent gesture not only spiritually waved but physically put the policeman on one side and continued his dissertation as though Parliament, and even the Monarchy, didn't exist.

On the subject of Robson my father was inexhaustible, declaring him to be very nearly the best actor he had ever set eyes on. Of this great little comedian and burlesque tragedian—he was no bigger in stature than Garrick—much has fortunately been recorded. Clement Scott has written of him :

> The only strictly serious part that I ever saw Robson play was Desmarets in *Plot and Passion*, a performance never to be forgotten ; but his burlesque was on the very borderline of tragedy. Such intensity he had, such power of sudden contrast, such quick changes from seriousness to fun, that he electrified one. In an instant he had the whole audience in his grasp, and communicated to them his magnetic personality. . . . He was a very little man, but in his inspired moments he became a giant. He seemed to swell and grow before our eyes. When he lifted himself up, his rage was awful ; when he wept, the whole house sobbed in sympathy.

Still more illuminating is a little-known account by George Augustus Sala :

> In *The Yellow Dwarf* Robson was the jaundiced embodiment of a spirit of Oriental evil ; crafty, malevolent, greedy, insatiate —full of mockery, mimicry, lubricity, spite—an Afrit, a Djinn, a Ghoul, a spawn of Sheitan. How that monstrous orange-tawny head grinned and wagged ! How those flaps of ears were projected forwards, like unto those of a dog ! How balefully those atrabilious eyes glistened ! You laughed, and yet you shuddered. He spoke in mere doggerel and slang. He sang trumpery songs to negro melodies. He danced the Lancashire clog hornpipe ; he rattled out puns and conundrums ; yet did he contrive to infuse into all this mummery and buffoonery, into this salmagundi of the

incongruous and the outré, an unmistakably tragic element—an element of depth and strength and passion, and almost of sublimity. The mountebank became inspired. The Jack Pudding suddenly drew the cothurnus over his clogs. You were awe-stricken by the intensity, the vehemence he threw into the mean balderdash of the ballad-monger. These qualities were even more apparent in his subsequent personation of Medea, in Robert Brough's parody of the Franco-Italian tragedy. The love, the hate, the scorn of the abandoned wife of Jason, the diabolic loathing in which she held Creusa, the tigerish affection with which she regarded the children whom she is afterwards to slay—all these were portrayed by Robson, through the medium, be it always remembered, of doggerel and slang, with astonishing force and vigour. The original Medea, the great Ristori herself, came to see Robson and was delighted with and amazed at him. She scarcely understood two words of English, but the actor's genius struck her home through the bull's-hide target of an unknown tongue. " *Uomo straordinario !* " she went away saying.

I have quoted thus much about Robson because I have a relic of him. This is the tobacco-box he used in *The Porter's Knot*. A letter goes with the box, dated February 12th, 1908, and written by Mrs Emily Combes. The letter says : " Dear Mr Tree, On the chance that you may collect theatrical relics, I am sending you the old ' baccy ' box used by the late Frederick Robson in *The Porter's Knot*, in the hope that you will do me the favour to accept it. It was given to Alfred Bryan the artist, by the widow of F. R. who gave it to my husband." The box was presented to me by the writer's nephew. I rank it third in what must be the smallest collection of theatrical relics in the country. The first two are a knife found under the floor of Shakespeare's house at the time of its restoration and Henry Irving's press-cutting scissors. Seymour Hicks gave me these, and I like his story that Irving, whenever he used the scissors to cut out the notice of some famous critic, would snarl, " What does he know about it ? " My fourth and fifth treasures are two photographs of Irving and Ellen Terry which, in their present frames, hung for twenty-five years on either side of Irving's dressing-table at the Lyceum. When Irving died his valet gave them to Lady Martin-Harvey, and she very kindly gave them to me.

My father was the most severe of critics and would come home after a performance of Irving's saying that the man had so many faults that he oughtn't to be on the stage at all! Yet at heart he admired him tremendously though he always said that Macaire was his best performance.

About Ellen Terry he held the opinion that she was the most exquisite of all human creatures, but not a great actress. Of all English actresses he placed Mrs Kendal first, one of her greatest feats in his opinion being to have turned her husband from a stick into a tolerably competent comedian. He had considerable admiration for Hare and Wyndham, and a strictly limited appreciation of the Bancrofts. But his view about Tree as a serious actor was that he ought to be whipped! Indeed, I remember his taking me to see Tree and Mrs Patrick Campbell in *Fédora* at the Haymarket and telling me afterwards that the age of the professional actor was gone, and that all I had seen that evening was a couple of talented amateurs!

My own conscious playgoing began just about the time that the English Drama was undergoing one of its many re-births. I mean, of course, the first night of Pinero's *The Second Mrs Tanqueray* in 1893, which is not very noticeably short of fifty years ago. Elsewhere I have named my theatrical gods of that period. Has the reader noticed the omission to make very much of Duse? Here undoubtedly the actress's nationality has stood in the way of my admiring her. I have always avoided setting up to be a judge of any player speaking a language of which I don't know enough to order a mutton chop. But that the English have never understood Italian has not prevented them from hailing the Italian actress as a world-genius. According to Maurice Baring, who can speak anything from Russian to Choctaw; Arthur Symons, who could translate Dante standing on his head; Shaw, who could lecture to Venetians in their own language on the function of drains in a water-logged city, and the omniscient Walkley, whose beard could laugh in any language it liked—according to all these, Duse was an undeniably great actress. Personally I never trusted my own opinion about her because, as I have already said, I know no Italian except the names of some of the arias in Mozart's operas. In consequence I was never able to tell whether, when Duse came on waving her lovely hands and looking like the back of the kitchen grate, she was bewailing the coldness of the cold mutton at lunch or proposing to enter a nunnery! Also she affected me exactly in the way in which she affected Max Beerbohm. Some of to-day's young people may not know Max's dramatic criticisms by heart, and therefore I shall remind them of this :

Am I overwhelmed by the personality of Duse ? Of course, I ought to be—there can be no question of that. But the wretched fact remains that I am not. True, I see power and nobility in her face ; and the little shrill soft voice, which is in such strange contrast with it, has a certain charm for me. I admire, too, her movements, full of grace and strength. But my prevailing emotion is hostile to her. I cannot surrender myself, and see in her the 'incarnate womanhood' and 'the very spirit of the world's tears' and all those other things which other critics see in her. My prevailing impression is that of a great egoistic force ; of a woman overriding, with an air of sombre unconcern, plays, mimes, critics, and public. In a man I would admire this tremendous egoism very much indeed. In a woman it only makes me uncomfortable. I dislike it. I resent it.

Oct. 11   In the evening took Jock to the first night of James
Friday.   Bridie's *The Black Eye*, for which I had suggested that
             he should write a practice dramatic criticism in way
of being a dress-rehearsal for his *Manchester Guardian* job, which starts next week. He was to write a notice in exactly the same time he will have for the paper—that is to say, between the end of the play and twelve midnight. He left me at the theatre, after which I went to supper at the Savoy.

Got home at ten past one and sat down to see what I could do in an hour. Only I cheated, because there was all that ruminating over supper, and in addition I took two hours, if you count getting up out of bed three times in order to add finishing touches !

Oct. 12   Jock's article arrived with the midnight postmark
Saturday.   showing he kept his word.   Excellent, though
                 bearing slight traces of stage-fright.   He confessed
this morning to having been momentarily tempted to return
to Scotland for good by the midnight train.   But he can teach
me nothing about fright, for I suffered from it in Manchester
for seven years *and never got any better*.   Never once throughout
the whole of those seven years did I go to a play without something written in advance, which I used or not according to
circumstances.   The difficulty, of course, is that of trying too
hard and attempting too much.   It takes pretty nearly the whole
of fifty minutes merely to write the number of words it takes
to make half a column, never mind the four-fold job of telling
the reader about the play as news, fulfilling the critical function,
using the right words, and—last infirmity of noble mind—
putting something of yourself into the whole thing.   Writers
either have this gift or they haven't, and a man is not the worse
critic for not possessing it.   Montague and Walkley had this
faculty absolutely, and so to-day have Charles Morgan and Ivor
Brown.   But I know one very distinguished critic, the possessor
of an exquisite mind and whose weekly outpourings are pure
joy, who has been tried at this nocturnal job and spent his hour
gaping like a fish at a blank sheet of paper.   If Jock fails, which
he may very well do, it won't be a failure in criticism or artistry.
It will simply mean that he lacks a facility often denied the best
brains and granted to the most commonplace.   The reason
I didn't altogether fail on the *Manchester Guardian* was that I
sedulously collected the London criticisms of each new play as
it appeared and so knew what it was about before it came to
Manchester.   From these I prepared my advance notices, and,
further, provincial papers go to press an hour later than the
London ones.   I therefore had two hours, and not one, for
the task—an immense difference.

However, Jock's first attempt was very much better than

I expected, though not so good as it would have been if the time-threat had been removed. Bits of it are very good indeed :

> One went to the new play hoping at last for Mr Bridie's rounded, complete thing, a play with a " total gesture." Alas, no ! It was evident early in the evening that he was going to make even more little gestures than usual, one gesture per scene and the whole totalling nothing.

Also :

> Mr Morland Graham's appearance was all too short ; he perfectly suggested the typical north-country father extremely nervous of allowing his heart to get nearer his sleeve than his elbow, so to speak.

Also :

> The moral of the whole thing, if it is a whole thing, is so trite that I cannot remember it.

These are not only good criticisms, but tellingly delivered, and only once does Jock go off into his preciosity as when he says that Shaw was in the audience, each particular hair of his beard *candid* with approbation ! He justified this nonsense by saying that he is using " candid " in its pristine sense, whereupon we trot out Webster. Jock claims a win on the strength of the quotation from Dryden :

> The box receives all black ; but, poured from thence,
> The stones come candid forth, the hue of innocence.

Whereupon I point to a small word in italics which he disingenuously overlooks. The word is *obs.* ! A great argument follows. He is to write this week about *Romeo and Juliet*, and I ask him if he thinks the *M.G.* will allow him to call this " the world's greatest venereal tragedy."

Oct. 31   Last night at the *M.G.* office Jock asked James
Thursday.   Bone whether George Mair had been a fastidious
               journalist. J. B. replied in a whisper, " Man, he
once telephoned a semicolon from Moscow."

Lunched at the Savage with Herman Finck, who was in terrific form. He showed me the programme for a forthcoming Sunday concert at Hastings, and when I objected to *Bacchanalia* as being too profane a subject, he said, "All right, we'll call it ' John Sebastian Bacchanalia.'"

Nov. 9   A hell of a week, of which I remember :
Saturday.   1. Broadcasting about Sybil, and on the theme
                that if she is great enough to be a Dame she must remain a *grande dame*. The point is not that S. should resist characters like Pinero's Lady Orreyed, but something much more subtle. If she went outside herself on such occasions I should have nothing to say. But there was a time when, although utterly free from any vulgarity of mind, S. had certain provincial elegances, mouth-twistings, arm-wavings and the like, *to which she returns for her comedy*. It is this that I find deplorable—the renewal of something long and successfully put behind her. Her performance in *Advertising April* and in *Madame Plays Nap* left me *bouche béante*, and here it is again.

2. After broadcasting, dinner at Isola Bella with Maurice Healy, a most amusing cove, brilliant talker, and author of this fine epigram :

To the Memory of the 29th Division

We failed ; but, when the sacrifice is needed,
Fail you as nobly. We shall have succeeded.

A grand meal—oysters, minute steak, and toasted cheese— and the talk best of all. Moray McLaren in fine Scots form, while M. H., who began talking in English, finished up in Arthur Sinclair's richest brogue.

3. The Opening Lunch of the *S.T.* Book Exhibition. Rose Macaulay coming up to me and saying, "Sir, a bone to pick with you," and me countering with the Hamlet-like, "Madam, a whole skeleton ! "

4. Talking at the Exhibition, with Sybil Thorndike in the chair. Charming to me, and looking and behaving like some female seraph, exactly what Coleridge meant by " a man all light."

5. Supper with James Bone at the Café Royal. J. B. in tremendous fettle. Stories about George Mair coming into the newly decorated Savoy Hotel, all white paint and panelling, and saying, "This place would be exactly like the Berengaria *if only it were a bit steadier*!" About T. W. H. Crosland refusing tea at one of Lady Londonderry's political fêtes, ordering a bottle of whiskey from the footman, writing his name on the label, and putting it on the drawing-room mantelpiece for his private use. About the late Sir Edward Hulton, who had in his library twelve sumptuously bound volumes lettered "Grand National Shakespeare."

6. A first-rate concert on my new wireless, *which works*! B.B.C. Symphony Orchestra, Hamilton Harty conducting:

> Strauss's *Don Juan.*
> Chopin Concerto No. 1 (Hoffmann).
> William Walton's 1st Symphony.

Why do pianists so seldom play the Chopin Concerto, which is lovely? Fascinated by the Walton, though one must not hear too much of this new stuff. Matisse & Co. make one look at Constable a shade patronisingly, and I'm not going to risk listening to Beethoven with amused contempt.

7. Swopping my old Dunlop and cheque for ten guineas against the best of the new Dunlops in the show at the Redfern Galleries, the portrait of a wistful little boy.

8. Hearing Richard Hearne, the amazing acrobat in the new Henson show, tell Duggie Furber that he couldn't stay late at the Savage Club unless he 'phoned his mother. Everybody admired this.

9. Agreeing with Jock that in comparison with Rosalind's pure flame Juliet is a man-struck little besom.

Dec. 3   Part of my broadcast last night:
Tuesday.

Since my last talk I have received any number of beauty hints which, since they appear in print, are presumably read. And that's the horror of it! Here is one: "Not every

woman realises that it is cruelty to faces to try to cover their
sorrowful 'hang-over' with rouge and powder without
first giving them the kind of pick-me-up which on these
occasions is indicated. . . . Spread a coat of feeding cream
over the skin. Massage with firm strokes upwards from the
throat, using a fan-like movement over the face. Flick rather
than stroke the skin, with a quick ' whippy ' rhythm. . . .
Then lie down with the feet raised on the pillows, a hard
cushion in the small of the back, *and the head slightly hanging
over the side of the bed*. Stay completely relaxed."

Some of you are probably wondering what on earth this
has got to do with the theatre. I will tell you. The other
evening I had an experience in the theatre of the kind of
fool who indulges in antics of this sort. The play was
Shakespeare's *Timon of Athens*—not a favourite play of mine
or of anybody's, but a play at the end of which Shakespeare's
poetic genius sounds the depths of pessimism.

Now, listeners, permit me to tell you that while this part
of the play was being performed in the revival at the Westminster Theatre, a woman in my neighbourhood opened
a vanity bag the size of an attaché-case, spread out a lot of
little pots and pans on her knee, and began to daub her face
with all kinds of pencils and cover it with powder. Am I
not right in suggesting that this is the kind of a woman who
spends the morning with her head hanging over the side of
a bed ? And that it is for such creatures that musical comedies
are written ?

The whole thing makes me boil with rage, and I warn
the entire sex that if at a serious play any tray of cosmetics
is again exposed within my reach I shall sweep it to the floor !
Alternatively, I have a small portable shaving-set which I
propose to fix on the back of the stall in front of me. But
there, it's no good getting cross, and I must cultivate a more
philosophic attitude.

This morning I received a letter from which I cull the
following :

The Navy . . . ordinary ratings . . . has been before you.
The other day, in the Portsmouth-London express, eight
jolly tars, when they saw a bright young thing begin to
cosmeticise, with one accord took combs from their pockets
and behaved like mermaids !

Dec. 19   A hurly-burly of a morning in which the follow-
Thursday.   ing alphabet of events occurs even before I get
                 up !

(*a*) Ivor, in the post, accepts my challenge, proposing to
dash off thirty lines or so of unmistakable Stephen Phillips
" in the dead vast and middle of Christmas afternoon."

(*b*) Henry Ainley, in the post, tells me in a charming letter
apropos of *Macbeth* at the Old Vic that he is not likely to return
to the stage for " Æons of Swinleys."

(*c*) Some ass, also in the post, has been cast for a part in
The Cherry Orchard at Tyrone or Guthrie or somewhere, and
will I tell him by return what the character means and what
the play is all about, since it didn't make sense when he read it.

(*d*) A paper rings up to say it wants a pantomime article at
once, and that it is sending a boy for it.

(*e*) A messenger arrives with an excellent photograph of
Teddy Baldock intended for my *Kingdoms for Horses*. Another
messenger brings the typescript of that masterpiece, which I
immediately start to revise.

(*f*) Jock meanwhile forces me to begin the pantomime article.

(*g*) The boy arrives and is asked to wait in the study.

(*h*) H. Steggles, the artist, arrives and has to be asked to
wait in my drawing-room. He is to do a painting which is to
be the frontispiece for *Kingdoms for Horses*.

(*i*) George Bishop rings up to coax me, wholly without
success, to attend a revival of *La Poupée* on Saturday night.

(*j*) Fred planks my breakfast on my bed.

(*k*) Jock brightens up and we finish the pantomime article
in a blaze of collaboration. Thus, concerning Nellie Wallace in
The Sleeping Beauty, I dictate the sentence : " Then comes a
modiste, clothed in black velvet, who is the epitome and
apotheosis of every genius in this line from Worth to Schiaparelli." Jock is good enough to alter this, even while taking
it down, to the following : " Then comes a modiste *clothed in
black samite, mystic, wonderful*, who is the epitome and apotheosis
of every genius in this line from Mantalini to Schiaparelli."
Have my revenge for this amendment by dictating : " Mr Bert

Coote, our one remaining tragi-comedian, sings what purports to be and ultimately becomes a chorus-song for children, entitled, ' Don't Tease the Bees, Please ! ' and his delivery of the first verse is wet with the shimmer of wings and eyelids ! "

J. A.   How many words have I done now, and what time is it ?

JOCK.   Eight hundred and it's one o'clock.

J. A.   Look here, Jock, be a darling and . . .

JOCK (*suddenly wildly Scotch*).   'A ken what's comin'. Be a darlin' and feenish the bluidy thing ! All right then, since it's nearin' Christmas.   Get up and get yer face washed and attend to yer visitor !

Still later, Jock's face comes round the bathroom door :

JOCK.   I suppose you've no objection to a comparison between your friend Bert Coote and my friend Aristophanes.

J. A. (*a little stiffly and nose full of soap*).   I fail to see any connection !

JOCK (*in scornful triumph*).   " The Wasps," ye haverin' gumph !

Jan. 10   Good party last night. Princess Marie-Louise, Mrs
Friday.   Adams, and Herbert Morgan. First night of Noel's
              To-night at 8.30. H.H. in great form. When, after
the play's 1860 funeral, the family drank Madeira she sniffed
and said, " Nonsense ! We never drank anything except sherry
and ham ! " Supper in the Savoy Grill. Couldn't get the table
I had ordered at midday because some actors who had begun
dinner at seven o'clock were still in possession and refused to
budge. Wouldn't have minded, only they were *repertory* actors.
Peter Page and Bill (Mrs Edward Hudson) joined us, and all very
jolly. Turtle soup, fillets of sole very plain, a rich mess of chicken,
foie gras, asparagus and mushroom sauce, ice with peaches, and
Bollinger N.V. Half-way through supper called to the telephone
to hear from James Bone that Allan Monkhouse is dying.

Jan. 11   Monkhouse died in the night. Told Bone I would
Saturday.   do something for Monday's *Guardian*. Two
              columns in to-day's issue written by Montague
ten years ago. Shan't enlarge here on the effect this made on
me. Jock, who never met either of them, greatly impressed.
Scott, Arnold, Montague, Monkhouse, Mair, Johnstone, Lang-
ford, Dixon Scott—what a roll-call !

Jan. 18   Have been more or less in bed all week with
Saturday.   bronchial catarrh. It started on Monday going up
              to Monkhouse's funeral. Travelled with Bone,
H. M. Tomlinson, and Cochran, who was going on to Manchester.
Very good talk and a bright, sunny day with lots of white frost.
Somebody remarked how Monkhouse would have enjoyed it.
The weather changed completely after Crewe, and the combined
effect of Stockport, black fog, sleet, and the purpose of our
journey was most depressing. During the ceremony my chest
crackled like a machine-gun. I think Allan would have hated
the way the clergyman at the crematorium pronounced God

" Gard." The psalm was " The Lord is my Shepherd," but in the prosaic version which goes on to say " I shall not lack anything," and the Lesson from Revelation had no particular relation to A. N. M. If I had had to arrange the service I should have wanted something Allan liked, some great passage from Meredith, or a Browning poem. At the end we had the most human bit out of *Gerontius*. But Allan did not care very much for music.

Kipling died early this morning. *Many Inventions* and *Life's Handicap* contain stories as good as anything by Maupassant, whom I have read in his entirety. I do not know enough of the short stories of Tchehov to justify comparison. As a boy I was a great Kipling fan. I remember, in 1898 when he was desperately ill in New York, making a solemn vow that if he died I would wear a black tie for the rest of my life !

One minute before midnight last night the dance music on the wireless was faded out and an announcer came to the microphone to broadcast news of the King's illness. Not the attack of bronchial catarrh which matters, but " signs of cardiac weakness which must be regarded with some disquiet." Four doctors at Sandringham.

Jan. 20   Fred Leigh's boy has got hold of a copy of *The*
Monday.   *Times* for November 7, 1805. The paper consists of
               four small sheets only, and as it was printed in the days when people 'read with their minds instead of their eyes there are, of course, no pictures. It begins with one sober column of advertisements and then launches straight away into the *London Gazette*. Beneath a heading taking up less than one inch of space, this gives Collingwood's dispatches containing the first account of the Battle of Trafalgar and the death of Nelson. The account goes on for three columns and then turns the page. The second page is entirely taken up with extracts from the foreign Press, after which there are two dignified leading articles, from the second of which I cull :

No ebullitions of popular transport, no demonstrations of public joy, marked this great and important event. The honest and manly feeling of the people appeared as it should have done : they felt an inward satisfaction at the triumph of their favourite arms ; they mourned with all the sincerity and poignancy of domestic grief, their Hero slain.

Fancy any modern newspaper holding that the honest and manly feelings of a people cannot be expressed except through the medium of streamers and paper caps, crowds, piano-accordions, and Trafalgar Square !

Yet the age was not wholly unalive to expediency. One of the advertisements announces the publication that day of an engraving of Hoppner's picture of Lord Nelson, while the dramatic critic tells the reader :

> After the Comedy of *She Would and She Would Not*, in which Miss Smith acted Hypolita with admirable spirit, the Proprietors of this Theatre, ever alive to the national glory, produced a hasty but elegant compliment to the memory of Lord Nelson.

Jan. 21 *Tuesday.* Yesterday was a moving day indoors. At 5.30 the wireless announced : " The condition of His Majesty the King shows diminishing strength." At 9.25 came the statement : " The King's life is moving peacefully towards its close." Heard afterwards that the Queen drafted this. At 10 o'clock there was a five-minutes' service beginning with the 23rd Psalm. Then every quarter of an hour the repetition of the last message. One couldn't read or do anything, so George Mathew and I sat and talked. News that the King was dead came through at 12.15.

Jan. 22 *Wednesday.* Every flag was at half-mast yesterday except at Buckingham Palace, where there was no flag at all, there being no sovereign. The town like a Sunday ; all theatres and cinemas closed and all public functions abandoned. Dined quietly at the Langham with Moray McLaren and Rose-Troup, and at 9.30 went across to Broadcasting House to hear the Prime Minister. Very good and well delivered. Moray said the speech was for all Europe as well as England—

"Hitler and the boys will be listening." When Baldwin spoke of the Prince of Wales and his tremendous responsibilities there came into his voice, or I thought so, just a hint of the Lord Chief Justice of *Henry IV*, Part 2, Act V, Sc. 2.

Feb. 1   A card from Brother Edward :
Saturday.

When am I to be invited to your new flat ? Ever ? Never ? Or may I come when I like ? I still have boots !

Feb. 11   The Chaplin film. Until last week there were four
Tuesday.   absolute silences—Outer Space, the grave, the Sphinx,
              and Charlie Chaplin's. To-day, Tuesday, February 11,
1936, the number of those silences was reduced to three, since in *Modern Times* Chaplin's voice was heard for the first time. It would not be true to say that Charlie spoke, because he didn't. He sang, and his singing was enough to destroy something which all the world had cherished. The point is not whether Chaplin sang well or ill ; he destroyed a mystery. This song of Chaplin's is forgivable only if it is unique, and if never again under any pretext whatever he utters spoken or singing word. *Loquor et qualis artifex pereo !* should be written in letters of gold on every wall in Charlie Chaplin's studio ; this may be dog-Latin, but it is good enough for a hang-dog little fellow who is, and must ever be, without a peer. Chaplin is, as all the world knows, a man of education, and probably knows Matthew Arnold's lines :

> And thou, who didst the stars and sunbeams know,
> Self-school'd, self-scann'd, self-honour'd, self-secure,
> Didst walk on earth unguess'd at. Better so !

Half the secret of that wistful tramp, that pilgrim of eternity in a finer sense than Byron ever knew, lies in the fact that he has walked the silent screen guessed at by all the world, yet never wholly revealed. Other film actors, Mr Chaplin, abide our question. You are free, on condition that you for ever hold your peace.

Feb. 13   Letter in to-day's *Times* :
Thursday.

   SIR :—I vouch for this, which happened to-day :
   TELEPHONE SUBSCRIBER.   I have been dialling " Operator "
for four minutes.   Suppose my house had been on fire ?
   OPERATOR.   Is it ?
   SUBSCRIBER.   No.
   OPERATOR.   Then what are you bothering about ?
                                                I am, etc.,
                                                      JAMES AGATE

      The Savage Club, Feb. 12

Feb. 21   The chauffeur having left, the old problem once
Friday.   again rises and is once more settled.   Garage sends
             round one Charles, alleged to be model of all the
virtues and a fine driver.   Believe the first but not the second.
He nearly fainted on hearing he was engaged, owing to 2½
months' semi-starvation.   Recovering, asked if he could have
afternoon off !   Why ?   To visit sick wife in hospital and arrange
disposition of baby during wife's illness.   Must therefore dis-
patch fruit and flowers to Missus, Glaxo and Allenbury's Food
to Baby, out of all proportion to mileage driven, which is nil.

April 18
Saturday.   MORNING CONCERT
                                     of
                              RECORDED MUSIC
                                     by
                          FIVE FAVOURITE COMPOSERS
                              ————
                                 JOCK DENT
                             APRIL 18th, 1936
                              ————

   1. Gigue for Strings   .   .   . *Baldassare Galuppi.*
   2. Nautical Moments   .   .   . *Charles Dibdin.*
   3. Overture to *Stradella* .   .   . *Friedrich von Flotow.*
   4. Two Tudor Madrigals   .   . *period circa Henry VIII.*
   5. Concerto for two Violins and
         Orchestra   .   .   .   . *J. S. Bach.*

This programme was performed by Jock on records he brought before I got up this morning. Why nothing by " Claribel"? He explained that he looked high and low for a record of her. But in vain.

April 19   " Sweet heaven, keep me in temper : I would not
Sunday.   be mad! " It would take Lear's vocabulary to deal
              with some of my correspondents. Here's one sends me a play to read with a demand to be informed as to its theatrical possibilities. Including the stage directions, it takes exactly four minutes to read. Yet I must be patient. It's only that our neuroses are different. I think I am going insane ; they think they are keeping all right. *The Times* to-day prints two newly discovered letters of Carlyle, whose neighbour at No. 4 Cheyne Row appears to have kept poultry, macaws, etc. "I have never in my life come athwart a tract of miserable grievances at once so contemptible and so intolerable, about which, except to men of delicate character, and acquainted like yourself with sedentary and studious ways, it is worse than useless to speak or to appeal." I have never known the point about nerves to be better made. What, to the sufferer, is a sky full of locusts the size of vultures is, to the onlooker, less than the buzzing of a gnat. But there are compensations. Nobody is more moved than I am at *The Times* Active Service In Memoriam Notices. Yet nobody could be quicker to spot the absurdity of " In memory of our darling, beloved Mamma, who flew away, etc., etc."

I wish this weather would fly away. Wet and cold, without any sentiment of spring. Oh, to be out of England now that April's here ! Played golf this morning with the new assistant at Thorpe Bay. Enormous hands, feet big enough for two policemen, leggy like a colt, he drives some 300 yards and should make a golfer some day. At present he is too loose and, as he rightly says, needs a bit of stomach to play his shots against. When he lets out, is inclined to swing round and face the wicket-keeper. Thanks to 3 twenty-yard putts and 2 dead stymies he beat me by 4 and 3, conceding 2 bisques. Am I coming back to health and form ? What a pity Lear didn't play golf ! A round a day with Kent would have made all the difference.

April 23   The *D.E.* cuts out a sentence in which I deprecate
Thursday.   the use of the word " bum."   On the other hand
it cheerfully prints a quotation from Miss Radclyffe Hall : " He had taken her almost reverently, pressing her down on the fertile soil as though on some primitive pagan altar." With my comment : " I do not know how Norwegian sailors do their love-making, but I doubt very much whether at primitive moments the pagan altar looms largely even in the Norse mind." Jock tells me that there is a subtle difference between fornication and bums. You may write about the former and photograph the latter—see any modish corset advertisement. Whereas to mention the second is as great a breach of taste as to photograph the first.

April 29   Millionaires-to-be spend their early years picking
Wednesday.   up thousands of pins.   Potential astronomers
spend their infancy with eyes glued to sixpenny telescopes. I myself wrote lengthy dramatic criticisms, complete with French quotations, long before I had entered any theatre. Last night was the twenty-first anniversary of Leslie Henson's first appearance at the Gaiety Theatre. This is a buffoon of genius. Ask Leslie to poke fun at the seaside fortune-teller. Easy. Or make game of your Harley Street psycho-analyst. Easier still. Or take the mike out of the Sphinx. A sitter. Our buffoon has one question for the lot : " Why must you be so ut-ter-ly absurd ? " I have been trying for fifteen years to do justice to Leslie, and the nearest I have ever been able to get was some seven years ago on the occasion of the production of *Follow Through* : " Leslie Henson will, in moments of ecstasy, look at you out of eyes bulging like those of a moth which has eaten too much tapestry." Only, of course, the next minute he will be looking like a goldfish somebody has forgotten to put back into its bowl, or a tortoise imprudently come out of

its shell. Since our collection of pet animals first appeared on the Gaiety stage, it or he has taken part in some seventeen musical comedies. It is an open secret of this trade that however good the " book," it is the business of the principal comedian to make it better. I suspect our Leslie's brain to have proved the female to a score of librettists' souls. Have librettists souls ? Don't be so utterly . . . but that's another story. The point is that wit springs eternal in the Hensonian breast. " Let those that play your clowns speak no more than is set down for them." But Hamlet was not thinking of musical comedy, or his advice would have been fatal. W. S. is always said to be universal ; it is certainly odd how, over and over again, he seems to fit the case. Alas, poor Yorick ! But don't we feel in our bones that Y.'s gibes, gambols, flashes of merriment, and all the rest of it were something more than smoking-room stories ? Leslie is another Yorick. In all the many plays I have seen him in I have never known him joke nearer the knuckle than good table-manners permit.

May 30   The Great Day has arrived, and the International
Saturday.   Horse Show opens at Olympia, with Ego showing
             at the first performance. Saw him in his box last night, and he looked grand. Albert Throup says that if he gives his show he can't lose. But I don't know, and the memory of last year's Olympia is very much with me this morning. Since waking have done everything possible to put the idea of winning out of mind. I have never had a success at Olympia, and to-day it is now or never. I have done all I can to discount the inevitable disappointment. I have been going about the house reciting, " Whate'er I prized, it ne'er was mine." I turned up Pinero's old *His House in Order* and read Hilary Jesson's speech about renunciation : " Nina, there are some people walking the earth who are wearing a halo . . . the glow of it sustains them through pain and tribulation . . . who've been offered a sceptre and passed on. They are the people who have renounced. Nina, be among those who wear the halo." All morning I have been saying, " James, be

among those who wear the halo." Yet I confess to opening
Ego at random to see if the gods were favourable. I opened it
at page 237, and read : " Tried to reproduce Ralph Richardson's
Bunyanesque manner, *and satisfied myself for the first time.*" And
then of course I couldn't let well alone. Edward having sent
me an old copy of Doran's *Table Traits*, I opened that at random
to see if I could get the favourable omen confirmed. The passage
I lighted on was St Luke's " When thou art bidden of any man
to a wedding, sit not down in the highest room, lest a more
honourable man than thou be bidden of him ; and he that
bade thee and him come and say unto thee, Give this man
place, and thou begin with shame to take the lower room."
Not so good !

Ego won ! Albert drove beautifully, and the horse put
up a cool, collected, self-possessed show with plenty up his
sleeve if any more had been wanted. The crowd quickly took
to him, and he at once became the talk and sensation of the
show.

June 2   A man apologising for having been laid out on the
Tuesday.   floor through drink for the greater part of the previous
             evening, Geoffrey Bennett said, " Nonsense, my dear
fellow, you were the still life of the party ! "
     Selwyn Jepson's contribution to a discussion on really good
earthly paradises : " A loaf of bread, a jug of wine, a book of
verses, and NO THOU ! "

June 5   Nobody realises that if I hadn't the Buddha-like
Friday.   capacity to ignore the play and withdraw to Bir-
             mingham and muse about Tulip and Ego's prospects
I should, on three evenings out of four, collapse with boredom,
and one fine night find myself in the asylum. I am much more
interested in what ponies are coming on than in what actresses
are going off ! At the same time I realise I must not quarrel
with my bread and butter. Also that they can't help being
bread-and-butter actresses.

June 14   Two exciting days at Leicester. On the first day
Sunday.   Hemingway's big horse rightly won the all heights
               class, All Trumps, the recent winner in the open class
under 15 hands at Olympia, being placed second, and Tulip,
who was throwing a temperament, an unsatisfactory third.
Later in the afternoon Ego romped home in the novice class.
Next day I had both Ego and Tulip entered but decided to
keep the gelding fresh for the National Show on Tuesday. As
the winner on the first day of this show cannot compete on
the second this meant challenging the earlier decision and, of
course, the odds on All Trumps winning again under the same
judge were enormous. However, Tulip came out in her very
best mood and went beautifully, with perfectly balanced action,
and I have no doubt the owner of the other mare would say
the same of his animal. Round and round they went, then a
good straight show and then another prolonged trial round and
round the immense ring. By this time the crowd had warmed
up and was cheering both horses. Finally the judge lined them
up and went over them for conformation, after which he pointed
to Tulip. It was a great battle, and young Haydon, who drove
his own mare, was extremely nice about it afterwards. Much
nicer than I should have been.

June 20   The National Hackney Show, held this year at
Saturday.   Worthing, has come and gone, and between them
               Ego and Albert have done what I have been trying
to do for twenty-three years—*i.e.*, again take first prize at this
Show. My first appearance at what was then called the London
Hackney Show was in 1913. I had bought an untried and
unshown three-year-old filly called Rusper Maryan, and with
her won first prize, both in hand and in harness. I remember
thinking it quite easy and taking the success rather lightly. But
I also remember Alexander Gemmell, who was sitting behind
me in the Agricultural Hall at Islington, saying, " Man, whatever horses ye may own it may be twenty years before ye do this
again ! " Actually it has been twenty-three years. Ego won
his class in harness as easily as he did at Olympia. He also won

the hand class and was awarded the Challenge Cup for the best young mare or gelding shown in hand.

June 21   At dinner to-night Monty delivered himself of the
Sunday.   following harangue :

My dear James, you and I have known each other for a good many years, and I am very fond of you. But I am also a little anxious. You say your new book is good, and your horse has certainly done well. But try to realise, my dear fellow, that you won't always be on the crest of the wave. You may be another Samuel Butler, and after you are dead the reading public may discover *Responsibility*. And, of course, *Ego* and its successors may show you to be another Pepys. But, with great respect, I don't think so. Your diary is in every way inferior to Arnold Bennett's, and you are not the writer he was. My advice to you is to consolidate. You can't last for ever ; we shall tire of you. The proper thing, in my opinion, is to take up a position like Saintsbury or Gosse and boom away once a week. Gosse did boomers in the *Sunday Times* for donkeys' years. Choose some nice little house near Godalming, to which people can make pilgrimages on Sunday afternoons. As the last man who knew Sarah Bernhardt you will always have a steady if limited vogue. Shall we take our coffee in the drawing-room ?

June 23
Tuesday.   *Edward's Journey*

The coffin came—a masterpiece of flummery,
Flashy outside, inlaid with cheapest lead ;
A pallet soft, as bolster to the mummery
Of Edward resting his unwanted head.

They washed him first ; and then, with snip-snap-snorum,
His nails were cut. In bib and tucker cosseted,—
Allons, c'est tout. Mais oui ! High cock-a-lorum !
Into his narrow crib he was deposited.

He had ignored the churl who measured him,
Jibed at the undertaker's jewelled hand ;
He had no friend who loved and treasured him
Save the Fagotto in a Fireman's Band.

Sechs Lieder lay serenely on his breast;
Seven un-Vocal Scores his hands caressed;
Into the coffin copyrights were flung,
Unbought, uncut, unnoticed, and unsung.

One hearse, one horse, no flow'rs, some *bonhomie*,
(Relatives venting *Vales*, much relieved),
All with an eye to strict economy,
" Which puts the lid on it," sighed Edward, grieved.

He lay quite still, rejoicing in the gloom
That had delivered him from Life's alarms,
Hoping the horse did wear a modest plume,
Doubting of Bach—but humming bars of Brahms.

He reached the Gates, and paused till Peter came,
Tendered his three-and-six with show of mirth;
Trusting, in Heaven it would be the same
For Bed and Breakfast, as upon the Earth.

But Peter spake, ridiculously proud:
" Of cash in hand we have sufficient hoard;
Please scan the notice on the entrance-board—
' No Hawkers or Musicians are allowed.' "

The Gates were shut, they echoed far and wide;
Sentence pronounced invited not to stay;
And Edward, though defeated, dignified,
Wrapping his shroud about him, went his way.

  . . . . . .

Whither, oh wand'ring Spirit, wilt thou go?
Where shall thy all too fretful Ghost be laid?
Thy pilgrimage on Earth long over-stayed,
Thy presence in the Firmament *de trop*!

              E. A.

Aug. 8   At the Royal Dublin Horse Show, Ego, a five-year-
Saturday. old bay gelding, the property of James Agate, beat
       Wensleydale Madge for first place in the Open
Class under 15 hands, and, on the same afternoon, was awarded
the supreme harness championship.

Aug. 9   As the train steamed slowly through Chester station on
Sunday.   Friday morning last the sun began to shine for almost
              the first time in this woebegone summer.   Monty
Shearman had never been to Ireland, and I was coming over for
the Horse Show.   Yesterday while I inspected the show-ground
M. explored Trinity College and Phœnix Park.   He is full of the
architecture of Dublin and its pictures, incidentally bores me to
the homicidal verge, and behaves generally like Shakespeare's
" pickèd man of countries."   Once, however, when I am thinking
about a plan of campaign for Ego—the horse, not the book—and
obviously not attending to Monty, he has a " Look, how our
partner's rapt," which makes me forgive his interminable
æsthetics.

   Lunch, to annoy my old friend, off lobster and Sparkling
Burgundy, and feel quite well afterwards.   He wakes me up
about four and insists on our driving to Glendalough.   Very
fine, including a fifth-century graveyard where the contrast
between the stones and a French officer and his mystically
scented, exotically taloned *petite amie* sets me Sparkenbroking
—ecstasy about death and all that nonsense.   After dinner
begin *Ego* 3 in the hotel writing-room, which I have to desert
in a hurry owing to a priest being sick.

Aug. 10   This is a land of Autolycuses.   Monty put down
Monday.   his spectacles, and they were at once picked up.
              I left my best stick, the gift of George Mair, in the
hotel cloakroom and never saw it again.   The odd thing was
that during the night of its disappearance I kept on dreaming
about the stick.   And the man who eats at the next table has
had his horse stolen.   But the charm excuses the dishonesty ;
one reads this nation's poverty in its smiling eyes.

Aug. 12   Newcastle, Co. Down.   On getting in yesterday
Wednesday. afternoon we at once had a round on the links,
              which I remember from twenty-eight years ago
as being absolutely first-class.   The 13th, where all those years
ago I holed a brassie shot from among the stones, is now a
velvet paradise, and the 9th, where once I nearly holed out

from the tee, is now a fine two- or even three-shotter. My golf, alas, is falling into the sere; I shan't mind if I can keep it out of the yellow! But the ball doesn't go as far as it used to, and I can see that I shall have to putt very well to break 85. Still, I agree with Monty that two elderly gentlemen, if they take it quietly, can get a lot of fun out of the game. M. said this with the perspiration streaming down his face, and his chin just showing over the edge of a sixty-foot precipice some two hundred yards off the line. It is only fair to state that M. S., in receipt of 11 strokes and 1 bisque—a complicated system of handicapping in vogue among Civil Servants—beat J. A. this afternoon by seven up and six to play.

Aug. 14   The death of Harry Preston, though expected, is
Friday.   still a shock, for I had got very fond of the little
            man during the last few years. He would fall back
on me whenever he came up to town unexpectedly and found himself without somebody to lunch with. At almost the last big dinner he attended, a motoring affair, I made his speech for him, as he wasn't feeling up to it. The 500 guests didn't know who I was or want to hear me, and I got out of it by talking entirely about H. P. and saying that, whatever buildings Brighton might pull down and reconstruct, it would never demolish H. P.'s memory or build another man to replace him.

In appearance Harry was exactly like a baby elephant; the very folds of his skin were pachydermatous. I think it was James Gunn who first discovered this, at the time he was painting him. For his own protection Harry put on an impenetrable armour of *fausse bonhomie*, which to him was what his part is to an actor. Without it he must have succumbed to the assaults of all the bores who had ever spent a night at his hotel. To his real friends he was sincerity itself. He had a quality which has become very rare. He was *merry*, and his laugh had a real tinkle. Early this year he told me that the end might come at any time and that he was ready. After which he crossed the floor to take out Lady Preston in the Blue Danube, which, he said, he had danced with her every night for thirty-nine years.

Aug. 15
Saturday.
M. insisting on returning *via* Stranraer, we spent yesterday in Belfast, whose beauties refuse themselves to the casual visitor. While Dublin is obviously a capital, though a seedy and impoverished one, Belfast is mean and provincial. Too many of its shops are branches of well-known London emporiums, the whole place is depressing, and the note is a dull opinionativeness. The things which struck me most were the number of swans and newsboys, the out-of-the-wayness of the obviously unwanted Parliament House, and the age of the taxi-cabs. The one in which we made the tour of the city was fusty with old leather, smelling of all the funerals it has ever attended. Intellectually the place is as backward as Spain. The R.C.'s insisting upon putting up a church in the middle of a Protestant slum, the devil's own disturbances are created, stones thrown, and the neighbourhood's lamp-posts decorated with Union Jacks.

My night was sleepless, owing to a bed concave in all directions, like a dish-cover. Also, hotel much too hot. I never left any place with so good a will, and Monty agrees. If ever I visit Ireland again I shall give Belfast a miss. Its petty ugliness is revolting.

Aug. 16
Sunday.
Postcard from Jock, who appears to be having a good time in Amsterdam :

DEAR JAAMS,
I think u would not mooch like this place. It is ver wicked but also ver dirty. It suits me well because I am ver mooch both.
                                             Your—JOEK

Aug. 17
Monday.
I shall never be a really *first-class* critic owing to my inability to wrap things up. I must blurt them out. This morning I cut the following out of Neville Cardus's *Manchester Guardian* notice about Henry Lytton :

Old men with long memories have been known to maintain that Lytton was not as great a comic actor in the Savoy operas as Grossmith was, or George Thorne. The truth is that Lytton could never be estimated purely and simply as an actor. There was indeed a touch about him of the inspired amateur; that is to say, he usually seemed able to win his audience without the help of the tricks of the footlights. On or off the stage he was the least theatrical of men; his art was indeed nothing but his nature. . . . In private life Lytton was very much as he was on the stage—he required only to dress himself for his parts and 'taste' them rather than present them in the technical gadgets of the theatre. In Jack Point he did, to some length, emulate a definitely histrionic art, and in the death scene his own personality was submerged by an emotional current of no little strength. Yet even here the expression was naïve, not of the greenroom's sophisticated texture. The great thing about Lytton was that you loved him first and then, by taking thought, admired the very absence of those technical adornments which are three parts of the equipment of most comic actors.

The truth is that Lytton was a poor actor; in my view he could not hold a candle to C. H. Workman, who played his parts in the provinces. Ernest Fenton, who was with him in *A Princess of Kensington*, *The Earl and the Girl*, and *The Talk of the Town*, said yesterday, "Lytton was like some small prehistoric bird hopping about the stage. He did it all by a catch in the voice, which he used for the humorous, the amorous, and the pathetic. This trick was always the same and pleased the audience, which knew exactly what to expect."

By the oddest chance, and going into the Savage Club about eleven o'clock to-night, I met Cardus.

J. A. Look here, Cardus. What would happen to a batsman who lacked those technical adornments which are three parts of the equipment of most cricketers?

N. C. Bowled all over his bloody wicket, old boy!

Aug. 23   George Mathew arrived last night. Golf at Lytham
Sunday.   and St Anne's in the morning with young Rawstron,
              who has greatly improved. He has not missed a holeable putt—up to 9 feet—since Thursday morning! I find I can always get *one* half of the course in 39. But the two halves, alas, don't fit! Receiving 9 strokes, my tally of matches with

Rawstron for last week is 1 win, 3 defeats, 1 halved match. This last had a grand finish. The 16th on this course is a most fascinating hole, especially with a following wind. You *must* place your drive on the left, for then the hole opens up beautifully. The least suspicion of slice and you are faced with a series of crevasses, the last of which bites into the green. With the wind behind, no niblick play of mine can carry the lot and stop. I was all square here and played a beautiful spoon shot, for safety, short, but well to the left. A full plonk with my big mashie left me four yards from the pin. In the meantime the boy had hit a terrific drive, but with a hint of cut right into the chain of bunkers. He got out with a marvellous shot which pitched on the very rim of green and crevasse, wavered, and rolled to the pin stone-dead. One down! At the seventeenth I saved my bacon with the last of my strokes and the best brassie shot I have ever hit or shall hit. That was all square, and as neither of us could get a three at the last hole we went in all square. I have not sunk a putt since I arrived. That admirable caddie Joe Hodgson keeps saying, " Left lip ! " and always my eye wants to borrow from the right. I believe that you must be able to see the line for yourself, and that putting *against* your eye must always fail. Hudibras's

> He that complies against his will
> Is of his own opinion still

holds true of golf.

Sept. 6   Exhibition match at Thorpe Hall. In the morning
Sunday.   Padgham and E. R. Whitcombe whacked the heads
             off Adams and Denny, the last of whom was fresh
from his 66 in the *News of the World* qualifying round at Frinton. I noticed that at the last hole, 210 yards long, all four indulged in the pitiful ambition of taking iron clubs off the tee. All were short and struggling for threes, whereas last night a miserable amateur with the sense to take wood was past the pin and putting for a two. The course is 6000 yards long, and a prize was offered for whoever should break Abe Mitchell's record of 69. Denny, out in 32, looked well set when he hooked his drive to the 11th,

and, in trying to pull round a tree, hit it. I know that tree!
The hole cost him 6, and at the 13th, a hole he invariably does
against me in 2, he three-putted, after which nothing would go
right. He finished in 69. The course was in grand condition,
the greens being fast and true, yet velvety enough to hold the
high-pitched shot. The four caddies singled out for the honour
of carrying for the great men had obviously been " barbered
three times o'er," and turned up in clothes one did not suspect
them of possessing.

Sept. 25   The talk at supper turning on stage folk and how
Friday.   they never think of anything except introductions
             to managers, Selwyn Jepson said, " I've given up
making love to actresses. They put their arms round your
neck and murmur, ' Do you know Sydney Carroll ? ' "

Sept. 26   Jock this morning : " When you die I shall be at
Saturday. the bedside with my notebook, leaning over you,
             ready to catch your last witty rattle, and saying,
' Finish the article first ! ' "

Oct. 14   Went last night to the *Romeo and Juliet* film. It
Wednesday. is monstrously over-produced. And for a very
             good reason, which is that two-dimensional acting
is just not good enough. Read Shakespeare, and you create for
yourself a three-dimensional world peopled by creatures of flesh
and blood. See a Shakespeare play on the stage proper, and you
behold a reasonable semblance of the three-dimensional world
peopled by actors of flesh and blood. The film is neither the
study nor the stage, but a wishy-washy, two-dimensional compromise. If *Romeo and Juliet* had been a silent film the London
Symphony Orchestra would have been called in to restore the
balance. But, says somebody, *Romeo and Juliet* could never have
been a silent film : what about Shakespeare's poetry ? The
answer is that even the talkies do not give us Shakespeare's
poetry. That, then, is the explanation of all the absurdities of
over-production. Last night's show began with a parade of

Montagues and Capulets reminding one of a Hollywood party. Now I just do not believe that the Capulet household contained forty page-boys, or that Juliet went about attended by forty tiring-maids. I do not believe that Juliet's bedroom was at the end of a passage containing as many doors as a floor in the Regent Palace Hotel. I do not believe that the Montague-Capulet brawl attained the same dimensions as the Battle of Agincourt. I do not believe that the entrance to the Capulets' tomb was as magnificent as the façade of Chartres Cathedral.

As always on these occasions, the programme was a mine of information: " Materials which would almost have built a small town went into the work. 60,000 square feet of plaster, 700,000 feet of heavy lumber, 35,000 square feet of composition board, 24,000 pounds of tiling." The critic's view of all this nonsense has been set down once and for all. It is contained in the poem of the Walrus and the Carpenter, who, you remember, wept like anything to see such quantites of sand. " If this were only cleared away," they said, " it *would* be grand." If only the film producers would clear away their junk ! The programme goes on : " Just to keep the ballroom floor swept clean was the constant job of seven men, and an equal number of brooms." This is handing it to one on a plate. " If seven maids with seven mops . . ."

Film programmes are notoriously immune from humour. Were they not it would be impossible for them to print such a passage as the following : " Informed that she would be tested, Miss Shearer balked at an immediate test. She asked for time in which to study. Then began *one of the most rigorous novitiates since the time of Ignatius Loyola*. [Italics mine.] Miss Shearer retired into the Italy of the fifteenth century. She read books on the etiquette of the day, instructions on the deportment of a young girl of the time. She studied the costumes of the period, and looked at hundreds of copies of the works of the painters of the time. Practically nothing that a girl of fourteen of that day would have thought, known, or done remained foreign to Miss Shearer." But one must not impute this goggle-eyed nonsense to American taste only. I have not forgotten the

English musical-comedy actress who, prior to essaying the
rôle of Cleopatra, made herself " personally acquainted with
every mummy in the British Museum." The programme then
tells us that, " completely steeped in the tradition of Juliet,
Miss Shearer had the courage to renounce it when the time
came for making her screen test. It might be simpler, she felt,
to play the part as Ellen Terry had." [Italics again mine.] Leslie
Howard's Romeo is hang-dog.

Oct. 19   Either you can't sell a horse at all or you can sell
Monday.   it twice over. As soon as Ego declared himself I
             knew it was all up with Tulip, who is exactly the
same height. And I realised that even if the little mare deserved
second place to Ego she would never get it, as judges don't
like giving too much to one exhibitor. I have known for over
a year I should have to sell Tulip, but could get nobody interested. Then, one day last week, I sold her to an American
millionaire, a coaching man who intends to show her in his
team at the New York Horse Show. The next day I had an
inquiry for her from Scotland ! I got exactly what I gave Albert
Throup for her, and as her prize-money just about paid for the
show expenses, all she has cost me is her keep for four years
and her entrance fees at the shows. At a generous estimate
I have had all my fun out of her at something under £500. She
gave me many a thrill, and I shall never forget her first show at
Oxford.

Oct. 22   Good talk at the Savage Club about the Infinities :
Thursday.

WARNER ALLEN. I am a mystic. Why be afraid of Death ?
Since Time is not absolute, but merely something invented
by Man for his convenience, we are already dead. Equally
when we are dead we shall be alive. We are both now. Past,
present, and future are one. (*Turning to his guest*) By the way,
what about lunching with me to-morrow ?
    GUEST. Sorry—I've got to attend the execution of Charles
the First.

Oct. 23   Motored Leo Pavia down to Brighton. He told me
Friday.   his smoked salmon story, of which I never tire.
          Old Mr Silverstone, a rich merchant, was accustomed
on leaving his house in the morning to bestow upon his poor
co-religionists assembled outside various sums of money. One
morning Mr S., being in an especially good humour, presented
a particularly seedy *schnorrer* with a half-sovereign. At eleven
o'clock the same morning, going into Sweeting's to eat a small
plate of smoked salmon according to his wont, he was staggered
to perceive the *schnorrer* indulging in a large plate of the same
delicacy. Accosting him, Mr S. said, " Are you the man to
whom I gave half a sovereign this morning ? " The *schnorrer*,
with his mouth full, nodded. " Why then," said Mr S., with
some heat, " do I find you here eating smoked salmon ? " The
schnorrer, swallowing rapidly, retorted, " Mr Silverstone, vill
you listen ? Ven I haf no money I can buy no smoked salmon.
Ven I haf money I must not buy smoked salmon. Vill you tell
me, Mr Silverstone, ven then shall I eat smoked salmon ? "
     The old thing was full of good stories.
     One was about a distinguished aurist, a notable bridge-fiend
who looks like a short-sighted walrus. One day in 1915 his
woman partner messed up a hand to such an extent that the
old man followed her about the room telling her how the hand
should have been played. A few days later the news arrived
of the death at the Front of the aurist's only son, with the result
that for some time he did not come to the club. When, some
weeks later, he did turn up he was met by the lady who had
ruined the hand. She, full of sympathy, exclaimed, " My dear
Doctor F——, I am so sorry. I am so very sorry ! " Whereat
the aurist, gazing vindictively at her, said, " That is all very well,
madam, but it's too late. Had you led the King of Spades and
followed it up with the Knave . . ."

Oct. 24   Golf at Littlehampton on top of too much lunch.
Saturday.   A wheezy, grunting, asthmatic, pot-bellied round
              which recalls all the nasty things Prince Hal said
to Falstaff about his stomach. I hold my own with young

Riseborough for nine holes, after which I go to pieces, physically and morally. I even very nearly lose my temper, and am glad the game is over at the sixteenth.

In the evening Leo and I drop in to a concert at the Dome by the Society of Symphonic Players. *Meistersinger* overture, a Mozart concerto with Szigeti, who butlers it very well, and Brahms' Fourth Symphony. The concert winds up with de Falla's dances from *The Three-cornered Hat*. It is rather fun to creep into " unprofessional " places like this and see how they carry on when, so to speak, nobody's listening. The orchestra does brilliantly in the de Falla, and some day, perhaps, I shall get over my prejudice against women leaders.

Leo is an extraordinary mine of out-of-the-way information. I mention casually that I have seen the *Mayerling* film at the Curzon. The old boy actually remembers the name of the coachman—Bratfisch ! He tells me at great length all about Frau Schratt, and reels off a list of her great parts. Now comes an extravagant coincidence. In this morning's paper I read that the old lady, now aged eighty-three, is dying in a little suburban villa in Vienna. In her heyday, says Leo, she was a first-class actress, an artist to her finger-tips, and a woman with a riotous sense of life and humour.

To-night Leo interrupted my writing to say, " Since you pretend, dear James, to like Chopin's little-played No. 1 Concerto "—he was reading an advance copy of *Ego* 2—" you'd better hear it." Whereupon he went to the piano and played it. All Leo's musical conversation is on a par with Mr Squeers's notions about practical spelling. Ask him how a piece is played, and he will play it to you. L. made his first appearance in London as a boy prodigy at the age of eleven. At fifteen he gave three recitals at the St James's Hall, and his name occurs in Shaw's *Music in London*. He then went to Vienna, where for four years he studied under Leschetizky, his fellow-students being Mark Hambourg, Ethel and Harold Bauer, Sapellnikoff, Ossip Gabrilowitsch, Katharine Goodson, and Artur Schnabel. At lunch to-day I said something about dishonourable conduct. " What is honourable, and what is dishonourable ? " Leo exclaimed. " Many years ago a friend of mine approached a young and starving poet with a business proposition. He would get a hundred pounds if he would go through the ceremony of marriage with a woman who was to inherit a considerable legacy provided she could produce a marriage certificate. The husband, of course, was to leave her at the door of the registry office. The poet flew into a violent rage, refused point-blank, borrowed a shilling, and walked out of the house, slamming the door. My friend followed him and saw him turn into a public-house. He waited five minutes and went in himself. There, if you please, was the poet standing a drink to somebody needier and seedier than himself."

Nov. 3
Tuesday.
From Brother Edward :

THE EPITAPH

Hic jacet was the customary form
The Ancients used, to start an epicedium,
Devoid of simple truth, replete with tedium,
On those who now are cold that once were warm.

To-day, in English tongue, the tag " Here lies "
Begins the roll of fame spectacular ;
" *Ci-gît*," in French—the meaning still applies,
In foreign phrase or the vernacular.

But on the slab, denoting Edward's tomb,
No tricksy blandishments shall they inscribe ;
For he, in person, hath pronounced his doom.
Beginning with a self-imposèd gibe :
" The elbow, once he lifted to imbibe,
He lifts no more, for lack of elbow-room."

Then, lower down, a comprehensive screed,
In hieroglyphic characters mysterious :
His history in full ; for prudes to read
And sticklers for convention, deleterious ;
Nay, at the sight, Catullus would have blushed,
Schiller recoiled, and even Goethe tushed.

Full well he knew, his family would meet,
Post-morteming in the approvèd way;
And each, in turn, propound the quaint conceit
Of hens so white they never laid astray.

He further was aware, his ample store
Of misdemeanours would not be condoned;
But rather dwelt upon and stressed, the more
To vilify a mem'ry unbemoaned.

" He's gone at last ! "   " Spent is the breath of him ! "
" Lived on us all for years, and thought it funny ! "
" Those Golden Cock'rels were the death of him ! "
" Why couldn't he be vulgar and make money ? "
And so on, in the well-established fashion;
Evidence of true Christian compassion.

And while this pleasant atmosphere persists,
Of Sanctimony-cum-vituperation;
And while these well-intentioned humanists
Are putting corpses in their proper station,

They find no will or testament exists—
In truth, no violence to expectation—
But, counting it as one of his offences,
They wrangle o'er the funeral expenses.

Vex not his spirit with th' unseemly sound !
With jarring notes no longer try his ears !
He'll come no more, the bones are underground
Of him who ever ate his bread with tears.

                                                          E. A.

Nov. 9   The night has been unruly; some say the earth
Monday.   was feverous and did shake. In non-Shakespearian
              English, *Ego* 2 was given to the world at midnight.
The *S.T.* had a discouraging review and a heartening advertisement yesterday. Gollancz, fishing for advance opinions, had
hauled in a noble catch. Eddie Marsh, Cedric Hardwicke,
Hugh Walpole, Noel Coward, E. M. Delafield, and Bob Sherriff
were all highly flattering. But the best of all was Rebecca's,
" I shall keep these journals as I keep the Goncourt Journals,
as records of their time more truly historical than history."

The Goncourt reference is wildly gratifying, and I like Hugh's notion that I am a character in the novel that Dickens and Dostoievsky would have written in collaboration. Add that in the *Observer* Humbert Wolfe, while using his most malicious pen, does me proud with a reference to Pepys. The fact that it is a backhanded one—" a winsome self-satisfaction unequalled since Pepys "—does not matter. The point is that he couples with it a " rich Balzacian love of life and self." It is the overtones which count. Goncourt, Dickens, Dostoievsky, Pepys, Balzac . . .

Nov. 14   The Empress Poppæa
Saturday.   Said, " Nero, you're queer ! "
                Nero said, " Like Caligula,
                I am a bit irrigula ! "

Dec. 6   It is a quarter-past seven, and I have been sitting
Sunday.   with the wireless half on all afternoon. There was
            to be a Cabinet Meeting at half-past five o'clock,
at which presumably the King's decision was to be made known.
So far nothing. If ever there was an occasion for a " solemn
musick " this was it. While waiting I tried to read a pamphlet
by J. Joseph Renaud entitled *Lagadière s'explique*. This discusses
whether *Le Bossu*, the famous Porte-Saint-Martin melodrama,
was written by Sardou or Paul Féval. The *Encyclopædia
Britannica* says : " *Le Bossu*, which Sardou wrote expressly for
Fechter, did not satisfy the actor ; and when the play was at
last successfully produced the nominal authorship, by some
unfortunate arrangement, had been transferred to other men."
Renaud proves that the piece had four incarnations. (1) It was
a piece by Féval and Sardou writing in collaboration. This
piece was rejected everywhere. (2) Féval, having obtained
S.'s consent, turned the unsuccessful play into a best-selling
novel. (3) Sardou and Féval started to turn the novel back
into a drama. (4) Sardou withdrew and Féval finished the job
with one Anicet Bourgeois. Normally all this would have
entranced me. To-day I found it dull.

8.56. The wireless news hints much, says little. The P.M. will not see the King to-night. To-morrow's Cabinet meeting has been cancelled, and the P.M. will make a statement in the House to-morrow. I thought I detected a defensive note in the plea that Ministers had neither threatened the King nor attempted unduly to hurry him, and that at no time had there been open or formal disagreement.

Dec. 7   Could not remain at home last night, so went down
Monday. to Fleet Street and found the *D.E.* gnawing its
           fingers up to the knuckle. It had issued a poster
with the words " No Decision." But a rival had gone one better with the placard

THE KING
A
DECISION

with the " a " in very small type. Naturally the newsboys cried, " King's decision." Which meant that the rival paper mopped up all the sales. Hence the chagrin.

Jock is not seeing eye to eye with me in all this—he likes his Shakespeare in the past, whereas I have a use for it in the present and find the drama going on under my nose more exciting in fact, if less so in poetry. After all, there are rules of drama, and you know more or less how a play must end. Whereas not only is this one being acted for the first time and we are spectators at a world-première, but also we can have no idea which ending the dramatist will choose. There isn't even a dramatist. We are looking on, so to speak, at a performance of the *commedia dell' arte*. Only this is a tragedy, or may be. Discussing this to-day, Jock admitted that three hundred years ago he would have been more interested in a rising Jacobean playwright than in a sinking Armada.

In his speech in the House this afternoon Baldwin added nothing to what we read last night, and again this morning, except that his Majesty had broached the subject of the

morganatic marriage " some weeks ago." The King is still at
Fort Belvedere, and the general impression is that the situation
is a little eased.

Dec. 8   I went last night to the Victoria Palace, leaving
Tuesday. there at ten minutes to twelve, going straight home,
            and therefore just missing the midnight specials
containing Mrs Simpson's statement that she is willing to withdraw from " a situation that has been rendered both unhappy
and untenable." This morning the *Express* announces in head-
lines " The End of the Crisis." I do not think so. The statement
says that the attitude is " unchanged," which can only mean
that nothing is now declared which was not known before.
The King, then, must still decide.

Two days ago my impulse was to hope the King would tell
Mr Baldwin to write, call, speechify, resign, and be damned.
I do not feel this now. I do not think anybody feels this now.
I have just come across the painter Haydon's description of the
Coronation of George IV. " Three or four of high rank appear
from behind the throne ; an interval is left ; the crowd scarce
breathe. Something rustles ; and a being buried in satin,
feathers and diamonds rolls gracefully into his seat. The room
rises with a sort of feathered, silken thunder."

But the King is not a feathered darling. He is not a bird of
paradise, but a man living in a world that is not paradise. His
name stands first before his country's, carved in granite on
enduring monuments throughout the length and breadth of the
land. It is a king's part to do a king's duty.

Since all this started I have had the greatest difficulty in
settling to my normal work. Jock openly opposes my writing
this detailed account of something so wildly out of my province.
Whereupon I charge him with puling æstheticism, which he
admits if by that I mean being concerned more with the local
than the world theatre : " My work, the arts, food and drink,
my own affections and not anybody else's—that's all I'm going
to bother about till the next war, when I shall probably be killed
fighting for a country I'm not particularly fond of against one

I probably like better ! " I tell him that I consider this attitude despicable but honest.

Dec. 9   Waste ! Waste ! Waste ! The secretary's cry
Wednesday.   which ends Granville-Barker's tragedy brings down
               the curtain on this one also. What of the King
himself ? " Dispute it like a man," says Malcolm to Macduff
in his extremity. And Macduff answers, " I shall do so ; but
I must also feel it as a man." If I write of this matter as a dramatic
critic, it is because I feel it as a dramatic critic. Therefore I see
the King as an actor in a world drama echoing Antony's

> Fall not a tear, I say ; one of them rates
> All that is won and lost : give me a kiss ;
> Even this repays me.

Dec. 11   So far as I am concerned, the King abdicated when
Friday.   the news was announced over the wireless at six
               o'clock last night. The ceremony, for such it was,
was moving. Baldwin came out of it very well. It entirely
cleared my mind of any possible doubts as to the way in which
this thing ought to be looked at. I see the affair now in terms
not of Shakespeare's Antony but of Wells's Mr Polly, who,
when Destiny tried to bully him, stood up to Destiny :

Man comes into life to seek and find his sufficient beauty,
to serve it, to win and increase it, to fight for it, to face anything and bear anything for it, counting death as nothing
so long as the dying eyes still turn to it. And fear and dullness
and indolence and appetite, which indeed are no more than
fear's three crippled brothers, who make ambushes and creep
by night, are against him, to delay him, to hold him off, to
hamper and beguile and kill him in that quest.

History will record that Edward VIII found the Kingship of
England to be insufficient beauty.

1937

Jan. 11
Monday.
An example of the amateur beating the professional. I devoured half a penholder trying to find out why Edna Best wasn't a good Cinderella. Imagine my disgust when somebody asked Gladys Henson what she thought of the performance, and Gladys replied, " She just didn't want to go to the ball ! "

Jan. 13
Wednesday.
Just as I was sallying forth to consume a digestive biscuit and a glass of milk prior to a medical examination for insurance purposes a 'phone message came for me to lunch with Herbert Morgan. Potted shrimps, boiled salmon, asparagus, Bollinger, brandy, and a foot of cigar. " It's a magnificent ruin ! " said the doctor, tapping at what I still call my chest. And again, " The quality's good, even if the fabric's impaired." This reminded me of what is almost my favourite quotation in the whole of Hazlitt : " In that prodigious prosing paper, *The Times*, which seems to be written as well as printed by a steam-engine, Mr Kemble is compared to the ruin of a magnificent temple, in which the divinity still resides. This is not the case. The temple is unimpaired ; but the divinity is sometimes from home." (I am conscious of having quoted this in an earlier volume. But if I have, I do not apologise. It will do nobody any harm to read this passage again ; I have read it fifty times.) The doctor asking me if my consumption of alcohol was moderate, I said, " My lord and jury, I won't deceive you " ; and he said, " You had better not ! " As I was driving home along the Goswell Road I wondered whether there is anything in Dunne's Theory of Time, and whether it was *because* I was going to be driven home along the Goswell Road that I thought of Mrs Cluppins. I noticed, also in the Goswell Road, a shop sign belonging to a firm of briar-pipe manufacturers—

"Vuillard and Strauss." Almost my favourite painter and almost my two favourite composers.

Jan. 16   Brother Edward, who is recovering from 'flu,
Saturday.   writes to say that he is going to make a change
                 in his post-'flu literary diet. Normally this is
a re-reading of *The Anatomy of Melancholy*. This time he promises
himself Donne's *Biathanatos, or Vindication of Suicide* (1651):
"I am convinced this is one of the finest books in the English
language."

Rooting about to-day in some of my old papers, Jock found
a page torn out of the *Musical Standard* for Nov. 2, 1907. This
has a two-column review by Joseph Holbrooke of Edward's
Sechs Lieder. These are the songs referred to in the fourth
stanza of "Edward's Journey" (see p. 127). Holbrooke says
that the composer of these songs "has, to my mind, a great
genius. It is revealed in his harmony, in his most original
atmosphere, and, greatest of all, in his melodies. . . . If I say
that the third song, *Parting*, rivals Mr Delius in passion, this
should be sufficient to those who know those works." I believe
John Coates sang one of the songs at a recital at the Bechstein
Hall in 1906. Now they are what Ethel Monticue calls "piffle
before the wind," and I don't suppose Edward ever thinks of
them. It is just like him to compose stuff which, at that date, only
Coates could sing—Ernest Newman in the *Manchester Guardian*
called his harmony "modern of the moderns"—and no amateurs
could play. Edward has always been very difficult to encourage.
How on earth is one to presume to encourage a man who, for
a New Year's card, sends you the fly-leaf of a pocket-diary
annotated like this:

PERSONAL MEMORANDA

Telegraphic Address.	MORT.
No. of Bank Book.	Ce que tu voudras.
No. of Watch.	J'ai le temps.
No. of Car.	Tu ris ?
No. of Stores Ticket.	Moi, je ris aussi.

INSURANCE (Qu'est-ce que c'est ?)

Accident.	Peu m'importe !
Burglary.	Mais voyons !
Fire.	Et l'Enfer ?
Motor-car.	On m'attribue deux jambes.
Servants.	Pour moi, tous les habitants de la terre.
Life.	Mais je suis mort !

Jan. 21
Thursday.

Dined last night at Scott's with Clifford Bax, Meum Stewart, and a Mrs Blanche, an artist. Best potted shrimps and talk I have tasted for a long time. Went back to C. B.'s flat in Albany and stayed till very late. They took me up to see some of the lady's paintings —women bisected lengthways and grafted on to halves of violoncellos ; wicker dummies fully crinolined, but with a punch-ball for head and boxing-gloves for hands ; cornucopias spilling ladies' gloves—the whole done in salmon pink, and *très* Regency. Asked if I liked it, I said it affected me like Sitwellian poetry. Asked if I liked Sitwellian poetry, I said it affected me like Alban Berg's music, and was no further harried. Clifford showed me his Sims picture, which he says he understands, as he knows the next world intimately. Was quite positive about the smallest details. Long talk about Buddhism. Clifford offered to put on a gramophone record of somebody dead speaking at a spiritualist séance. As it was two in the morning I flatly refused to hear it. Happening to mention having read some new theory, according to which Cause and Effect, not directly connected, rotate round one another like spots on a rapidly revolving cone and result in no more than a confluence of probabilities, I said this would mess up one's notions of morality. Clifford said, " Some of us have done that already, James."

Jan. 30
Saturday.

Part of a letter from Brother Edward :

You who are such a devotee of Samuel Johnson should dip into his Dictionary. There you will find such definitions as :

Pension : An allowance made to anyone without an equivalent. Pay given to a state-hireling for treason to his country.

For the sake of this, I have almost forgiven the author his coarse insensibility to Gray, his denial of the efficacy of travel as a mind-broadener, his pronouncement about the barbarity of the Greeks, and his opinion of Leibnitz—" as paltry a fellow as I know." And I have quite forgiven him all the fuss he made about a flea-jump to the Hebrides, which he considered a more prodigious feat than Marco Polo's travels to Tartary or Herodotus's world-wanderings, for such remarks as : " *The Courtier*, by Castiglione, is the best book that was ever written upon good breeding," or " Edinburgh Castle would make a good prison in England." And this leads to the question of Boswell. Let us give Macaulay a rest and read Carlyle's essay on Boswell. As the Doctor would say : " I have never read it : but I intend to read it ; and you may read it."

Feb. 2   Eiluned Lewis's wedding, before which Hamish
Tuesday.   Hamilton gave a luncheon party at the Jardin des
             Gourmets.   Jimmie Horsnell said he thought that curtains should fall at the end of the ceremony and the bride be whisked out of sight, as at the other place.   Somebody said, " Into an ardentorium."   Eiluned, looking with her red hair the perfect Rossetti, came down the aisle chattering like a magpie.   I had to make a speech at the reception, and fortunately remembered a recent story which ended, " Everybody lived happily ever after except the bride and bridegroom."

Feb. 22   Albert showed me the last number of the American
Monday.   magazine *Sportologue*.   This has an account of the
             four-year-old pony mare Highland Cora : " This grand young filly has, besides the carriage of a queen, unusually balanced action, and an indescribable ' it,' which is essential in the general make-up of a show-horse champion."   Highland Cora is by that great pony King of the Plain.   But what interests me is that her dam is Skirbeck Cora, which I bought as she came out of the ring at the Olympia Show of 1919.   This makes the third of my animals which have done well for other people. I gave £150 for my first show pony, Talke Princess, whose first foal, Axholme Venus, was sold for £2500 !   Vortez, bought

by me for 14 guineas, got Rainbow, sold for £3000. And now
Cora, for whom I paid £200, at the age of seventeen does herself
proud by giving birth to Highland Cora, who, if she is as good
as *Sportologue*'s description, and goes as well as her photograph,
should be worth a mint of money.

April 6   Just back from the Old Vic. Olivier as Henry V.
Tuesday.   I annoyed Jock very much by telling him what a
             relief this or any of the histories, not to mention
the tragedies, is after the too frequent revivals of the comedies.
I have got to the stage that whenever the curtain goes up on a
Shakespeare comedy what I hear is something like this :

> As I remember, 'twas upon this fashion.
> Now, fair Hippolyta, our nuptial hour
> Draws on apace ; it wearies me, you say
> It wearies you, and there begins my sadness.
> In sooth I know not why I am so sad.
> If music be the food of love, play on,
> And fame, that all hunt after in their lives,
> Live registered upon our brazen tombs.

April 18   Last of the season's Sunday concerts at Queen's
Sunday.   Hall. Took Julian Phillipson, who knows two
             tunes only—" I've Got You Under My Skin " and the
big theme in the last movement of Sibelius No. 2. Mark came
on to the platform with one stick and in his oldest suit, and got
a great reception. I hate the people who don't like Mark ; if
they played bridge with him they would better understand his
piano playing. Mark talks before, during, and after every hand,
and when he forces himself to silence his mind continues to
ferment ; this is why he has *fortissimos* and *pianissimos*, but
disdains mezzo-fortes. This afternoon he played Rubinstein's D
minor Piano Concerto with admirable truculence in the first
and third movements, and a laudable attempt at tenderness in
the middle one. I now know that Brahms' Fourth Symphony
is permanently too dry for me. I think I can get something
out of the first three movements, but confess to finding the
Passacaglia a bore. The programme says that the thirty-two

variations show Brahms' "complete mastery of the technique of his art." A fat lot I care! Repeating a dull thing thirty-two times doesn't make it less dull.

MY AMERICAN VISIT

April 26
Monday.
The *Sunday Times* has been dangling America before me! *Pourparlers* are now finished, and I leave on the *Bremen* on Wednesday. The idea is to write about the New York scene, with the theatre as pivot. I was a little nervous about this until in Borrow's *Celebrated Trials*—my present bed-book—I came across this: "It is no easy thing to tell a story plainly and distinctly by mouth; but to tell one on paper is difficult indeed, so many snares lie in the way. People are afraid to put down what is common on paper; they seek to embellish their narratives, as they think, by philosophic speculations and reflections; they are anxious to shine, and people who are anxious to shine can never tell a plain story." Jumping at the tip, I have decided to treat the whole thing as diary.

April 27
Tuesday.
A jolly doctor friend of mine comes with me. As B. looks like a Jewish Traddles, I have asked the shipping company whether there will be any Nazi nonsense on board. The clerk replies that the company does not allow politics to interfere with business. An admirable Jewish maxim! In the middle of some hectic packing—I am convinced that spare collar-studs are not obtainable in America—the 'phone rings. Will I tell a perfect stranger all about the French actress Rachel? I reply that she was Napoleon's last mistress, who lived to a great age, and married Buffalo Bill! (Actually she was born in the year Napoleon died.) An odd thing has happened about the luggage. Having dispatched our cabin trunks, suitcases, and my golf-bag through the ordinary office on Waterloo station, I get home to read that all baggage "*must* be registered at the Norddeutscher Lloyd Office." Panic! Hamlet's "You shall know I am set naked on your kingdom"

is not going to be much fun in New York. So I rush hysterically
down to Waterloo again and give a perfect performance of
Mr Magnus, who was satisfied from the ostler's manner that the
leather hat-box was *not* in the Ipswich coach. Am told the
luggage will be all right.

April 28   Alan Dent—*i.e.*, Jock—who is to hold the *Sunday*
Wednesday. *Times* fort, makes me a platform offering of his
                 own copy of *Le Voyage de M. Perrichon*. Remem-
bering Madame P.'s " Vous faites des phrases dans une gare,"
I refrain from effusiveness, merely recommending him while
I am away to shine, but not outshine. Wanting to know how
good a doctor B. is, I ask him during breakfast if he can do a
tracheotomy. He replies, " Yes, if you've a penknife." A
Baron Something, whose name I do not catch, but whom I take
to be a Director of the N.D.L. Company, is extremely civil to
both of us. The Southampton Sewage Works are gay with
flower-beds and a bowling-green. Otherwise nothing of note
until we go on board, to find the luggage snug in our cabins.
I think the N.D.L. should take a tip from the Rules of Golf
Committee and alter " must " to " may."

As we cast off the band strikes up *Eine Seefahrt die ist lustig*.
Lots of telegrams, and a letter from John Gielgud in his exquisite,
absurdly tiny handwriting, telling me all the things I should
do and the people I must meet : " The nicest person of all is
Lillian Gish." The boat is about half full, with nobody on
board I have ever heard of except Max Schmeling, the boxer.
The food is excellent beyond belief. For lunch we have the
most decorative hors-d'œuvres, including a delicious, velvety
herring known as " Swedish Appetiser," langouste, and a German
family dish of chopped beef. A good bottle of Eitelsbacher
Sonnenberg at 4 marks. Am struck not so much by the extreme
attentiveness of the stewards as by their spick-and-spanness,
and above all, their noiselessness. This is dream waiting. The
lazy man need never trouble his pockets ; when he wants matches
there is always a silent presence to put them into his hand, like
the ghost in the story. A bandbox smartness pervades the

ship. The lift-boys in their white uniforms suggest tap-dancers in a revue; the stewardesses have the rectitude of hospital nurses.

Leaving Cherbourg, we meet the *Queen Mary* coming in. She left Southampton two hours after us, but is faster by three knots. I ought to be able to calculate when she will catch us up, but even at school could never do this kind of sum. And now I have not the vaguest idea how to employ the time. I have put on an Elia-like quality of superannuation. I am Retired Leisure. I am to be met with on trim decks. I grow into gentility perceptibly. I am like a dog which, having been on a leash for years, is suddenly liberated and has forgotten how to frisk.

April 29   It is just untrue that on the first night out one
Thursday.   doesn't dress for dinner. Nearly everybody
              dressed last night, including Schmeling, elegant
as a prize-fighter can be who really wins prize-fights. Handsome is as handsome does is truer in the boxing-ring than anywhere else. George Bishop, who is *persona grata* with everybody at sight, would by this time have made Schmeling promise to attend the Malvern Festival. If I get introduced to him I shan't bore him with questions about Braddock and Joe Louis. I shall ask him about Salzburg, and tell him as much as I can remember of Ernest Newman's views on Glyndebourne.

Lunch-time. No sign of the *Queen Mary*.

How these Germans eat! A man at the next table breakfasted off grape-fruit, haddock, a dish which the menu described as " Sauté'd chicken liver in claret with mushrooms," and fresh strawberries. At eleven o'clock they bring round soup and rich-looking delicatessen, after which you are supposed to be ready for lunch at twelve-thirty. At two o'clock they begin again with coffee and cakes, tea at four, and the rest of the day is a thick-coming procession of kickshaws, with, at seven o'clock, an eight-course dinner to relieve the monotony.

Just received a radio-telegram from Sam Eckman, the London head of Metro-Goldwyn-Mayer. " Hope Neptune will be as kind to you as you will be to us." That's just it. I have always found Americans enchanting, while rather boggling at their country. This is probably because it frightens me; I am afraid of its slang, efficiency, bustle, and stark cruelty. No English critic would want to write, and no English editor consent to print, Robert Benchley's notice of a new play in the current number of the *New Yorker* : " There must have been a play called *Bet Your Life* which opened last week, for I have it on my list. However, as I can't find it anywhere in the advertisements and nobody seems to know anything about it now, we might as well let the whole matter drop." Against this my reason suggests that the American hurly-burly may conceal an inferiority complex. But does that help ? What about mine ? Can there be anything more dangerous to mutual understanding than a clash of inferiority complexes ?

And on what, pray, do I base my prejudices ? On some Sunday-school Longfellow, sickly Hawthorne, priggish Emerson. A handful of modern novels, some plays, all the Hollywood nonsense. The only American book I have ever really liked is Louisa M. Alcott's *Little Women.* Or am I worried by the lack of great dramatic and singing poets ? Walt Whitman has written sound sense about this. His first point is America's *material* preoccupation, which in any new country must come before the arts. His second point is about Shakespeare and Tennyson. He calls the plays " the very pomp and dazzle of the sunset," while the poetry is " feudalism's lush-ripening culmination and last honey of decay." Just before sailing I threw into my bag W. W.'s *Complete Prose.* " Meanwhile democracy [meaning American democracy] waits the coming of the bards in silence and in twilight—but 'tis the twilight of the dawn." A fine passage which ought to put the English visitor to the States on his guard against uppishness.

April 30   I know now why B. was so eager to get me alone
Friday.   in the middle of the ocean. He has written a light
              comedy, which, it appears, has raised laughs in
Leeds, and will I read it ? How can I refuse ? As well might
Ravaillac, the murderer of Henri Quatre, have refused his limbs

to the torture of the boot. I will say this for B.'s dialogue—that it isn't wooden. The play itself? When I was a young man there was a cake-walk entitled *All Coons Look Alike to Me*. After thirty years of dramatic criticism all light comedies have come to be the same to me. Still, this one is not without a certain preposterous sparkle, or seems in mid-Atlantic to be so endowed. There is an excellent bookshop on board, whose earnest attendant is much impressed when I tell him that I know the author of *The Fountain*.

Still no sign of the *Queen Mary*. I believe the officers know where she is but won't say. There is a rumour that we are trying, vulgarly speaking, to do it on her; our best chance is to hope for bad weather, which the *Bremen* likes. At the moment we are just passing a tramp steamer so close that we can almost hear Masefield's " cheap tin trays " banging in her hold.

May 1   A misty, moisty morning. A thin deck-steward
Saturday.   thinks the *Q.M.* passed us in the night; his fat
              colleague is of opinion that she is still miles behind
and that we shan't see her before New York. If this is so I shall be disappointed. I want to know whether, with neither shore nor shipping to measure her by, she looks impressive or negligible.

Already foresee that I shall be defeated by America's sheer incalculableness. Here is a paragraph from to-day's issue of the *Lloyd Post*, published on board, being an item in the News Service wirelessed from New Brunswick :

> Stooping Oak, Tennessee. After keeping silence for fifty-two days while Jackson Withlow starved himself to the verge of death, the Lord told the mountaineer Friday night to take a little wine for your stomach's sake and suggested orange juice as a chaser.

May 2   A heavy sea running, and I watch my toothbrush
Sunday.   veer from port to starboard and back again in dis-
              quieting fashion. I shall not be ill, though I shall
refuse the invitation to visit the engine-room after breakfast.

All such places are hot, greasy, smelly, noisy, and alarming. And I am glad I did not tackle too much of the buffet at last night's Farewell Ball. It wanted a Rubens to paint not the cooks but the dishes. The women put on all their finery, resulting in a flamboyant frumpishness. Why do Hausfraus, built on Brünn-hilde lines, imagine they can wear pale blue georgette? Hence-forth I shall associate the word " gala " with a dancer more massive than Gilbert's Lady Jane and wearing a print frock of blue chrysanthemums tied with vermilion love-knots. Her husband told me in one breath that he had " two factories and three daughters all like their mother." I have not spoken to Schmeling.

A word about ship life. Judging by the novels, plays, and films on the subject, life on a liner should be a maze of card-sharping, jewel-thieving, expensive vamping, and cheap flirtation under an obliging moon. The fact lags far behind the fancy. There is only one bridge table, and this is monopolised by a quartet so bellicose that I don't like to cut in. Also they don't appear to play for anything. Instead I teach B. piquet—with the usual beginner's luck he holds all the cards and beats me. I have seen no jewellery worth stealing. There are no unattached ladies, and no flirting couples. Perhaps flirting is not feasible in German. As a conscientious reporter I made one midnight tour of what seemed the likeliest deck, fell over a hose-pipe, and was told by its gruff manipulator to hop it. (The German word escapes me.) The day-time distraction is to walk endlessly round the ship, the alternative being liver which I prefer. The brass band has vanished into the *Ewigkeit*, to be replaced by a well-meant twitter of strings. These discourse the kind of music which makes me agree with the man who wrote, " Music is an accessory, not an object in life. To make an object of it is sensuality. It is on all fours with worshipping the wallpaper." There is a good cinema, but my friend Sam Eckman knows I can see better, or at least bigger, pictures nearer home. After five days of physical, intellectual, spiritual, and almost moral disintegration I resolve never again to look down on a drunken sailor. I know why he gets drunk. It is to make up for the

utter boredom of the sea. As I feel now, I too would give the
whole of the Atlantic Ocean for the Waterloo Road at opening
time.

May 3   A brilliant morning with a slight haze. The first
Monday.   discernible thing after passing the Ambrose Lightship
             is the Brooklyn gasometer. This is on the right.
Next, on the left, the Statue of Liberty, a big girl who is obviously
going to have a baby. The Birth of a Nation, I suppose. Next
a factory marked " Wrigley's." Now, very slowly, the famous
Manhattan skyline comes through the mist. At first it looks like
one of those scenes in stencilled cardboard fashionable in the
London theatre just after the last war. Here I have the same
experience as M. Bergeret's little dog Riquet : " As I approach
an object I grow less." Soon the spectacle becomes overwhelm-
ingly grand : I am now no size at all. Almost every skyscraper
has its feather of white smoke ; I had expected electricity everywhere. Entering the river, we pass the *Leviathan*, all dirty with
nowhere to go—I am told she will never put to sea again. The
Queen Mary is just being pulled and shoved into dock—she has
gained one and a half hours only on the voyage. At noon we
too are berthed, and it may be permitted to a landlubber to ask
why the docks are at right-angles instead of slant-wise. Through
the Customs in something under an hour.

Arrived at a famous but not luxury hotel, my confidence
begins to return. A messenger-boy has to wait while I scribble
a note, and I ask him one or two questions. No, he does not
know what New York looks like from the river. No, he does
not know how long it takes to get to Harlem, where he was
born. I reflect that at least there is one person in New York
who is not my intellectual superior. The hotel has two lifts,
one of which is not working. This also makes me feel at home.
I have seen three chambermaids, one Irish, one German, and
one, I presume, American. They are as old as the witches in
Macbeth, and not much better-looking. Prices are staggering.
This moderate-sized suite, on the sixth floor, consisting of
sitting-room, two bedrooms, and two bathrooms, costs sixteen

pounds a week without breakfast. Champagne is anything from thirty shillings to two pounds a bottle, proprietary brands of whiskey twenty-eight shillings.

After lunch take a stroll down Broadway, which is tawdry, like a film-producer's notion of the Place Clichy, with a hint of Shepherd's Bush. Drive round Central Park, which is a smaller and shabbier Hampstead Heath, with bits of the Serpentine and Rotten Row thrown in. Not a single flower, and the grass brown and patchy. The astonishing thing is still the skyscrapers; the Park is the crater of which they are the walls. From far away and in the near distance they are enormously impressive; when one gets right under them they vanish, and one regains one's normal size.

Dine at the Twenty-one, which I am told is a great place for actors and critics. Discreet lighting, so discreet that you can hardly see the food or read the prices. Ultimately it turns out that a steak which you would get for 4s. 6d. in any London grill-room here costs 8s., and a tournedos 10s. A bottle of champagne with coffee and a modest cigar brings the bill for two to just under £4. Later we stroll along Broadway, which, now that the lights are on, is exciting, like Blackpool at illumination time.

I am afraid all this is extremely tame, especially about money. I have, of course, *carte blanche* from the *S.T.* to spend what I like. But the interesting thing is to see how one would fare if one had saved up a few pounds for a holiday and were using one's own cash. B., whose tastes are simpler than mine, pretends that he will be ruined, but I tell him to look forward to next winter's influenza.

May 4   A sweltering day. Matinée of *Victoria Regina* at
Tuesday.   the dignified Broadhurst Theatre. The Americans
            are an amazing people. Shubert's publicity manager, one Greneker, a delightful fellow, is arranging for me to see not only all his firm's plays, but every other management's as well. Hearing I want to go into Massachusetts to look at a pony, he has sent alternative itineraries by road and rail. I know

it's business, but I'm afraid we should let an American critic who came over to London fend for himself. I called on Lee Shubert, whom I had never seen before out of the Savoy Grill Room. He too heaped attentions on me. Offered to lend me money !

The theatre was crowded, 95 per cent. women. An enchanting play, and a very clever actress. Lots of people could give the early scenes the Janet Gaynor quality, and extreme old age is never very difficult. The Beaconsfield episode, with the Queen approaching sixty, is another pair of shoes, and Helen Hayes quite took my breath away with her picture of the dragonsome old lady, lidless even when half asleep. An excellent Prince Consort by an actor called Vincent Price. Abraham Sofaer was a good Disraeli ; Housman has left it uncertain to what extent that fluent Eastern courtier had his tongue in his cheek, and Sofaer cleverly left us in the same doubt. Delicious scenery by Rex Whistler, heavily and handsomely realistic, thank heaven ! *The Show is On*, at the Winter Garden, with Beatrice Lillie, Bert Lahr, and Reginald Gardiner, is New York's fashionable riot of the moment. About as good as all but the best Cochran. Twenty-three people have had a hand in this. B. Lillie has enormously improved. She has now become a " socialite " Gracie Fields ; New York sees in her what we see in Gracie. Her work in this revue is brilliant throughout ; the Atlantic itself couldn't be as unruffled as her Society dame chattering throughout Gielgud's Hamlet.

May 5   J. Mason Brown, of the *New York Post*, took me
Wednesday.   to lunch at the Harvard Club. He is delightful.
                  But all the better-class Americans appear to be this—and from now on I shall leave it to be understood. The negro taxi-drivers also have charming manners. The non-charming people in this country are the in-betweens—the waiters, lift-boys, and particularly box-office attendants, who hand people their tickets like bones thrown to a dog. This annoys the dog who has paid for the bone. With me, who have not paid, the attendants are politeness itself. I suppose it is just

American independence which makes the middle American what we should call rude.

Lunch was prefaced by two enormous cocktails, and accompanied by iced water and coffee. I looked round the vast room and couldn't spy a drink anywhere! I begin to perceive that Americans regard food as something to sober up with. "Ces gens-là ne mangent pas; ils se nourissent." But my host's conversation was dry and sparkling. He told me about some of my predecessors over here. How St John Ervine had achieved a *succès d'animosité*: "But New York was sorry when he left; it missed its morning bile." The talk ranged all over the place, and I kept reminding myself that I had come to America principally to listen. About Mrs Patrick Campbell: "She is committing the wittiest form of hari-kari." About Beatrice Lillie: "Each of her eyebrows is an R.S.V.P." After lunch I was taken over the Century Club—an exquisite period house, with lovely, august furniture. I shall not see anything better over here. Am made a temporary member of the Harvard.

Went to *Babes in Arms* at the Shubert Theatre. This is a fresh, inventive musical comedy played by a sixteen-year-old cast headed by Mitzi Green and Duke McHale. The girl is clever, and the boy is a budding Richard Bird who can sing and dance as well as act. I enjoyed every moment of this; the music by Hart and Rodgers is written in a fascinating idiom which is theirs and nobody else's. Haunting! The show cost comparatively little to stage—fifty-five thousand dollars only—and could be put on in London for a quarter of that sum. But I doubt whether it would be a profitable experiment; seeing that it has been put together with many brains, I foresee flattering notices and empty houses. London likes its musical comedy to be solid, substantial, and thick; *Babes in Arms* is airy and fanciful, and the scenery is of the sketchiest. This is as it should be, since the whole notion is that a lot of actors' orphans will be sent to work on the land if they don't make good with a revue of their own concocting. The bill for the kids' scenery is forty-two dollars, which Sam, son of the orphanage master, puts up in return for 49 per cent. of the profits. "Just like the real thing."

I find myself at variance with New York opinion about its best stuff. (The contemptible is the contemptible all the world over.) For example, Clare Boothe's *The Women* is said by Benchley to be "pretty amusing." I think it is more than that. At least, I was seated between two very fat men on an intensely hot night in the densely packed Ethel Barrymore Theatre, and watched and listened to the intoxicated full of my eyes and ears. A venomous comedy on an old theme beautifully summed up by the remark of this play's cook to the parlourmaid : "The man who can think out an answer to that one about the husband who adores his wife while going around with another woman is going to win that prize they're always dishing out in Sweden." The cast of thirty-five consists entirely of women, each of whom makes you see her man as though she were a Ruth Draper, which very nearly each is. The playing of these American companies is superb, and I doubt very much whether we could match this one individually or collectively. This is nonsense. I am in no doubt at all ; we hardly have the actresses, and certainly we haven't the team.

At least, if I were to present this in London I should want Norah Howard, Marda Vanne, Marie Ney, Jean Cadell, Martita Hunt, Olga Lindo, Margaret Rawlings, Isabel Jeans, Greer Garson, and twenty more, including somebody who can suggest a discomfited giraffe. I should also insist on thirty-five American producers, one to each actress to give her the pace ! Thirty-five Olive Blakeneys would do fine. What this play won't stand is your English leading lady laboriously making her effects while the rest of the company yawn and look on. Some of the actresses who did magnificently to-night are Margalo Gillmore, Ilka Chase, Adrienne Marden, and Phyllis Povah, although in fairness I should give the whole cast. These women do not play themselves in ; they come on and there is your character, as sharp as if Rebecca West had described her. The scenes include a sitting-room, a hairdresser's, a boudoir, a dress-shop, an exercise parlour, a pantry, a nursing home, an hotel bedroom at Reno, a bathroom, another bedroom, and the ladies' room on the Casino Roof.

May 6   Called on Mrs Patrick Campbell, who is living
Thursday.   at a clean little hotel in West 49th Street. Took
               her to lunch at a place she insisted was called the
Vendôme, but which turned out to be Voisin's. Didn't notice
what we ate or drank, and don't remember paying. Probably
very good. After lunch went for a drive across Washington
Bridge. This also, I dare say, is very nice, but my attention
was entirely taken up by Mrs Pat, who radiated quicksilver.
Saw the *Hindenburg* nosing majestically between the skyscrapers
on its way to Lakehurst, and had the taxi turn round so as to
follow it and get a better view. By the time we had rounded
a block it had disappeared, and we couldn't catch it again. This
made Mrs P. pretend it had never been there, and that I needed
psycho-analysing. I think I have never been in contact with a
mind so frivolous and at the same time so big. She talked a
great deal about " flight " in acting as being the first quality of a
great actor. For four hours I listened to chatter about everything,
from Moses to Schnabel. About the former : " He probably
said to himself, ' Must stop or I shall be getting silly.' That
is why there are only ten commandments." She described
Schnabel's playing of Beethoven as being " like the winds of
the air and the waves of the sea, without shape." As she said
this I heard again the crooning of Mélisande.

Of a well-known English novelist : " He has never met a
great actress. No actress could be great in his presence. He
has a worm in his brain. He lives in hell and likes it." About
an American actress : " She has a Siamese forehead and a mouth
like a golosh." About another actress : " She is the great lady
of the American stage. Her voice is so beautiful that you won't
understand a word she says." About the same actress : " She's
such a nice woman. If you knew her you'd even admire her
acting." With a smile, about *Ego* : " I did so enjoy your book.
Everything that everybody writes in it is so good." About
Washington Bridge : " The world's greatest piece of architecture
after *Hedda Gabler*." About Hedda : " You have always been
right. I never could play her because I could never get the
Latin out of my blood. I have had Swedish masseuses who were

ten times better Heddas." About herself: "Many people say
I have an ugly mind. That isn't true. I say ugly things, which
is different." And again: "My voice at least has not gone,
and Brenda can always make me another face." About her
future: "I don't think I want to return to London. They
seem quite satisfied with Miss B." The whole of this was
punctuated with stories of her white Pekinese, Moonbeam,
and melodious altercations with the taxi-driver, who failed
to convince her that a certain monument was not Grant's Tomb.
About Sarah Bernhardt she said: "I toured with her for five
months, sat on her bed till five o'clock in the morning, and
never heard her say a word to which a child could not have
listened." She told me how she dined with Sarah three nights
before she died. Sarah was wearing a dress of pink Venetian
velvet with long sleeves, sent for the occasion by Sacha
Guitry. Knowing that she had not long to live, she sat
there with a white face eating nothing and infinitely gracious.
Her son Maurice was at the table, paralysed, and fed by
his wife. At the end of the meal Sarah was carried upstairs
in her chair; turning the bend of the staircase, she kissed
one finger and held it out. Both knew they would not meet
again.

When I got back to the hotel I found I was holding a
velvet geranium which, in one of the altercations with the taxi-
driver, had become detached from Mrs Pat's headgear. We had
chattered and chunnered for four hours.

May 7   I had just written the foregoing when a terrific
Friday.   thunderstorm broke. Great crashes and a lot of
             lightning, which made me fear for the skyscrapers.
These were said to be in no danger. I suppose it is that, the
sides being sheer, the stuff shins down them without opposition. In spite of the torrents, it was unbearably hot, so I took
off my clothes and lay on the bed.

At twenty to eight I went downstairs, and the middle-aged,
motherly receptionist said, with a telephone to her ear, " Sakes
alive, Mr Agate, my daughter has just called me to say she's

heard on the radio that there's been an explosion in the *Hindenburg* with everybody killed."

Within a minute people were saying " Sabotage." Somebody in the lounge who appeared to know about these things said that normally the ship would have avoided the storm and delayed making her moorings, but that she couldn't afford to do this as she had to return to England last night with a full complement of passengers for the Coronation, and to pick up films. The special editions of the newspapers struck me as being slow in coming out, but the electric news-signs got busy at once and Times Square was almost impassable. I was intending to see Katherine Cornell, and there meet B., who had spent the afternoon with his brother. As it was Cornell I particularly wanted to see, and *Candida* has nothing important till the last act, I delayed going, and listened to the radio's version of the disaster. I noticed that the announcers were very careful to qualify each and every statement, and to say that this was the nearest that could be guessed. A grim touch of realism was given by the command to all owners of motor-cars proceeding to Lakehurst to turn back and leave the road clear for doctors and ambulances. There was also a stern order to sightseers to keep away. New York is deeply moved by the tragedy, and nobody can understand why hydrogen was used. It is thought that if not lightning, then some electric friction in the air—supposing there is such a thing—was the cause. If it wasn't, then the disaster happening at the same time as the storm is an extravagant coincidence. I had forgotten how short a play *Candida* is, with the result that I got there in time to see the curtain descend upon a beautiful apparition bowing more lavishly than ever Bernhardt acted.

Called for Maurice Evans after his show. He has made tremendously good here, the view being that if he is not the best English-speaking actor he will have to do till the next comes along. He told me that Mrs Pat said after his first night, " I liked it all except the honey-coloured hair," and then, turning to an immaculate blonde, " I always think fair hair destroys personality, don't you ? " Wound up the evening at the Cotton Club. This is the place to hear swing music as the negroes like it. What I personally think about it doesn't matter; it stirs American audiences to frenzy. Duke Ellington conducts, presuming conducting is the word. A first-class cabaret follows. This takes place in a purplish penumbra, in which the dancers, naked except for diamond girdle and breastplate, are a twilit salmon-pink. They are extraordinarily attractive. The principal star is one Ethel Waters, and her enthusiastic reception argues talent. The Nicholas Brothers are here, tinier and skinnier and cheekier than ever. The waiters share the general frenzy; the very plates, as they are put before you, shimmy. Our waiter is a magnificent fellow with blue-black hair; the chap at the next table is pure ivory. A delightful little lady, like a drawing in sepia, persuades me to buy two toy dogs on the plea that they come from Manchester, though whether the English or the American Manchester she doesn't say. We regale ourselves with broiled lamb chops, chickened rice, and sausages with scrambled eggs. I drink half a bottle of champagne, the other two insist on whiskey —and the bill comes to five pounds. All that was yesterday!

Lunched to-day in the Persian Room at the Plaza Hotel on Fifth Avenue, an opulent place like our own Ritz Hotel, except that the women are not so well dressed. As we come out I am struck by the dazzling whiteness of the street, some greenery, and a woman suckling a child. Over the way are four sky-scrapers of great beauty. Each has its own shape, and B. points out how the eye, when it has done climbing, is rewarded, since each has a top which is designed to be something more than a roof. In comparison the London to be seen through our hotel doorways is a collection of native huts at the Wembley Exhibition. I have now entirely altered my view of this city, and warn everybody that Broadway is as much representative of New York as the Elephant and Castle is representative of London.

In the evening to Madison Square Garden to watch Tony Canzoneri fail to win back the lightweight title from Lou Ambers, to whom he lost it last year. As usual in these world championships, there was too much at stake for the men to go out for larks. A rather dull affair, the Italian losing on points after taking a lot of punishment. Canzoneri, who has a real name like an old master—Luigi d'Ambrosio—was originally a shoe-shine boy who in 1928 started to take the shine out of all the other lightweights. For ten years he has been recognised as one of the great masters of the glove. Now at twenty-seven he is old, and they tell me that the spring is gone from his legs, the snap from his blows, the resiliency from his body, the alertness from his mind. The previous bout, between one Paul Junior of Maine and one Al Casimiri of Corona, was very nearly the best fight I have ever seen. Sheer spectacular hitting, Junior winning by dint of a series of right uppercuts like Woolley's off-drive. The building is enormous, all concrete and steel, fire-proof and air-conditioned. What I didn't like were the refreshment vendors who continually moved about between the seats, interrupted the view, and were a nuisance generally. There must have been some hundreds of them.

Supper at the Howdy Club in Greenwich Village. According to Rian James, author of the informative and amusing *Dining in New York*, the Village is a lotus-land in which " gaiety is synthetic, poverty is fashionable and real, hilarity is forced, honour is infrequent, purpose is pie-eyed, ambition is asleep, and art is merely an excuse for everything." The Howdy Club is a night resort so dark and crowded that everybody eats off everybody else's plate. The entertainment is clever, witty, and wholly impermissible.

May 8   Motor to New Marlboro partly to see New England,
Saturday.   partly to visit the famous Hackney pony stud of
            Mr and Mrs J. Macy Willets. Take about three
hours each way. Admirable highway, in one place skirting a lake-reservoir reasonably like Thirlmere. The scenery consists principally of gay Swiss chalets and sordid little golf-courses poorly kept. The odd thing about the chalets is that they are obviously put up on the Wemmick principle : " Here's a bit of ground. Let's build something." There are neither walls nor fences, which gives the landscape the air of being unfinished yet derelict. The washing-up, the car-tinkering, the tea-taking, all are conducted in full view of the passer-by. " Come right in "

is the mode of invitation in this country, and every house seems
to be saying it.   This applies also to the great State Insane
Asylum, which is within fifty yards of the road, unfenced and
unwalled, so that you can see the inmates standing at the windows
and clutching the bars.   B., who has been clinical assistant in
an asylum, says that they are only standing, and that 90 per cent.
of the inmates are perfectly happy and in no need of pity.   Later
the skyline offers a big school, bare, bleak, and penitential-
looking.   Manners vary.   At one place an old man who tells
us the way doffs his bonnet with a sweep of courtesy that is
almost Shakespearian ; at another a youth makes his thumb
do the talking.   This isn't the " dumb insolence " it looks like.
Americans refuse to be rattled, and what looks like casualness
is really equanimity.

Willets is a distinguished-looking man, very like Norman
O'Neill with some of the same silvery charm.   His lady is one
of the managing sort, I guess a Candida, but with more style
than Shaw's.   In two minutes I realise that she knows all about
ponies, and this puts me on my mettle.   They pull out the pick
of the stud for me, famous little stallions whose names I have
known for years.   The brood mares are out in the paddocks,
and it is a thrill to renew acquaintance with old favourites like
Bricket Fuchsia and Colne Marvel which I knew in their young
days in the English show-ring.   Here too is the little mare
Eastertide, one of the greatest winners in America as at home.
She is being got ready to show and retains all her old brilliance.

Get back about seven o'clock, and agree to take pot-luck
at any restaurant B. likes the look of.   The place he chooses is
clean, the service amiable, and the food revolting.   *Dead End*
at the Belasco Theatre is a Galsworthian essay on the tendency
of the law to turn youthful wrongdoers into hardened criminals.
Very moving.   Principals in the cast mostly children.

May 8   Am writing this on the veranda of a builder's hut
Sunday.   on the slope of a hill overlooking the Croton Lakes,
              some forty miles from New York.   The Grenekers
have motored us here.   Mrs G. is a provocative little creature

and hair's-breadth image of the Bergner. Heavenly day. Apple-blossom and the décor of Viennese opérette with Lea Seidl in the wings preparing to warble. There are five workmen, Italians from Trieste, though they prefer to call themselves Austrians. All are of an incredible *Gemütlichkeit* ; the one named Rudi is the perfect Joe Gargery. The hillside belongs to Greneker, who has already built three houses on it, and is busy on a fourth. Or rather it is Mrs G. who is busy ; she is architect, builder, engineer, plumber, decorator, and foreman of works. The land is terraced as in Provence, and one of the feats of this extraordinary little lady, as practical as she is fascinating, has been to make a road 800 feet long, 16 feet wide, and in places 20 feet deep, without any engineering training whatever. She builds, without plans, large airy rooms of sweet-smelling pine. I do a lot of scrambling, holding on by the scaffold-poles, and wonder what it is in the New York air that enables me to sit up till all hours of the night in an atmosphere which in London would make a horse dizzy, but here merely clears the brain.

Lunch in the open air consists of salami, raw Italian ham and cheese, followed by chicken soup, chicken and spinach, iced beer, coffee, and crême-de-menthe frappé. This was the workmen's meal, cooked by them and smelling so good that we jumped at the invitation to share it. Where it all comes from even the Grenekers don't know, as this is a wilderness apparently without hotels, restaurants, or shops. We are an extraordinarily gay little party, and I feel I am nearer to American life than I have yet got. Mrs G., who as the day wears on becomes more and more like the Bergner, has the same child-like *mutinerie* masking colossal intelligence. She has invented finger-stalls with brushes at the end of them; these are for the use of painters, enabling them to work on their canvases with five or, I suppose, ten fingers at once. She combats the suggestion that this is painting *à la* Lewis Carroll by the statement that the method is psychologically and functionally more correct. I refrain from retorting that I shall look forward to listening to a painting by Mark Hambourg.

After lunch B. goes in the car to advise in the purchase of

timber, and I am left on the veranda with the diary, a friendly spaniel, the apple-blossom, and the workmen's wireless celebrating Mothers' Day. A quarter of a mile below me the cars pass and re-pass on the ribbon of road. Presently on the hill across the lake a fire breaks out, and there is the momentary excitement of a cream fire-engine dashing across the grey steel bridge. Then the afternoon settles down, and I am left alone with the apple-blossom and the musical-comedy décor. As I have now had a sufficiency of American mothers, I turn off the wireless and go to sleep.

May 10   Wall Street. Utter peace. The holy place is quiet as
Monday.   a nun. Breathless with, I suppose, adoration of the
              almighty dollar. Anyhow nobody seems to be worrying. A few people are chatting quietly on the kerb, the rest are lazing along. No messengers butt into me at breakneck speed. A leisurely calm pervades the scene, and I am conducted unemotionally into the pile-carpeted, onyx-chandeliered, rosewood-furnished withdrawing-rooms of Messrs Brown, Brothers, Harriman and Co., foreign correspondents of my bank. One feels that in this country Mr Micawber's manners, which so peculiarly qualified him for the banking business, would here have found their scope and outlet. To my amazement the young gentleman who " takes care of " me has never heard the phrase " ten grand," which every English chit knows is the sum you are held up for in these parts. However, I get what money I want, and return to a street that is ambling to lunch. The American bustle is all ballyhoo carefully fostered for consumption abroad. I have seen Greneker conduct two telephone conversations, dictate to a secretary, talk to me, and indulge in a nap all at the same time.

My meal is taken at a famous hotel. The lamb chop has the consistency of indiarubber. Nothing in America tastes of anything.

> Let beeves and home-bred kine partake
> The sweets of Burn-mill meadow,

occurs in, I think, *Yarrow Unvisited*. Let me revisit Yarrow, or even Barrow, and partake of home-bred beeves ! Iced water to drink, or so it is proposed till J. A. puts in his little oar. Nobody else drinks anything, and it is explained to me that no American can take a drink during business hours for fear of being over-reached.

The other guests are Cedric Hardwicke, the English actor, and Winston Paul, the first man in America to make ice by electricity and therefore a millionaire. Our host is Eddie Dowling, lessee of the St James's Theatre and Maurice Evans's partner. Cedric has the idea of a floating deck half-way between New York and London on which to stage plays striking a compromise between their conscienceless professionalism and our own aspiring amateurism. According to Cedric the English are playwrights who cannot finish off plays, like trainers who can do everything with a horse except make it win, whereas the Americans are up to every dodge of putting plays together without being able to write them. The ice man is typical, I imagine, of all American millionaires ; that is to say, his clothes make you wonder how often he can afford to lunch at sumptuous places like this. Hearing that I may be going to Philadelphia, he says he regrets he hasn't a place there, but will telegraph this afternoon, putting at my disposal a friend's apartment, car, and chauffeur. If, on the other hand, I have a mind to visit Idaho, he will be delighted to offer me the same facilities plus a ranch in the Rockies to which from time to time he runs down. A warning to me not to despise strange Americans, for I do not hear about the ice and the millions till later ! Our host, Eddie, was originally a music-hall artist who toured England some years ago, without, as he himself admits, achieving any particular fame. His wife is Ray Dooley, who was at one time a partner in vaudeville with W. C. Fields—music-hall is music-hall all the world over. Eddie, who called me Jimmie at sight, is an infectious little man who looks like a member of the Lupino family. He takes to you, you take to him, and you are bosom friends before you sit down. He told me some astonishing things about Maurice Evans's success over here. How a total stranger to Maurice, having seen him in *Romeo and Juliet* and *St*

Helena, wrote to him asking if he had another play and wanted money for it. If so, would he meet him in a bar? Maurice, having nothing better to do, turned up, and the man said, " I'm sorry, but since I wrote you I've engaged my capital elsewhere. Would twenty-five thousand dollars be any use, and what's the play? " Maurice stammered out, " Shakespeare's *Richard II*." But the man did not blench, and, calling for pen and ink, wrote out a cheque then and there. Maurice then went round to most of the other managers and brokers, and in each case was politely bowed off the premises. At last he fell in with Dowling, who first enacted an amusing little comedy in which he pretended to be his own secretary, and so played Jorkins to his own Spenlow. Before the interview was over the pretence was abandoned, and another twenty-five thousand dollars was forthcoming. When the time came to pay back the first twenty-five thousand dollars, the original philanthropist was asked what share of the profits to date he thought he ought to have. He replied that he hadn't been out for profit and would be satisfied with 6 per cent. interest ! The result is that our young actor is now a rich man. Maurice modestly told me as much himself, and added that he had a permanent offer from Hollywood at a thousand pounds a week, which he intended to go on turning down. Coming back from lunch, I was driven past the Waldorf-Astoria. This is a stone building as impressive as a Sibelius symphony, and I have a notion to try the cooking there.

At five o'clock George Jean Nathan called to take me out for cocktails. As I do not want to drink too much—for what little drink there is in America is immensely potent—I order tea and crumpets, and get some very poor tea and very mean crumpets. The place is expensive, and I note one or two little ladies who look exactly like white toy poms. They are accompanied and obviously of the highest respectability, though only Peter Arno could do justice to their utter inability to open their mouths, and, when they do, to produce anything resembling human speech. Amazing children.

Nathan has not changed. He has still the same delicate features and beautiful hands, the look of the fallen cherub, and the smile which breaks out when you say something malicious and he thinks of something to cap it. After a bit we are joined by Richard Watts, the dramatic critic of the *Herald-Tribune*, and I listen while they tell me about the greatness of Maurice Evans, who, I am rather shocked to find, is over here rated above Gielgud. From what these boys say I judge that Maurice must have made enormous strides, for if we are to talk about greatness I begin, as always, with first things, and must therefore contrast Maurice's baby-face with the august masks of Irving, Forbes-Robertson, Benson. A great actor must include the forbidding in his facial range : when last I saw Maurice he could do no better in this line than fob me off with impudence.

Excursion, by Victor Wolfson, at the Vanderbilt Theatre, is a fantasy about a Coney Island steamer that put out to sea with all its passengers on board and found an island. When I woke up the steamer with its passengers was coming back. A mixture of *Outward Bound* and *The Passing of the Third Floor Back.* We could act this and probably will.

May 11   Lunch with the Drama League. The Leaguers
Tuesday.   contrive to be overdressed and dowdy. Hardly
            a man to be seen, and none who dares to be heard.
I sit between Peggy Wood, of *Bitter Sweet* fame, and the little lady who is Richard II's Queen. Peggy tells me that she is to play Portia again " in order to have a finger in the Shakespeare racket." Her view about Nathan is that it is not playing the game to make so much money out of a thing you despise, that thing being the theatre. Richard's Queen is the most appealing, sensitive little lady I have met in this continent. She has a Plantagenet coiffure and wears a frock of red silk on which the figure " 83 " is printed some hundred and fifty times. I ask what this means. Richard's Queen says she hasn't noticed it.

The object of the lunch is to present the medal for the year's best acting performance, won in previous years by Katherine Cornell and Helen Hayes. This time it goes to Maurice, who turns up an hour and a quarter late ! Among the celebrities present are Mrs Richard Mansfield, who, it appears, gives readings from Shakespeare with her late husband's annotations, and Ruth St Denis, formerly a great dancer and now an exquisite figure with white hair and the first approach I have seen to anything one can call a manner. There is a lot of introducing from the chair, and each person as she is named stands up and bobs. I am introduced as the Dean of English Criticism! In the course of the speech-making we are told that Gielgud during the last week of *Hamlet* took eighteen thousand dollars and that Evans's run of *Richard II* up to date *averages* eighteen thousand. I am twitted with these figures, and asked what London can show against them. I speak for a good ten minutes, in the sort of cathedral hush which befits a dean, the difficulty of praising Evans to his face being got over by the fact that the face is no longer there, its owner having grabbed his prize and gone. In the matter of the figures I tell the League with a well-simulated air of conviction that if America will send us two Shakespearian actors as good as Gielgud and Evans we will . . . I don't need to finish the sentence. An American audience though dull-looking is quick-witted.

Called on Helen Hayes and found her to be a very bright, extremely intelligent little woman full of an inner distinction which looks out through a woebegone pair of grey eyes set wide apart from the nose. We were not there very long, as Helen wanted to listen to Alexander Woollcott on the radio reading Edward VIII's abdication speech. She disapproved of Woollcott doing this eve-of-Coronation stunt, but intended to listen all the same.

May 12   Coronation Day. Cable from my sister May:
Wednesday.   "London is empty without you!" Claud Greneker
                rang up before breakfast to ask what I had thought of the proceedings, which here started at 5 A.M. It appears that Mrs Greneker is also a wireless expert and had connected up the whole show. G. sounded very weary, and I refrained from asking the poor man whether he had got up to listen or had been kept up.

Dined last night at Voisin's. Now that Mrs Patrick Campbell

was not with me and I could give some attention to the food, I found I had discovered a restaurant which is the equal of anything in Paris. The service was both attentive and understanding, and the habitués looked as though they were accustomed to food. Attended première of *Orchids Preferred* at the Imperial Theatre. As my views of musical comedy are known, I shall reproduce what Brooks Atkinson of the *New York Times* says :

> For the antiquarians it might be reported that the story, in its graceful and airy summer fashion, deals with the adventures of some amiable girl prostitutes. There is, of course, an ingénue who really doesn't know what her friends are up to and is much shocked when the hero, thinking she is no better than her companions, makes love to her. . . . Tastefulness is not one of the outstanding qualities of *Orchids Preferred*, but it isn't the vulgarity that is likely to bother you. It is the excessive tediousness of the proceedings that will probably send you screaming into the streets, or, preferably, into *Babes in Arms*, which is playing near by and will help you forget some of the horrors of this little spring catastrophe.

I have spent the whole morning writing, and this being Coronation Day propose to do no more work. Seeing New York is not all beer and skittles. I would rather say that it is very little beer and very fatiguing skittles. I am therefore going to take the afternoon off prior to attending the Coronation Ball to-night.

May 13   Listened to the King's speech immediately after
Thursday.   lunch yesterday. It came through perfectly.
                Good-bye, alas, to my afternoon off ! A. proposed, but B. disposed. He insisted on my going to the film at the Belmont Theatre, *The King's People*. This is a chronicle affair made up by Drinkwater with Shaw's help out of a lot of news-reels. The papers here are rather hard on Shaw :

> The world's greatest playwright, it seems, is also the world's greatest ham. Though he photographs poorly—something like a badly neglected faun—Mr Shaw knows how to deliver lines as well as write them, and the dialogue, in which he claims that Ireland created the new British Commonwealth

of Nations by stubbornly refusing to take any part in the old discredited empire, is theatrically successful, though the paradoxes do seem a little tired. Incidentally, the only reference in the film to Edward VIII is couched in the vaguest and most politic terms. " Circumstances," the commentator remarks, " which are now part of British history, led to his abdication from the throne." The word seems a dull, pedantic and unpardonably British way of spelling L-O-V-E.

Took our Coronation dinner at the Ritz-Carlton. Quite good. One of the many head waiters agreed that Americans have no palate, or have successfully destroyed it with cigarettes and cocktails.

The Ball was a grand affair, or, at least, that was the intention. Personally I cannot reconcile opera-hats with burberrys, in which I saw many men arrive. The women's frocks suggested a tennis dance at Upper Norwood, and it could be maintained that American women do not dress but merely clothe themselves. All the same it was a gay affair, with a well-meant pageant. This was a procession of nations with a tail of British and British-American societies, and I suppose one ought not to smile at bespectacled matrons carrying banners. But it was all a little funny. The Seventh Regiment Armoury is much bigger than the Albert Hall, and the way to the refreshment-room was through a huge canvas of Westminster Abbey ! Some of the girls were lovely in spite of the pains their dressmakers had taken to hide the fact ; in so far as my observation goes the smart American woman simply does not exist. Perhaps there are smarter places than I have yet discovered. Next week I propose to tackle the Colony Club, which is so expensive that revue comedians make jokes about it. After all, before you can pluck your hot-house flower you must first catch your hot-house.

May 14   *You Can't Take It With You*, a farcical comedy by
Friday.   Moss Hart and George S. Kaufman at the Booth
              Theatre, is the smash hit of the season and this year's
winner of the Pulitzer Prize. It is an American jumble of *After
October*, *French without Tears*, and *George and Margaret*, and it is

very funny. They call it " a madhouse which has all the comforts of home," and perhaps a home with the discomforts of a madhouse would amount to pretty much the same thing. The home is that of Martin Vanderhof, retired from business, full to the brim with the philosophy of contentment, bubbling over with its humorous, pawky expression. The story ? This, if I surmise correctly, is about Martin's daughter, who works in a store and has fallen in love with the boss's son. The boy invites his parents to dinner at the girl's home, but they mistake the date and arrive at a place which they can only conclude to be the equivalent of our Bedlam. For all the inmates are border-line cases. The girl's mother has the overpowering silliness of Dickens's Flora without her vitality ; she is a crushed strawberry who insists on wearing heliotrope. There is a son who writes anarchist tracts, not because he has any sympathy with anarchy, but because he likes to see the stuff in print. There is a gauche young woman who affects ballet-dancing. There is a Russian exile whose friend is a Grand Duchess earning her living as a waitress. (Kaufman is a first-rate hand at taking the good where others have already found it.) There is an Aged P. who is partial to inventions that go off making a noise like bombs. There is a woman who lies on a sofa in a state of intoxication. There is a comic negro servant. There are a few people I cannot account for. And I must believe that it is all extremely funny, though a foreigner cannot tell what will amuse another race. " I wouldn't deceive you for all the rice in China," says the boy. " Is there much rice in China ? " asks the girl. This is good Noel Coward, and to my surprise nobody laughed. But they laughed at a Russian refugee : " You do not know what following is. In Russia *everybody* is followed. I was followed right out of Russia." And " The reason Mother writes plays is that eight years ago a typewriter was delivered here by mistake ! " went with a roar. But American audiences laugh very little, and are quite undemonstrative. The young woman in front of me may have been full of inward merriment. Her hat— a straw sloop with a bowsprit of holly and a rudder of tulle— showed no tremor.

May 15   Oscar Wilde called the Atlantic Ocean "dis-
Saturday.   appointing." Out-of-season Atlantic City, whither
               we have come for the week-end, is complete and
summary disillusion. Blackpool without its crowds. The
station called Pennsylvania is a most impressive place—immense,
lofty as a cathedral, finely proportioned, noble, marble-flagged,
clean, and very nearly noiseless. The trains start from a hole
underground. Ours is an abominable train, hot, stuffy, with
windows both impossible and unlawful to open. There is an
almost continuous whistle from the engine, a brain-splitting
shriek, which is one of the tortures left out of Octave Mirbeau's
Le Jardin des Supplices. Three hours of flat, deadly dull country-
side like Essex without its trimness.

On the way to Atlantic City I read Maxwell Anderson's *High
Tor*. I must be careful about this one, to which even the *New
Yorker* is respectful. It is a poetic fantasy. The place is the
top of a mountain, the time the present, the weather Macbeth's,
the *dramatis personæ* mostly dead, the medium blank verse, and
the plot a jumble of Barrie's *Dear Brutus* and *Peter Pan* and Susan
Glaspell's *The Verge*, except that Anderson's characters have toppled
over. I doubt very much whether it is my cup of tea.

Atlantic City turns out to be completely empty, swept,
garnished, and not a mouse stirring. Not a soul on the nine
miles of boardwalk, which is the name for the promenade made
out of planks like a pier. Nine miles of hotels, casinos, fun-
palaces, and the like. No roadway. The hotels give directly
on to the boardwalk, or would do so if the doors were not
locked. Windows locked also. To-day is scorching hot, and
all the radiators are turned on full. Our hotel is a splurge of
orange, pink, and black, the food exactly as everywhere else.
They try so hard, go through the most touching preliminaries,
give you Gargantuan helpings, rush up trimmings and sauces
with the urgency of reinforcements, and the result is something
that tastes like the inside of a sofa cushion—the steak I had for
luncheon was obviously a bit of padded armchair. Pathetic!
But B. doesn't seem to mind; he stokes up at each meal like a
famished walrus.

The Horse Show, which is in full swing here, is excellent, and on the same scale as Olympia. I was very anxious to see the famous five-gaited horses, which have even better and longer fronts than the English thoroughbred. The long, flowing tails are miracles of science and adjustment, like huge interrogation marks. In classes for five-gaited horses the required gaits are walk, trot, canter, what is known as " slow gait," and the rack. In these last two gaits the horse has the same way of going, which is not exactly pacing (where both legs on each side move simultaneously), but combines a trot with the forelegs and a pace with the rear legs. This movement they do slowly and at speed, the first being the slow gait, the second the rack. Both methods of progression are uglier than anything devised by the animal for itself. The big harness horses are poor, the ponies superb, the champion being Highland Cora, by King of the Plain out of my little mare Skirbeck Cora. The jumping is very much better than ours, and the prize-money bigger. At home we are content with a fifteen-pound first prize and a challenge cup to be held for one year. Here the class prizes are the same, but there are championship classes for horses and ponies where the prizes are $400, $200, $160, $100, $80, and $60. The same applies to the hunter classes, in which the women ride magnificently.

I was wheeled to the show to-night in a thing called a rolling chair. This contraption plies for hire along the boardwalk and is the only mode of conveyance. It is a combination of bath-chair, sedan-chair, and rickshaw, is propelled from behind by a negro, and may be used either open or closed. The cost is $1 per hour or any portion thereof. As I was wheeled solemnly along there was not a soul in sight in as much as could be seen of the nine miles of boardwalk. Yet the auditorium was full of immensely smart and obviously wealthy people. The men were wearing silk hats, tails, and buttonholes ; the women struck me as orchid-and-husband-conscious. I have sensed all along that their rule is iron, and that every American woman has two souls to call her own, the other being her husband's. The young men, all looking exactly like Robert Taylor, abase themselves before innumerable Loretta Youngs; I conclude that the much-vaunted American independence obtains outside the home only. Five minutes after the show closed everybody had disappeared, the boardwalk again became empty, and the world was left to me and darkness in the person of my chairman. Or would have been but for the neon lights illuminating the regardless ocean. (Excuse the Andersonese!) The place is terrifically expensive. For a haircut and shave the hotel barber demanded a dollar and a half, which with the tip came to seven shillings. I do not think Americans pay these prices.

May 16   A lovely day of glorious sun, cool wind, and a
Sunday.   sparkling blue sea which does not seem to go either
            in or out. White sands peopled with donkey-boys, only the donkeys are horses and the boys full-grown negroes of great stature. It is odd how few boys and girls I have seen; the children here seem to be born round the age of sixteen. I left Atlantic City with regret. During the night it had become crowded with a light-hearted, orderly, and considerate mob. I bought a blue china horse, some hand and a half high. They told me at the shop that it was an exact model of the American agricultural horse. I don't believe this, but it is a delicious blue.

The return journey was much more comfortable, the train being cool and extremely clean. I saw a notice saying that last year these Pullmans carried 1,475,000 passengers 1,500,000,000 miles without a fatal accident. Lunch was simple and good. By the way, the railways ignore daylight saving; you just make the train one hour after its scheduled time. These trains go through the middle of the streets of towns and villages like motor-cars; if they stopped, you could shop from the windows, provided you could open them. All the streets are at right-angles to the line, and the smallest places have the air of being planned. But the country still retains its unfinished look. I note one house and a tennis lawn which have apparently dropped from the skies into the middle of nowhere. Here, in the middle of untenanted plains, is a baseball ground with a game in progress. Suddenly a lake, with a tiny motor-yacht as fresh as paint, and a huge, burned-out barge high and dry on the shore. Nothing much else to be seen, so I settle down to read the Sunday papers. To-day's *New York Times* weighs two ounces short of two pounds. It has 14 sections—New York news, general news, finance and business, editorials including letters and special articles, sport, society, book reviews, magazines, the news in pictures, drama and music, science (which includes aviation and motoring), real estate, classified advertisements, and pictures of the Coronation in rotogravure. 220 pages in all. Eight narrow columns to a page, each containing some 800 words. The pictures and the classified advertisements take up 26 pages, leaving 194 pages. Cut this in half to allow for the unclassified advertisements, and the result is roughly 100 pages of 8 columns. This means 640,000 words per issue, or somewhere about the length of seven average-sized novels. The price is 10 cents, or roughly 5*d*. The *New York Herald-Tribune* weighs 1 lb. 10 oz., and is made up in similar fashion, but with a comic section in colour. Any attempt to read these papers as a whole must fail because it would take more than a week; you choose the section you want.

May 18   Seeing is believing. I have heard of tree-squatters,
Tuesday.   but never believed in them until this morning, when
            I saw Shipwreck Kelly, " The World's Champion Flagpole Sitter," perched high above a music-hall and now in the fourth day of a squat which is to run thirteen days, thirteen nights, thirteen hours, and thirteen minutes !

Lunch at a French open-air café, where a green hedge, half a dozen shrubs in tubs, and the accent of the waiters transport one into the Pyrenees. After lunch explore Radio City. It is a world in itself. Magnanimity's purest poetry, making the reduction to the prose of fact is a sorry business, though a little of it must be attempted. The underground part of it covers four blocks. The ground floor is Burlington Arcade in excelsis. I concentrate on the music-hall section ; the entertainment here is a combination of stage and screen. First I am amazed at the foyer, easily ten times the size of the Empire's. The dominant

decorative note is Ezra Winter's 60 × 30-foot mural: "Based
on an Oregon Indian legend, this Shows the Upward March of
Man toward the Golden Mountain where the Author of Life
dwells beside the Fountain of Eternal Youth." (The prose is
American.)   The two twenty-nine-foot chandeliers weigh two
tons each. I am indebted for this and a mass of other information
to the page-boy detailed to show me round, who looks as though
he had come out of a Richard Strauss opera. All the ushers
are men in livery, and there is a complete absence of the cow-
girls, Quakeresses, little Miss Muffetts who enliven our cinemas
at home. We are taken through banqueting halls, kitchens,
and into the Celebrity Room, where we sign the visitors' book.
Presently we attain the Balcony, so high that looking down
into the foyer is a giddy business. A panel slides back discreetly
and we find ourselves in Radio City Music-hall, which is exactly
like the interior of an airship hangar. What light there is filters
through hundreds of slats. There are six thousand two hundred
seats. The screen measures seventy feet by forty. The drop-
curtain weighs three tons. A news-budget is in progress with
the house in darkness. This over, the lights go up and we
become aware of a symphony orchestra ; I reflect that here is
the concert hall of which Berlioz dreamt. The orchestra plays
an overture with Beechamesque punctilio, while changes of
lighting bathe the audience in a glow of tender dawn warming
to wanton sunset. The band returns hydraulically to the place
whence it came, having done great execution. A lady clad entirely
in diamonds now goes through the motions of the haute école
with the assistance of a dazzlingly white horse. This concluded,
we arrive at the Rockettes. There are thirty-six of them. They
are as good as the Tiller Girls. Then comes the new Fred Astaire-
Ginger Rogers picture *Shall We Dance?* which I permit myself to
refrain from seeing. We emerge, having looked on something
that is potentially the greatest show on earth. One says
potentially, because a show needs an audience, and there do
not seem to be more than a couple of hundred people present.
But the place is so vast that these two hundred may actually be
two thousand. If you can't see an orchestra of seventy players

you can hardly expect to estimate the number of human dots scattered about the floors of this measureless cavern.

Dine with Nathan at the Colony, said to be New York's last word in cooking, but the first I have heard about this art. We eat Canapé Colony, which is crab meat on pastry with a bisque sauce, cold soup, a filet mignon Henri-Quatre, and a chocolate ice. To drink there is Zeltinger 1931 and half a bottle of champagne, the brand of which I cannot see through the napkin. This place is firmly confident of itself, and the crowd too; both are justified. Not as guest but as an observer of social conditions I ask the cost, and Nathan is forced to show me a bill of just over £8.

Tobacco Road at the Forrest Theatre. This drama of Georgia's back of beyond is utterly and entirely American, and I am warned that I shall not make much of it. All the actors speak in undertones; it takes me half an hour to hear, and another half-hour to understand what I hear. The nearest thing is the plays of Synge, except that there is no poetry, actual or implied; the humanity is as remote as the statues on Easter Island. Jeeter Lester is the owner of what was once a tobacco farm and now grows so little cotton that he and his family are starving. He is married to a wife of whom he says, " When she was young she was that ugly it didn't make sense." The play is a maze of frustration, incest, and decay. We are shown some home-made nuptials between a semi-idiot and a revivalist female who has become possessed of an automobile; the boy will not hear of a honeymoon because he wants to joy-ride! James Barton plays Jeeter rather in the manner of Joe Jackson, the English music-hall comedian in trouble with a bicycle. The audience rocks with laughter throughout, taking no notice of the grandmother who hobbles through the play without saying a word; she is the counterpart of Firs in Tchehov's *Cherry Orchard*. This extraordinary mixture of grim, sordid drama and riotous fooling has been running for four years.

Supper with Maurice Evans at Sardi's, the equivalent of Rules, after which we are escorted to Harlem. Except in the matter of complexions, Harlem looks exactly like Pimlico.

We drink beer and eat mutton bones drenched with pepper
in a resort called Moon-Glow. This is a dingy little cubby-
hole crowded with darkies carrying on like a scene in a Cochran
revue staged by Professor Stern. The waiters handle their
platters after the manner of Salome. The heat is terrific, and
the noise so great that I cannot hear a single word of a saucy
song composed in my honour and bawled into my ear by a
dusky gigolo. For some time B. has been trying to say something
to me. But there's no opportunity of hearing what it is until
about three o'clock, when he seizes a moment of comparative
silence to yell : " You don't appear to be getting much golf."
At four o'clock some idiotic drink restrictions come into play,
and we make a move.

Lunched at a chop-house. Very comfortable and cheap.
I appear to have lunched twice to-day ! This is not so, but
due to writing and living a diary simultaneously. To-day's
entry up to now was all about yesterday ; with this lunch I
catch up. In New York it is almost impossible to keep events
from telescoping. This is due to the *slow* American hustle. I
once had a horse that ran away at a walk. Here the hustle takes
the form of not letting you alone ; a continual, relentless button-
holing goes on all the time. B. has his hands full, less in making
contacts we want than in avoiding those we don't want. It doesn't
seem to occur to anybody that one may like occasionally to be left
alone for five minutes, if only to think over what one has seen.

Went in blazing sunshine to the top of the Empire State
Building and hated it. There is a glass cage in which I felt
fairly safe, but anywhere near the parapet was impossible.
Something sways, but whether it is you or the building is as
moot a point as I know. The visibility to-day was charted
at 25 miles, and for the first time I realised how small the island
is and why the skyscrapers came into being. The view includes
the Manhattan skyline seen from behind, the Statue of Liberty,
the encircling Hudson with its scores of fussy little tugs, the
Normandie, which has just arrived and looks, as the fellow in
Lear says, " diminished to her cock," the great bridges, Central
Park, the rule-made avenues and streets, rival monsters like the

Chrysler Building and Radio City, and hundreds of lesser
pinnacles in stone like marzipan. Perhaps Man is not so inferior
to the ants after all. I am, of course, not surprised to find that
none of the Americans I meet up here is a New-Yorker; no
Londoner ever climbs the Monument. The people I talk to on
the roof answer me in French, German, Swedish, Italian, Russian,
and broad Lancashire.

Once more on terra firma we went to the pictures and saw
the Coronation and *Hindenburg* films. The shots of Queen
Mary made a great impression, the people near me crying out,
" Isn't she lovely ? " But the whole film was received with
the greatest enthusiasm. The *Hindenburg* picture included some
of the evidence of Captain Rosedahl, the head of aviation at
Lakehurst, who said that it was well known that airships generate
electricity. This is discharged as soon as the landing-ropes
touch earth, and members of the crew handling them before
establishing contact have been known to suffer severe shocks.
All this electricity runs wild in the immediate proximity of seven
million cubic feet of extremely inflammable hydrogen! The
Germans say they can't afford to buy helium, which can only
be got from America, though here I am given another explanation. This is that German airships are not designed for helium.
If they change their design they will be unfitted for hydrogen,
which is the gas they must use in the event of war since they
would not be able to get the other from America.

Dinner at the Grenekers' apartment, twenty-three stories
high and overlooking Central Park. Down below there is a
constant stream of motors, and four games of baseball are in
progress in a space the size of the Oval, but grassless. I had
asked to be given a typically American meal, as this is probably
the only private house in New York in which I shall eat. The
menu consisted of cream of mushroom soup, duck, asparagus,
fresh rice, and for dessert a grape salad with hot cheese rolls.
As a concession to British taste a bottle of Beaune.

The play to-night was *Yes, my Darling Daughter*. It is being
played to packed houses, all of which endorse the maternal
sanction to a young girl to behave as she likes.

May 19   Opening of the Renoir Exhibition at the Metro-
Wednesday.   politan Museum of Art.   A large, well-dressed
                crowd possessing a distinction I have not met
anywhere else. This magnificent collection of over sixty pictures
has been got together through the courtesy of several other
galleries and some twenty private owners, including Helen
Hayes and Edward G. Robinson, the film actor.   Here is the
glorious *Déjeuner des Canotiers*, an amazing piece of sheer paint.
About this Harry B. Wehle writes : " None of the girls or young
men present is smiling, none is definitely flirting.   A striped
awning shields them from the sun, and they sit there over the
remains of their luncheon, some of them chatting, one playing
with a lap dog, others doing nothing whatever.   Gentle breezes
from the river seem to caress them—and they are completely
happy.   The picture is a hymn to youth and summer-time."

Here, too, is *By the Seashore*, a picture of a lady sitting in a
basket-chair with a background of cliffs.   But the loveliest
canvas of all is *Le Bal à Bougival*, painted in 1883.   A pen drawing
of this runs as follows : " Elle valsait délicieusement abandonée
entre les bras d'un blond aux allures de canotier."   I came back
to this picture half a dozen times.   The grave innocence of
the girl, the eyes wide apart like a kitten's, the swirl of the
white dress, the red of the hat, the blue of her partner's rough
suit, the animation of the scene which is yet not without
melancholy—all this makes up a composition brilliant yet tender,
like Sarah's playing in the first act of *La Dame aux Camélias*.
Even when I got outside I went back to have one more look at
a picture owned by the Museum of Fine Arts, Boston, and which
is going to be one of my best excuses for returning to America
as soon as possible.

The foyer of the Astor Hotel is as full of people coming
and going as is Charing Cross Railway Station.   We lunched
with Milton Shubert, and I was asked a lot of questions about
the English stage.   I began to answer these with the freedom
imparted by two thousand miles, when I saw B. making frantic
signals for me to shut up.   Nothing escapes him, whereas I in
my simplicity had not recognised an interviewer.   The room

in which the meal happened was a combination of box-office, bookstall, flower-shop, and motor sales-room. The appearance of food was a surprise. Matinée of *Richard II*. A packed house and great enthusiasm for Maurice. I still have the impression that his features are too boyish for the conveyance of tragedy, though this view would be very unpopular here, and I do not give expression to it.

In the evening *High Tor* at the Martin Beck Theatre. Defeat with heavy slaughter. The difficulty is to see this play through American eyes, which I suppose one should try to do. As an Englishman I feel that it is high fudge interlarded with bleak, totally unfunny humour. But I am alive to the danger of regarding this as criticism. That a Japanese might not be tickled by the fun in *Juno and the Paycock* would be no criticism of Sean O'Casey's play. The fact that B. and I sat glum while the audience roared its head off tells me that I am no closer to an American than a Japanese is to an Irishman. Renoir once said, " After all, if you are going in for oil-painting you may as well use oil-paint." If a poet is going to write a fantasy he may as well be fantastic. I don't boggle about the non-realistic part of this play—high-faluting is the same all the world over. It is the comic interludes which strike me as inexpressibly dreary. I can only suppose that they awake echoes in the American mind which escape me, though I can find no hint of them in the text. The production has *Theatre Arts Monthly* written all over it, and the play would probably do very well in London if cut in two and produced in two theatres—the guff at the Mercury and the larks at the Gate. Nothing in either text or production could prevent one from recognising a potentially very fine actor in Burgess Meredith. This young man has an immense amount of vigour and a tremendous honesty, and I guess that he represents pretty exactly what young America is thinking. He has a fine voice, an excellent presence, and an open countenance conveying a backwoods likeableness. I should very much like to see him in something other than the backwoods idiom, something to be spoken instead of snarled. But I am in no doubt about his acting powers.

Here is raised a question of vital interest in the American Theatre—how to keep its young actors. Meredith's success means that next year he will be entirely absorbed by Hollywood. As this process will be repeated in the case of every promising young player, the result can only be the complete dearth of grown-up players. The theatres are very much worried about this.

May 20   New York declares against the proposed dramatic
Thursday.   censorship. Here is Governor Lehman's decision :

> While fully appreciative of the high purpose of those supporting this bill and while warmly joining in the desire to maintain the theatre on a proper moral plane, it nevertheless seems to me that the specific provisions of this bill are too broad and too susceptible of abuse in administration.

Was given luncheon to-day by the critics. These were Brooks Atkinson of the *New York Times*, John Mason Brown of the *New York Post*, Burns Mantle of the *News*, Joseph Wood Krutch of the *Nation*, John Anderson of the *New York Journal*, and George Jean Nathan, who writes for all the other papers. Very jolly. They want to know who are the heads of the English stage, meaning the present-day Irving and Ellen Terry. I reply John Gielgud and Edith Evans, with a reservation in favour of Laurence Olivier as the most promising young actor. It appears that I am right about *High Tor*, which nevertheless was awarded the Drama Critics' Prize by a majority, Nathan voting against it ; right about Burgess Meredith ; wrong about Maurice Evans. But I gather that, generally speaking, first principles are the same here as in London. Atkinson is austere and Morganesque, Mason Brown is the New York Darlington, and Burns Mantle reminds me very much of Baughan. Krutch is the Ivor Brown, I cannot quite fit in Anderson, and Nathan is his mischievous self. Mason Brown says, " Nathan is a good game, but you've got to know the rules." Was told a lot of lovely stories, the best being the remark of the French lady at the six-day bicycle race : " Ah nuts, alors ! "

Worked all afternoon, then taken for cocktails to the Fort Belvedere in West 55th Street, a newly opened bar lavishly decorated with frescoes of the Duke of Windsor, who if he wanted could be crowned King of America to-morrow, the Prince of Wales's feathers, and an escort of Life Guards. The wits congregate here. I asked one of them what he most wanted to see in England. He said, " Oxford." And the second thing ? " Lady Oxford." Dined in logical sequence at the Queen Mary in East 58th Street. This is laid out shipwise with an illuminated model of the boat. Swedish hors-d'œuvres are spread on a refectory table and you help yourself. One plateful is a meal. B. had two platefuls, and but for my innate decency would have attempted a third. Decide to have an evening of real drama instead of make-believe. Arrange therefore to be taken to a night court in West 54th Street, where we have seats in the front row. The performance starts at 8.30 ; the décor is that of any English police-court. The players are almost as inaudible as English actors. Police, burly as all-in wrestlers, shepherd their prisoners with a kind of rough gentleness. The magistrate, who wears neither wig nor gown, is thirty-five, keen-faced, looks *fortiter in modo* and turns out to be *suaviter in re*. The offences have all been committed since five o'clock this afternoon. Men and youths accused of peddling without a licence. They carry their wares with them. One batch is eleven strong, all Italians; they are discharged with a caution. Street-betting cases, a string of fourteen vagrants, old, some of them with heads which look definitely imbecile, all indescribably filthy, might be the inmates of one of Gogol's doss-houses. Pitiful. All are discharged. Most of these cases have taken less than a minute ; the longest five minutes.

An old Jew, who should be a figure in Italian comedy, pleads that he was not begging but selling umbrellas. These, produced, are obviously unsaleable. Old Jew says they are saleable if it rains hard enough. Acquitted. A young man with the air of a shabby Narcissus pleads not guilty to a charge we cannot hear. A whispered colloquy between judge and prisoner, at the end of which the young man is told to go away and behave himself.

There are no more prisoners at the moment, and an interval is taken. It is a Gilbertian court which waits for crime to be committed!

The shriek of a police-van as in the films. A young man has beaten up his wife for spending his wages on silk stockings. The magistrate tells the young man he is exceeding his authority. Will he promise no more beatings? Yes, if there is no more buying of stockings. A bargain is struck. Another young man is accused of violently assaulting his neighbour's wife! Will he desist? No, he will assault her again the moment he is out of this jam. She is a bitch, and has brought it on herself. The magistrate keeps him in cells till the morning, for his own protection. The neighbour seems wholly disinterested. The next is a drunk. "You're soused," says the magistrate. "I'm not sure you're not canned. Cells till morning." A voluble Japanese has refused to pay a taxi-driver $1.75. He has no money, but if he can go home on the subway he will return with the cash before the court rises. "But since you have no money how are you going to get the fare for the subway?" The Jap points to the taxi-driver: "He will lend it me!" The court dissolves in laughter, and the pair leave amicably. Another wait, then more peddlers, more vagrants, more drunks. It is midnight, and we go to supper. B. in his capacity as medical adviser sends me home soon after two. He insists on my having an early night, himself being all for another spot of Harlem's Moon-Glow.

May 21   B. is a fellow-traveller of genius. His latest notion
Friday.   is that while I am writing he should look at the
things which it would be disgraceful to leave New York without one of us having seen. This is splendid of him. Came in this morning to report that Shipwreck Kelly was still sitting on his pole; when he saw him he was eating the luncheon he had presumably taken out of the basket on which he sits.

Have come down to Coney Island in lovely weather, first calling for money in Wall Street, which to-day is distinctly livelier. Our chauffeur, who is second cousin to Kid Lewis, points out J. P. Morgan's home and library, the Law Courts, and Tombs Prison. The view from Manhattan Bridge is superb. To the left it might be the Thames. To the right is Brooklyn Bridge, beyond which we glimpse the Statue of Liberty. Behind us is still the Manhattan skyline, which keeps all its glamour. We proceed through slums, then suburbs which might be Tufnell Park. Then a long stretch of shady avenue, very like Bournemouth. Coney Island is like Southend Kursaal, only on a bigger scale. The season has not yet begun, and very few of the fun-fairs are functioning, though we manage to catch a glimpse of a Creature with a Human Head and the Legs of a Horse, and a Woman whose Body is Turning into Stone. We are introduced to Jack Johnson. Lunch at the Half Moon Hotel, on a balcony overlooking the boardwalk, narrow sands, and a lazy sea. Nobody about.

May 24   Spent yesterday exploring New Jersey. The place
Monday.   is as unfinished as everywhere else, and impresses
          me as being unfinishable. Like Slough, only less tidy. The Pulaski Bridge is a miracle of engineering. Two miles of steel switchbacks over stinking swamps, which still stink. The driving here is five times more expert than ours ; it is quicker and safer. I have done a fair amount of motoring and have not seen a single case of dangerous cutting-in. By comparison English drivers are bank-holiday lunatics. They have huge notices : " This is a highway, not a speedway." Lunched off hot dogs and iced beer served by white-coated attendants at a bar by the roadside and very nearly on the road itself, the radio in the car—it was a taxi, and most taxis have radios—discoursing Bach, Beethoven, Scriabin, and Stravinsky. Coming back I notice a Drive-in Theatre : " Sit in the car and see and hear the pictures." In the evening dropped into Radio City Music-hall again, and saw a short film about John D. Rockefeller, whose death had been announced in the morning.

To-day has been almost my busiest, and I begin to feel that there is a saturation point even in being entertained. Got caught in a traffic jam this morning. Swelteringly hot, and sitting in cab with braces off. Train passing on railroad overhead. Five yards to the left road-drills are hollowing out a subway. (At night the drill stops, and miners wearing steel helmets explode dynamite charges.) In other cabs also jammed two radios are tuned in to two different stations. So as not to be left out of it the horn in the car behind us jams. And I am trying to think out what sort of presents A, B, and C expect me to bring back. Have just bought my sister May a white leather bag which I feel convinced will turn out to be leatherette.

Lunched at an open-air café which looked extremely chic. It was in fact so chic that the waiter, having brought the menu, disappeared for twenty-five minutes. As I had only half an hour for lunch, this put me in an atrocious temper, in which I refused to write three articles on the American Woman.

Dined with Lucius Beebe at the Twenty-one. Lucius is a luscious Beckfordian figure. He is said to be fabulously wealthy, write a daily column for fun, and change his clothes seven times a day. Proud of being called the American Bayard, " sans peur mais avec beaucoup de reproche." Dog-French, but it conveys what I mean. Afterwards to *Room Service*, the new farce at the Cort Theatre. This is a riot, and New York theatre-world talks of nothing else. The credit is all given to George Abbott, who has produced this, though the authors, John Murray and Allen Boretz, deserve some of it. Abbott is part-author of *Three Men on a Horse* and the producer of *Boy meets Girl*. *Room Service* is funnier than both these put together. It is the American counterpart of our Aldwych farces. The pace at which it is taken is terrific, and even your Broadwayite can hardly keep up with the jokes, which are peller and meller than in any farce I remember. The plot ? All about a theatrical company which is stranded in a hotel and cannot pay its bill unless the play is a success. The hotel manager is about to throw everybody out neck and crop, but this is countered by the manager of the theatre company, who knows his hotel law. A person who is sick cannot be turned out of a hotel, wherefore the author of the play must be sick. The hotel manager is informed that it is a case of tapeworm. " The tapeworm must register," he says with authority. (Yes, taste over here is not our English taste.) Earlier on the author had appeared in a preposterous dress-suit, whereupon the lowest comedian said, " I wore a dress-suit like that in a juggling act." But that joke got no laugh except from me, who felt painfully English throughout the entire farce. Over here they are more graphic. " Feel like I've swallowed a couple of holes," means that you're hungry. The gag which got most laughs was : " I'm like Hercules. I think I've finished cleaning up, and there it is again ! " In the third act the fun got furiouser and furiouser. The pseudo-invalid had pretended to die from drinking too much disin-fectant. But a dead man is no longer sick, and the body could therefore be taken out of the hotel. This had to be delayed at all costs, the curtain having gone up on the piece, which was showing signs of being a wow. Whereby prayers had to be said, and orations made, and a hymn sung with one eye on the clock and the other on the corpse, who upset all arrangements by getting up and going to the lavatory. By this time, however, there was no doubt about the piece. As it was being played in the theatre belonging to the hotel, the curtain descended on the hotel manager's triumphant " Perhaps this will be the first hotel to win the Pulitzer ! " But even in the thick of the fooling one or two quiet strokes of wit had gone home. There was one about a new form of theatre : " A play without actors, a theatre without audience, only scenery and critics."

Went on to supper at El Morocco, a place so swagger that literally all you do is to sup. Eating appears to be out of the question. Like the woman who dresses with extreme simplicity, the place is ruinously expensive. It seems that the proprietor some years ago discovered that his guests, if of the right sort, would provide better entertainment for each other than he could provide for them. Therefore there is nothing whatever in the restaurant except a floor and a band. As the crowd increases the floor-space decreases, and on really witty nights the dancers are squeezed out altogether. The décor changes from time to time, which is to say that while it remains Moorish the shrubs in the pots are changed. One thing is changeless, and that is the zebra-striped upholstery. This is so well known that in the illustrated papers the name of the place is never mentioned; everybody who sees the stripes recognises El Morocco. As Beebe put it, " In the season everybody has to come here or they think you're dead. Or out of town, which is worse." Coming out, I heard a cad expostulating with the management. He didn't see why he should pay fourteen dollars for a coupla drinks for himself and the wife. I thought the man was clearly mad. Drinks or no drinks, fourteen dollars is surely not excessive for sitting in a room in which Noel Coward once waved to Beatrice Lillie !

May 25   Tuesday.   Had a look round Philadelphia, which I like very much. Imagine Birmingham encircled with a ring of Streatham-like suburbs and set down in the middle of Surrey. The surrounding country is enchanting, and perhaps the reason I find it enchanting is that it is more nearly English. Here are to be found walls, palings, and neatly trimmed hedges, though I apologise to Streatham in the matter of the suburbs. The houses in the immediate vicinity of the town are of an appalling and uniform hideousness. All of them appear to nave been built out of a child's box of bricks, each one having its pair of inane little pillars supporting nothing. Lunched at the Bellevue-Stratford, a palatial hotel and far bigger than anything in London. When I got to Philadelphia I found that the Devon Horse Show was happening only twenty miles away, so I took the afternoon off and discovered a toy Richmond, and that one of the judges was Bernard Mills, the son of Bertram Mills. Over here the stud-grooms are called managers, and one of them turned out to be Willie Black, who was with me when I bought Skirbeck Cora. America is large, but the horse-world is small.

In the evening sampled the Dance Theatre, which is W.P.A.'s essay in ballet. Frankly, I do not think W.P.A. is essaying very well. I am not a judge of this art, and the fact that I am in another country is not going to alter my determination not to write critically about it. The programme was in two parts. First a dance drama entitled *How Long, Brethren?* This is made up from six or seven " Negro Songs of Protest." The second part was a dance interpretation of Voltaire's *Candide*. One understands why niggers should have no shoes. But why Candide and Dr Pangloss and the rest of the Voltaireans should wear period costume all but the feet, and then insist on baring these, is, as Americans say, " just one of those things." B., who is a balletomane, tells me that while the applause was up to Sadler's Wells standard the dancing fell a long way below it. I think it only fair to the New York critics to make their point again here. This is that the revue called *Power* is easily the best thing W.P.A. have done in the theatre, and that the general level is much more truly represented by the Dance Theatre. They concede the ambition, but deny the achievement.

Afterwards B., a friend of his, and I adjourned to the Rainbow Room at the Plaza. This is the resort of the High Muck-a-muck. Must dress. It is solemn, grandiose, and dull, and not the less so because it is all happening on a sixty-fifth storey in Rockefeller Centre. Below us the New York floor is thick inlaid with patines of bright gold. These are the city lights. The imposing twin-steepled Cathedral looks the size of a play-producer's model. Town mapped out in gold ink, white and cream taxis crawling like gilded beetles, the twinkling Hudson—all this is sublime provided your stomach can stand sublimity at this height.

Inside is something which not all the evening dress in the world can keep me from recognising as Blackpool Tower dolled up. We sit at a table remote from the dance floor and order cocktails. Can we have supper? M'yes, but only when the show, now starting, is over. Two dancers we remember from a Cochran revue. A girl with what Mrs Campbell would call a mouth like Tesman's bedroom slippers sings interminable songs by Cole Porter. A pianist plays a rainbow effusion of his own composing, not unlike the " Rainbow Trout " of Cyril Scott. Will somebody sing out five notes? Somebody does, and I reject the notion of possible collusion. The five notes are then used in an improvisation in the pianist's own manner, and then Bach's, followed by Gershwin's. How many

combinations are there of twelve notes taken five at a time ?
My theory is that the pianist has worked them all out and has
them up his sleeve. Will somebody sing out four tunes to be
worked into a medley ? " Pennies from Heaven," " St Louis
Blues," Chopin's " Nocturne " (no need to specify the number),
and Brahms' " Cradle Song," here called " Lullaby." The
medley consists of playing these in turn. We cannot leave
because the pianist is blind and English. The lights go up,
and we observe that nobody has been eating anything. We ask
the damage, and are told seven dollars fifty cents. Say eight
dollars. One pound twelve shillings and sixpence for three
cocktails. Steep ? B. says it's the covers, and I urge that we
don't see any covers, and that you can't eat a floor show, however
good it may be. We descend the sixty-five sick-making storeys
and sup brilliantly at Tony's Bar in West 52nd Street, a tiny,
well-conducted café with good food, quick service, and a Café
Royal atmosphere. As this is our last night, we have foie gras,
caviare, chicken à la King, and a really good bottle of Piper
Heidsieck. But for my Restraining Influence, B., it would
have been two bottles. Bed soon after three.

May 26   This has been our last day. We sail to-morrow
Wednesday.   literally at the earliest possible moment, one minute
               after midnight to-night. Farewell lunch at Passy's
to Claud Greneker. I refuse to believe that he has had spies
sitting next to us in the theatres to overhear and report our
lightest whisper. I do not think he is as Machiavellian as people
here try to make out. Yet when that slow, sweet smile of his
subsides I see what they mean ; the residue is something cut
in lean grey stone. Everybody insists that in comparison with
Shubert's intelligence organisation the Ogpu is sissy. I tell
Greneker this ; his smile is slower to come than usual and quicker
to go. It is only proper to say that wherever we have been we
have found him at our elbow. I think of him now as a combination of sheet-anchor, shepherd, and dragon—a mentor to whom
we are infinitely obliged.

Next, packing. Have had to buy another trunk, which still

leaves me with eight huge parcels. Tips are difficult. There is a Swedish valet who looks as though he had not seen a sixpence since leaving Stockholm. There are three foreign floorwaiters, but none so imbecile as to be untippable. Four liftboys. Two of these are Welsh—one pines for Blaenau Festiniog, in which he was born, the other for the Rhondda Valley, which he has never seen. Both have kept their accent. Five bell-hops. (By the way, the bell-hop is a myth. There are no bells and nobody hops. Errands here are run slower than in England.) Two porters, one of whom does our motor-bargaining for us. The receptionist, who will accept flowers. Macbeth's Three Witches, early risers who want to make our beds before we have got into them. That makes nineteen people to be tipped, twenty if we include the telephone girl. As a working rule we decide to give five dollars to any of those who smile at us, and ten to those who scowl. (Actually we got off with something under eighty dollars. This may seem excessive, but we got a lot done for it.)

Nathan called this afternoon to take me to tea with Lillian Gish. She came into the room looking exactly as she did in *Way Down East*. A sad, pinched little face, with woebegone eyes looking out from under a hat like a squashed Chinese pagoda. A trim, tiny figure very plainly dressed; the whole apparition strangely reminiscent of Vesta Tilley. Since she left films she has played Shakespeare, Tchehov, and Dumas *fils*: " I came from the theatre, and I am glad to go back to it." Nathan has a theory that acting has nothing to do with the film or the film with acting, and that the proper function of the screen is to exploit the exuberant vitality of the Robert Taylors and Loretta Youngs, and discard all players as soon as they cease to exuberate. He thinks Lillian was the last screen-actress. I talked a bit about her old pictures, and she seemed to like it. Anyhow she sat there silently, nodding like some grave flower.

May 27   I think it was Wilde who said, " It is a terrible
Thursday.   thing to part from people one has known a very
           short time." The same holds true of countries;
though no truer, I suppose, of New York than of anywhere

else. *Partir, c'est mourir un peu* was probably first said by Ulysses. Still, leaving New York is an emotional business. As B. was spending the last evening with his brother, I proposed to seek out the Stork Club, said to be the centre of the younger and rowdier fashionables—the kind of place to which in 1926 Evelyn Waugh's characters would have betaken their vile bodies. When it came to the point I couldn't face it, and instead went for a last drive round Central Park, with a snack at Tony's to finish with. Would have had another look at Harlem if I had not paid off my guide. Left Tony's at 10.45 and was on the Hamburg-Amerika liner *Deutschland* by eleven. This boat is half the size of the *Bremen* and prettily done up in *rose tendre* and old gold. Full of Germans, whereby frumpishness sets in again. If Schiaparelli herself dressed these women they would revert to German before she got out of the room. A great crowd to see us off and a great waving of handkerchiefs, which begins at the first sign of departure and lasts till we actually move off. It is stiflingly hot with that curious quality of steam-heat I shall always associate with New York. This accounts for the mist, at first pierced only by the Neon tower of the Empire State Building, and later by a weak glimmer which is probably Radio City. Farther down the river and leaving the docks the mist clears, and we see some of the lesser skyscrapers, whose alternating panes of light and dark give them the air of cosmic crossword puzzles. (For three weeks I have been wondering what familiar thing they are like.) Twenty minutes later we drop the pilot—a bit of routine which the spotlight of the parent ship turns into a shot from a film. And now New York begins to fade from my consciousness. Or would do if B. were not whistling " Where or When " from *Babes in Arms*, the best piece we saw and the one I enjoyed most, musical comedy though it is ! I think its sixteen-year-old naïveté gave me some foretaste of this still new and still raw country.

But a country which made an immediate and immense effect on both of us. I suppose I ought to be ashamed to confess it, but the truth is that the thing which has interested me least in America is the theatre. Montague once said of a certain actress's

Juliet that he was glad to get out into the street again : " It was
jolly to look at the carts ! " Similarly I found New York's
streets more exciting than its plays, its skyscrapers more heart-
shaking than its stage décor, its manners quainter than their
stage simulation. But since to find the Beefeaters at the Tower
and the pearlies of Poplar more novel than the London stage
would be no criticism of that stage, so I must put novelty on
one side and try to take an unstartled view of the American
theatre.

First as to the playhouses. These are drab and forbidding.
Wherever you note a lull in the street's excitement, be sure
your eye is resting on a theatre. The floors of the inadequate
foyers are invariably littered with envelopes discarded by ticket-
holders. Box-office manners are those of booking-offices at
English railway stations. Americans go to the theatre as unceremoni-
ously as to the cinema. Except on first nights they do not
dress. Programmes are free. Applause is grudging. There
are many exits, and after each act everybody pours out from the
Turkish bath atmosphere into the draughty street. No smoking
anywhere, even at revues.

Let me summarise what of the season's programme is left
to run through the summer. 1. Last year's farce about Boy
meeting Girl. 2. A farce about life at a military institute.
3. A serious play acted principally by youngsters and showing
how gangsters are made. 4. A fantasy about excursionists and
an island. 5. A romantic comedy about campers. 6. A poetic
fantasy about ghosts on a mountain. 7. Shakespeare's *Richard II.*
8. A drama about natives of Georgia. 9. *Tovarich.* 10. *Victoria
Regina.* 11. A bitchy—the word is current and legitimate here—
comedy at the expense of New York's smart women. 12. A light
comedy about Free Love. 13. A domestic farce. 14. A musical
comedy. 15. A revue. 16. A musical comedy called *Sea Legs*
and which appears not to have found them. 17. W.P.A. pro-
ductions. From this list one might argue a drama barren of
heart. Let me put aside the Shakespeare and the Housman,
Tovarich, which is French, and *High Tor,* which is fake. (It's out
at last !) This leaves only two plays which appeal to the emotions

—a lean feast for those who, like myself, belong to the lump-in-the-throat school of playgoing.

Americans hold the expression of direct emotion to be ham, and devote their energies half to shunning emotion and half to attaining it by implication. This is why their tragedies are written in the key of farce. Robert Sherwood's *Idiot's Delight*, which I have read but not seen, since it is playing 1000 miles away, is the stuff Shaw would be writing to-day if he were sixty years younger. Does this mean that I regard Sherwood as the most significant young playwright on either side of the Atlantic? I do. I find the American public to be more theatre-minded than the English. It is alive to its theatre. It is at once receptive and critical.

About the American stage as a whole I feel that it is immensely vital and open to new forms. Not only open, but questing. This springs out of the American sensitiveness to lack of a past. That which cannot vie with yesterday must be the surer of to-morrow. That which has never learned to walk must be the first to run. The tree which has no roots must flower earlier. This may be poor physics and worse botany. But it is good human nature and doubly good American human nature. Direct Emotion belongs to your old world, America says, and we cannot beat you at it. But what about Indirect Emotion? Have the Tragic Muse chew gum! Have the next Hamlet say:

O what a louse and sonofabitch am I!

And now about one or two other matters. Production is invariably good. The general level of acting among women is higher than in London, though I cannot hear of, and certainly have not seen, an Edith Evans. The quickfire comedians beat ours, but otherwise, and apart from Alfred Lunt, there are no actors. There is nobody over here with the quality of Charles Laughton, John Gielgud, Laurence Olivier, Ralph Richardson, Stephen Haggard, Robert Eddison, Alec Clunes, to mention only a few. Of the older school there is no sign of a Martin-Harvey, a Seymour Hicks, or a Godfrey Tearle. The one exception to the foregoing is Burgess Meredith, an arresting young actor. But they tell me he is limited to the type of romantic hick or hobo, and can speak no English outside the idiom of " Now what the hell ya suppose is eatin' them two guys ? "

This is the last sentence in a little book recommended me by Brentano's and called *Of Mice and Men*, by John Steinbeck. This heart-rending tragedy of two tramps—one is an idiot shot by his crony that he may not be lynched—has extraordinary power and beauty. This and *Idiot's Delight*—a book I could have read at home and a play I did not see—have been the high-spots of my visit. Add, in lighter vein, the lilt of Hart and Rodgers' score, which has danced its way through everything I have seen, and which has given this hard-boiled city a dreamlike quality.

Or is it nightmare ? The sum of my impressions is like one of those kaleidoscopic, catherine-wheel shots with which the film depicts the mind of a man reeling under the bludgeon. Here let me offer a hint. The newcomer to this country should take care not to arrive in the morning, or to choose some hotel remote from Broadway. At night the lighting—a blaze and a frenzy exceeding Piccadilly Circus and reaching to Knightsbridge —gives Broadway a certain garish splendour. By day it is a dreary succession of candy-stores, drug-stores, cheap eating-houses, shoe-shine parlours, hot-dog stalls, newspaper-stalls, bars, tailors' shops, gambling-booths, photographers, cheap jewellers, and gimcrackery of all sorts. You have to wash the mind clean of Broadway before you can appreciate all that dignity and grace upon which it is a blot. For New York has been superbly planned. The streets are endless glades and the skyscrapers giant trees in a super-seemly forest.

Harlem also has a unity. You are aware of the sense of family as soon as you turn out of Central Park into 7th Avenue. Not a white face to be seen, and even the policemen are coloured. Brown niggers, yellow niggers, pale niggers, black niggers. Gay niggers and sad niggers. Old niggers with white hair and spectacles, young niggers dressed to kill with their yellow shirts, lavender suits, patent-leather shoes, huge cigars, and carnations in their buttonholes. The girls are often extremely pretty, delicious little creatures with melting eyes and crimped, blue-black hair. That part of the population which does not live out of doors hangs out of windows. It is largely vocal. The bucks lolling on the doorsteps chaff passing bucks ; coal-black mammies exchange window confidences ; piccaninnies play their shrill games under everybody's feet. A childlike, innocuous gaiety pervades the place, expressed in terms of rhythm through the radio pouring out of cafés, bars, taxis, beauty-parlours, and houses it would be absurd to call private. Everywhere the burr of soft speech and that sensuous appreciation which at night-time bathes the whole place in heliotrope lighting. An untinted glare is a solecism the Negro never commits. The American view of him ? This is simplicity itself. The Negro does not exist.

The vaudeville artist in Sherwood's play asks the vamp whether she knows America and receives the reply : " Oh, yes. I've seen it all. New York, Washington, Palm Beach—" The man interrupts, " I said America." I too have seen it all—Broadway, Park Avenue, Central Park, Harlem. But I do not presume to deduce America from these. Or from a few theatre managers, actors, actresses, critics, night-club devotees, bar-tenders, taxi-drivers, waiters, shoe-blacks. New England has nothing in common with Old England except the name. And I am told that New England is not at all repre-sentative of America proper. Whatever this last may be, it is something which has already created in me its own nostalgia.

July 9   The Royal Show. Ego went superbly to-day, and in
Friday.   every opinion except that of the judge won the class
            from Spotlight and Nanette with any amount to spare.
Whereas their action was fighting and laboured, his was as effortless as a breaker in the Atlantic. He looked absolutely lovely and satisfied the most captious, the judge coming up to me afterwards and saying it was a pity he is half a hand smaller than the others. I didn't in the least mind going down once again to established reputations. When an animal goes as Ego went to-day there is, as Montague said about Duse and Bernhardt,

" no less or more, but only a sense of boundless release of heart and mind."

July 16   Canterbury. Ego second to Nanette in the under
Friday.   15 hands class. Both went superbly, and the judges
             were a long time about it, sending us out together
several times. Ego is the more beautiful pulled up, and his action is always the purer. But Nanette at her best is a more extravagant goer, her additional six years help her, and that other inch and a half in height counts a lot when it comes to a near thing. She *fills the eye* more. Also she has a genius for single shows up and down the grand stand that I have never seen equalled. I told the judges I was perfectly satisfied, which I was ; I should, in their place, have done exactly the same. The championship class was contested equally hotly. Nanette won, with Ego reserve. Next came Pollux, this year's Olympia winner in the over 15.2 class. Then the pony High and Mighty, winner at the National. Holywell Squire, this year's novice winner at Olympia and the National, was fifth. Supper at the Savage Club, where I tried to tell Victor MacClure all about Ego. Instead of which he insisted on my listening to something about fish, and fish are not interesting.

July 20   Leo said, " After forty-five only two things matter—
Tuesday.   to be amused if you've got money, and amusing if you
             haven't." He has found a name for Charles Morgan's
criticisms in *The Times*. He calls them Morgan Voluntaries.

July 22   Feeling strangely well on Tuesday morning, I rose
Thursday. with the lark, and while I was shaving composed
             this poem, which will duly appear in my review of
Lord Horder's *Health and a Day* :

> Mister Korda
> Sent for Lord Horder
> Because of the strictures
> People pass on his pictures !

Highly pleased with this ebullition of unmitigated jollity.

Aug. 1   On holiday. Blackpool manners are super-normal,
Sunday.   and in the matter of raiment the return to nature is
             striking. The gay colours are worn by the men, and
I saw one young male dazzling his female in a get-up consisting
of black shirt and collar, trousers and suède shoes of black,
relieved by a white jacket and white tie. Another favourite
combination is baby-blue and canary. I saw one party of six
males set off for a jaunt in a landau ; their sweethearts were
told to sit down, do nowt, and await their return.

Played eleven holes of golf yesterday with young Rawstron.
The first time I have touched a club this year, and am surprised
to find I never hit the ball better. The sort of game which would
have bucked me up tremendously a year or two ago. But it's
too late now, and renunciation begins. Proof of this is in the
fact that I *forgot to bring my clubs*, and that I could limit myself to
less than the full round. What this means is that the days of
stern matches with assistant pros., who used not to be able to
give me 4 bisques, are now over. And I think I would rather
give up the game altogether than play with amateurs of no style.
Half my fun in golf has been the intense pleasure I have got out
of watching the professional stuff. But then I have never been
able to stick amateurism in any form. I loathe amateur acting,
and any golf-swing in which I cannot detect the caddie. Leo
says that Cleopatra made a mess of her love-making the day she
turned amateur. I shall probably not really give up golf so
long as I can break 90 ; yesterday my score for 11 holes was 52.
My excuse for recording all this is that it is of intense interest to
me, and that as a fanatic for Arnold Bennett's Journal I am
prepared to be absorbed in an entry telling me which sock he
put on first. There are occasional weak moments when I pretend
that I am writing for my old age. That wise old bird Leo quickly
disposes of this : " Nonsense, James ! You'll always be too
busy writing *Ego* to read it. You remember what George Moore
prophesied of Zola : ' One day he'll be found dead, *le nez dans
le boudin*.' One day you'll be found dead, with your nose in
Ego 25."

Later. This afternoon's golf much better, with a grand last

hole. All square. Two perfect drives, J. A.'s slightly the longer.
R. puts iron shot ten yards from pin.   J. A. pulls into bunker
biting into green ; finds ball lying on hard, baked sand, plays
explosion shot *à la* Hagen, so that ball sits down where it pitches
eight feet from pin. R. is dead in three, half-closing the hole.
J. A. squeezes past and in like a master, and for half an hour
walks on air.

Aug. 8   So Lady Tree has gone. A kindly soul and a delicious
Sunday.   wit. It is always said that the line in Barrie's play
                apropos of boiler-scraping—" What fun men have ! "
—was one of her dress-rehearsal impromptus. I remember how,
about to recite at a charity matinée, she advanced to a gold chair,
and, swathed in heliotrope tulle, said smilingly, " I want you
all to imagine I am a plumber's mate ! "   In her early years her
extreme plainness was a handicap. In later life her face became
her fortune ; it was that of a benevolent horse. In her old age
she was an admirable actress who made the most of a good part,
and got a lot that wasn't there out of a bad one.

Aug. 11   A day of extreme gloom, unprintable things
Wednesday.   happening to Ego at a little show near here. It
                was only to be expected, since every owner of a
good horse knows that it is always at the little, unsuspecting
places that it gets dumped. The Henriques, whom I had entertained to an *al fresco* luncheon of hock and wasps, were more
than sympathetic. But, alas, melancholy overcame me during
the drive back to Southport ! This was not improved by an
article in the *M.G.* on " The Discipline of Obscurity." There it
all was—Emerson's

> It is time to be old,
> To take in sail,

and Christina Rossetti's

> . . . the dark hair changing to gray
> That hath won neither laurel nor bay.

Tennyson and Bunyan too—in short, the whole caboodle,

omitting only the line in English hymnology which, from my childhood up, I have most resented. This is the line :

Whate'er I prized, it ne'er was mine.

In the evening made a moody tour of the Marine Lake, and at sight of its fairy lamps, Bridges of Sighs, illuminated gondolas, and what-not, something recovered my spirits.

Aug. 12   To-day began elegiacally enough. Garstang is
Thursday.   one of the prettiest little show-grounds I know,
              squeezed in between church and river. The field
slopes gently towards the stand—which is rickety rather than grand—and from the top side of the ring the little show is spread out before you like a map. Jock would tell me which English poet is best fitted to paint the admirable English scene, which is too much *alive* for Gray. Refreshment tent against churchyard wall, to which toothless greybeards turn their backs in supreme unconcern. Cheapjacks offering to turn base metal into gold. Children patting meek, immemorial bulls, or struggling with wilful calves. Not an inch of room anywhere. The local band.

Sat next to Mrs Henriques and debated how far the judge, who yesterday was chief ring-steward, would be affected by the Lytham awards, seeing that to-day's entries are the same animals which yesterday had what Mrs Gamp called the " bragian imperence " to beat Ego. He turned out to be totally unaffected, thereby proving himself an honest and an upright arbiter, and not one of those judges who, as Ernest said, are not to be trusted without a jury. In other words, Ego won.

Dined at the Henriques' and talked Hackneys till the early hours of the morning. As it was very hot and thundery, with no actual peals, but a great deal of summer lightning, went for a spin round the Marine Drive. Behind us the skeleton of the deserted Pleasure Park, with the steelwork of the *montagnes russes* showing against the sky like giant ribs. In front a nothingness of sand, pierced by a powerful car speeding in the wake of its own spear-head of light along the rim of where, if there be sea at Southport, that sea must be.

Aug. 23   Brother Edward dropped into Antrim Mansions one
Monday.   day last week to tell me my mind was too narrow.
              What educated man ever went to Blackpool? Why
didn't I spend my holidays in Munich? Why don't I go to
Russia? I made some feeble answer about a winter holiday
with a peep at Egypt. Whereat Edward rubbed the end of his
long, disapproving nose. " There's been no culture in Egypt
for three thousand years ! " he said icily. And departed.

Obedient to reproof, came down to Folkestone on Saturday.
George Mathew staying here. On Sunday, still anxious to
widen my mind, went to Boulogne, where I remember spending
one of the happiest days of the War. I was with a man called
Whymper, nephew of the famous climber who broke his leg
in an after-dinner attempt to mount a lecture platform. We were
on the way from Marseilles, reporting about something or other,
and there was so much sea running that the boat service was
cancelled, and we spent the day on the front shouting metaphysics through the gale. Yesterday the town seemed completely unchanged, except that on the previous night a fire had
gutted the Casino, whose ruins still smoked. In the afternoon
was a religious fête with processions of children and so forth,
the entire population turning out to sit on kitchen chairs. The
odd thing about French widows is that they are always accompanied by a brother of the deceased, a walking blob of ink.
We lunched at Mony's, not, I thought, quite so good as it
used to be. But perhaps that was because it was Sunday and the
place crowded. Spent the afternoon on the beach, reading
next week's review books, George poring over what he calls
The Unpoetical Works of George Meredith.

Sept. 9   Sixty to-day. Asked Leo what he did on the same
Thursday.   occasion. He said, " Stayed indoors and read the
               Book of Job." Had a very good day, if not quite
so austere. Luncheon-party at the Ivy. Guests were Marie
Tempest, Gladys Calthrop, my sister May, Hugh Walpole,
Harold Dearden, Hamish Hamilton, and Jock. Mary was
looking ridiculously young, Gladys magnificently apache-like

with a scarf printed like a newspaper, May quiet and mouse-like, Hugh pink and flourishing, Dearden macabre and genial, the result of Irvingesque eyebrows beetling over a bright blue hunting-stock, Hamish composed and self-effacing, Jock plump after his French, Dutch, and German holiday and obviously bursting with travel secrets. Sibelius Concert at Queen's Hall, including my favourite second symphony, and the sixth, which I find bleak. Left at half-time and looked in at the Queen's Theatre for the last act of Gielgud's *Richard*, conscience having pricked me. Rather boisterous supper-party at home. My presents included a drawing by Gladys Calthrop which was part of the décor for Noel's production of *Mademoiselle*. This shows a pink stallion prancing before a white ditto and trailing a black tail like the train of a court frock. The setting is half ancient Greece and half peppermint rock, and the whole is in the manner of Chirico, and may even be a copy. Gladys gave me this, and it is so large in its white frame that I shall have to take a new flat !

Sept. 10   Came across this in Sir Thomas Browne's *Religio*
Friday.   *Medici* : " I can look a whole day with delight upon
                   a handsome Picture, though it be but of an Horse."

Nov. 5   Saw this notice in a pub in the Charing Cross Road :
Friday.

LADIES UNACCOMPANIED ARE
RESPECTFULLY REQUESTED
TO USE TABLES FOR THEIR
REFRESHMENTS AND NOT TO
STAND AT THE BAR AND OBLIGE

Nov. 12   A day of successes :
Friday.

(1) Jock invents a name for a film star—Vomica Nux.
(2) Highly metaphysical letter from Brother Edward dated
     " Nov. 11, in a thick fog " and with the postscript, " I am
     deep in Sydney Horler."

(3) Monty telephones that the car of the British Ambassador in Paris is numbered EGO 2.

(4) Letter from a daughter of Clement Scott asking if I will accept her father's scrap-book of *memoranda dramatica*: " The first cutting is from the *Morning Post* for Dec. 30th, 1811. *Venice Preserved* at Covent Garden Theatre. The last entry is dated 1833, and is a notice of Kean's *Othello*."

Dec. 23 *Thursday.* Brother Edward's Christmas present is a half-sheet of notepaper with the quotation : " Like the patriarch who ran from the altar in St Sophia to his stable, in all his pontificals, to see a colt newly fallen from his beloved and much-valued mare, Phorbante." (Jeremy Taylor, *Holy Living and Dying*.)

Christmas Day. This began by being brilliantly fine and sunny. At eleven o'clock Lady Macbeth's blanket of the dark had nothing on the fog at Belsize Park, which by eleven-thirty rivalled the dunnest smoke of hell. It was so thick that taxis declined to leave their ranks. As everybody had gone on leave, I was marooned and should have starved had Fred not left a note saying I should find a cold turkey in the kitchen cupboard. Spent the day improvising a wine-cellar for a dozen bottles of brandy, being a Christmas present from Lee Shubert, tidying up the diary, playing two of the more Ibsenite Sibelius symphonies, and reading Matthew Arnold. In the evening the fog cleared and I was able to keep my engagement to dine at Monty's, which I have done every Christmas but one for ten years.

An excellent party, which it was bound to be considering the wit of the host and the blending of the guests—Herschel Johnson, a member of the American diplomatic corps, Maurice Ingram, now back from Rome, John Deverell the actor, Pat Kevan, a very promising young player, Alan Dent, that very promising young dramatic critic, and me. Monty is becoming higher than highbrow. At the Christmas party six years ago he would not have Logan Pearsall Smith because La Roche-foucauld is better, and to-night Matthew Arnold was dismissed

as a bastard Milton. Herschel told us about a friend who heard
the Dowager Empress of China interrupt a political conversation
to say, " That reminds me—I must have Lotus Fragrance thrown
down the well." After dinner we tackled the *Times* General
Knowledge Paper, which is becoming too snobbish. Too many
questions of the " What Old Wykehamist is whipper-in to the
Chiltern Hundreds ? " order. Wound up with games.

Afterwards Jock would have me drink a glass of brandy in
his flat. This is the first time in eleven years that I have been
bidden to any of Jock's abodes. We clomb to an eyrie in Covent
Garden consisting of three rooms and a " loggia "—a bedroom-
kitchen, spare and spotless, a library with shelves much better
furnished than my own and including a magnificent set of
Steevens's edition of Shakespeare with Fuseli's plates, and a
music-room with a superb collection of gramophone records.
Delightful playbills and old pictures, with one of Malibran
picked up at Southend and which Jock had not dared to disclose
to me on jealous grounds. The " loggia " is closed in winter ;
in summer I gather that it is the resort of Covent Garden's dart
champions. Jock insisted, at five in the morning, on my hearing
a Mozart symphony unperformed in this country, and I could
only get away by pleading that I had to-day's diary to write up.
To which " alibi " he was forced to yield !

Dec. 27   Did a lot of tidying up in view of proposed move
Monday.   to a bigger flat, my work having outgrown the
            present one. I hardly dare open the door lest a
parcel of review books should fall out. Spent the entire day
going through old papers till the dustbin was full. Made some
extraordinary discoveries, largely grotesque, but one or two
that I found moving. Let me tabulate :

1. Set of extremely lugubrious verses composed by me at
the age of five.

2. School group taken in 1887 and showing me standing
next to Fred Kenyon, afterwards known as Gerald Cumberland.

3. School report for the summer term of 1888, showing

that I was Present 81 times, Absent (illness) 5 times, Late 0 times !!
Position in form : 1st in English, Latin, History, Geography,
but only 3rd in French, 7th in Algebra, and 9th in Arithmetic.
In the following term I fell to 7th in Geography, but was 1st in
French, where I remained.

4. Letter from Brother Edward, at the age of eleven, to me
at Giggleswick :

> My sore throat is much better and I have been able to
> go for a walk. I wonder if you have such green trees as we
> have now. Surrey is playing Hampshire. Surrey goes in
> first and makes 494. Abel 46, M. Read 41, W. W. Read 80,
> Lockwood 100, Henderson 105. Then poor Hampshire goes
> in and as the scores are so little I will not detail them. Lanca-
> shire is going to play Oxford University. The team is Messrs
> S. M. Crosfield and A. T. Kemble, with Baker, Barlow,
> Briggs, Mold, Sugg, A. Ward, Watson, Paul and Yates. The
> influenza is something dreadful, hundreds of people are
> dying around us. Mr Birch came as usual on Friday afternoon.
> Sydney had drawn a face leaving out the ear, mouth and hair,
> and Mr Birch said it was charming, sweet, and there could
> not be anything better. He gave us two flat irons to draw
> that day, one ten lbs and the other the billiard-table one but
> we only drew the billiard-table one. How many runs have
> you made, how many fellows have you bowled, and how many
> chaps have you stumped ? You ought to bat, bowl and stump
> pretty well after our little pitch at Skipton that you did such
> wonders on. No, no flattery, you ought to be able to do
> something like Crosfield that you pretended to be. . . .

5. Letter to Edward from Sarah Bernhardt, presented by
him to me as a Christmas present some years ago. The envelope
has no stamp because it was given, May tells me, to my mother
to give Edward, Sarah at the same time scrabbling in her bag
and producing ten pounds. The piece which Sarah was to have
recited was Rostand's *La Brouette*, a little poem for which she
had commissioned Edward to write a piano accompaniment :

MON CHER AGATE,
     Je reçois à l'instant un mot de la Maison Royale me de-
mandant de dire devant Leurs Majestés " La Prière pour

Nos Ennemis " dont je disais quelques vers dans la petite pièce, " Du Théâtre au Champs d'Honneur." Je crois que c'est notre Ambassadeur qui leur a parlé de ces vers. Je ne puis refuser. Donc voilà notre " Brouette " reculée ; mais je la dirai dans un autre concert ! Ne vous dérangez donc pas ce matin, mon cher Edouard. Je vous envoie avec tous mes remerciments mes excuses pour le petit retard involontaire et mes grandes amitiés.

SARAH BERNHARDT

6. Letter from Allan Monkhouse dated Nov. 11, 1924, after the London production of *The Hayling Family* :

Meadow Bank
Disley
Cheshire

DEAR J. E. A.,

You'll think it queer but I haven't seen what you said about *The Hayling Family*. I've been in bed for three weeks with some return of my old trouble. As usual they're all kindness and consideration at the office and I can do a bit of work. But I can't get any work of my own done. Lack of energy and invention and some discouragement.

I should like to see what you said about *The H. Family* : I received cuttings of the daily papers and then my press cutting subscription ran out and I had told them before that I wasn't renewing it. The dailies were almost uniformly down on it, and, if I may say so of your colleagues, almost uniformly idiotic. I didn't seem to want any more but I thought the *S. Times* would somehow come my way, though it hasn't. There was nothing to show what was wrong with the play. These dramatic critics are, of course, experts of a sort. They are men of the world who may know a success when they see it. They don't want to go into anything. They said that the last act was ridiculous, preposterous, farcical melodrama. They all thought that the play was written to display Hayling. Not one perceived that the three young people were the play, that John pushed his idealism to a tragical and almost monstrous extreme, that this broke their unity, that the play poised for a moment on Bobby's " I don't know what to do," that the intolerable strain of the rupture is mitigated or exalted by the last line.

But of course I see that I haven't fitted the play for an audience, unless it be a very exceptional one. It's the first play I wrote, barring two one-acters, and in my inexperience I've left too much implicit rather than explicit. The implications seem clear enough to me, but the play is evidently more obscure than I thought. I never have accepted your contention that I'm a closet playwright. All my plays that I've seen acted have been stage plays. Ivor Brown, in a letter, told me you said it should have been a novel. I have sometimes thought of making it into a novel, but I'm afraid that this would merely amount to padding essentials. I think the trouble is that the last act is too much for any company that isn't composed exclusively of great tragedians! From what I heard I don't think I have any serious cause for complaint against the actors.

However, I've written one successful play—*The Grand Cham's Diamond.* I get an application from amateurs about it nearly every day. Dean was to have done it before another play but these damned managers never do what they say they will. Another book! Bravo! And many thanks.

Your proposal to come for a week-end is received with acclamation. Rachel says, "Make him come." But I think it would be best to defer it a little. I intend to get into better form soon. We have family assemblages in my bedroom but we'd like to improve on that.

Ever yours,
A. N. M.

P.S. (Parting Shot.) I don't think those London fellows know what a family is.

7. The *second* letter which I received from Jock before meeting him face to face. The first was a short note handed to my servant, Freddie Webster, to be passed on to me in bed. Here is the second letter:

21st Sept., 1926

This book I handed to your man three weeks ago, with the entreaty that he might ask you to peruse it. Two days later, he returned it to me describing his master as "up to the neck in work," and saying that I should return in three weeks. As I am very anxious to be up even to the waist in similar employment, I beg to return the book for your consideration. Can you not kindly recommend me, in writing, to some one ? Or will you not kindly scribble some advice or some remarks opposite some of these notices ? I have about sufficient wherewithal for another three weeks' existence in London. The past three I spent on tramp in Hardy's Wessex—intensely enjoying my varied experiences. And I have returned to London—lacking all influence but my own—with no other ambition than to conjugate in practice and in the first person singular the two verbs " to write " and " to starve." Would you tell me, meanwhile and immediately, where Grub Street is ? I want to find lodging there and I am all " moithered " in this vast city.

Expectantly and youthfully yours,
Alan Dent

8. Hundreds of iron-throated bills with a whisper of receipts.

9. Statements of " J. A.'s Financial Position " dated 1921, 1927, and 1932, all in Pip's best manner and with plenty of that hero's Margin. I note that as income increased so too did indebtedness. Likewise Margin. Pure Dickens !

1938

New Year's Day. My relations with my bank continue to be friendly.

Jan. 5 Wednesday. The English instinctively admire any man who has no talent and is modest about it.

Jan. 24 Monday. Tony Baerlein is back from Spain. I gather that the war was not such good fun as he expected. Most of the friends he made there have been executed since, and he has sold less than 5 per cent. of his films. The two sides are now so close to one another politically that there's nothing left for them to fight about. This means that the end of the war is further off than ever.

Jan. 25 Tuesday. Pavia was in great form to-day : " Every good deed brings its own punishment."

Jan. 26 Wednesday. I hear from a source which ought to be reliable that the Government is nervous about war in April. In which case publication of *Ego* 3 will have to be deferred till it is all over. It appears that the Navy cannot guarantee to defend Hong Kong and the Suez Canal and look after the North Sea. Any two, they say, but not three. As against an alliance between Japan, Italy, and Germany, that age-old cocotte France will not say what she will do, we do not know what use Russia would be, and America is indifferent. All the staff at the Foreign Office had their gas-masks tried on last week, and spent some time in a gas-filled chamber. Our Air Force is said to be pretty good, though reprisals seem to me to be mere baby-talk. If Germany is as ruthless as I believe, she will sacrifice Berlin for London in the way the chess-player with the stronger position will force an exchange of queens. I have not the slightest interest in any of the foregoing, except, of course, in respect of the deferred publication.

Feb. 10   Sorting out my papers before the removal to
Thursday.   Fairfax Road, which is now complete, I came
                across this letter :

Savage Club
1 *Carlton House Terrace, S.W.*1
9th April, 1936

DEAR MR AGATE,
    Enclosed is a copy of the letter which George Bernard
Shaw sent to George Alexander in answer to the invitation
which had been sent to G. B. S. as a representative dramatic
author to attend Irving's funeral in Westminster Abbey.
C. Aubrey Smith would, if necessary, confirm its authenticity
as he was present when I opened it. I have often quoted it,
but it has never been published.
    I, personally, destroyed the original in Adelphi Terrace
soon after the funeral, when Lionel Belmore and I—in our
youth—were looking for G. B. S. to " tan " him.

Yours faithfully,
[Sd.] RALPH KIMPTON

And here is G. B. S.'s letter :

Adelphi Terrace
November 1905

MY DEAR ALEXANDER,
    I return the ticket for the Irving funeral. Literature,
alas, has no place at his death as it had no place in his life.
Irving would turn in his coffin if I came, just as Shakespear
will turn in his coffin when Irving comes.

Yours very truly,
[Sd.] GEORGE BERNARD SHAW

    This being too good to be lost, I wrote to G. B. S. asking
his permission to publish, with the result that this morning
Mrs Shaw rang me up and asked me to lunch. I went, primed
with silence. Which was a good job, since from the moment
I entered Whitehall Court to the moment of leaving it G. B. S.
talked wittily, weightily, garrulously, informatively, charmingly.
He has an odd way of not looking at anybody while he talks,
sitting upright in a chair which is frail, spindly, and altogether
beautiful like himself. I have no notion what we ate and drank.

At the back of my mind was a letter I received this morning from Doris Thorne, Henry Arthur Jones's daughter, saying she wants to tell me " G. B. S.'s story of how it was entirely due to him that Irving was buried in Westminster Abbey ! " Obviously, to hear from G. B. S.'s own lips how he arranged for the Abbey funeral and then declined to go to it must be a piece of Shavianism which any collector would want to bag. Going down to Whitehall, I had pondered what conversational fly to use. Needlessly. The old man landed himself before I had put the rod together; it was like picnicking on some delicious bank and leaving the fish to do the rest. What G. B. S. said went something like this, and if I paragraph it, it is only to mark the sense and not because there was ever anything like a pause :

" It's time somebody wrote an article to let the British public into the secret of that old humbug Irving. In his lifetime he was looked up to not only as an actor, but as a great figure of literature and what not, the fact being that he was entirely illiterate and didn't know Shakespeare's best lines from his worst. As a producer he was deplorable, and as a manager he was never any use to me. His principal merit was in making the public believe that a man who had none of the essential qualifications for an actor was a great actor. The reason that Irving when he first appeared in Dublin was hissed for three weeks was that Barry Sullivan had taught Dublin what to look for in an actor, and Irving was nothing like it. He had no voice, and, when you looked closely at him, no face. He set to work to make himself both, and there was never a moment when he wasn't studying how to impress himself on the public. He set about this as relentlessly as any Hitler or Mussolini.

" It was the fashion at that time for actor-managers to bribe critics, and Irving tried it on me by proposing to buy *The Man of Destiny*. As the best part was written to suit Ellen Terry I consented, only stipulating for a date, as it was a youthful work and I didn't want it producing in forty years' time as my latest. Irving hum'd and ha'd, and said there could always be a paragraph in the Press. Dropping his voice, he said mysteriously,

'There's a man who does that sort of thing.' I said, 'Yes, I know him.' But he would make no promises, and presently I got a letter from Bram Stoker saying that while no date could be arranged I could always draw on account of royalties at any time I wanted. Shortly after this I went to see Irving's Richard III, and it seemed to me that something was wrong. At one point the house was electrified to hear Richard roar at Lady Anne, 'Get up-stage, woman!' In my article I said that Irving didn't seem to be answering his helm. A week later I met Bram Stoker, who asked why I had written so violently : 'Surely you knew the old man was drunk.' And do you know, my dear Mr Agate, it had not occurred to me. It is only fair to say that later on Harry Irving said he was glad I had written that article as it might do the old man some good and teach him to keep sober. Anyhow next day *The Man of Destiny* was returned to me with a note to say there was no further question of production. Most of the letters Irving sent out were written by his retinue. But I remember one in his own handwriting. The first sentence contained one of those simple grammatical errors which Queen Victoria used to make. The last sentence was 'For God's sake leave me alone.'

"The day after Irving died I got a letter from Lady Irving asking me to go and see her. She was an Irishwoman, and "— with a twinkle—" the Irish are very good at living on hate. She said that General Booth and Dr Clifford were trying to arrange for an Abbey funeral, and that she was determined that her disgusting beast of a husband should not have any such honour thrust upon him. It appears that Irving had made a will leaving his property in three equal parts to his two sons and Mrs Aria, that he had not left her even his second-best bedstead, and that she intended to have her revenge. Would I help her to stop the Abbey funeral? I was terrified. I wanted an Abbey funeral, not for Irving's sake, but for the profession's, and I knew that she had only to send a postcard to Booth or Clifford to have the whole thing dropped and Irving cast into obloquy worse than Parnell's or Dilke's. So I went home and wrote her a long letter full of sympathy, at the end of which

I said I felt bound to advise her as her lawyer would. I told her that when Irving caught a cold in Manchester and wanted to go to the seaside, the hat had to be sent round, that this sort of thing was always happening in the profession, and might at any time happen to Harry and Laurence. I went on : ' If this should happen, you, as the widow of a great actor buried in Westminster Abbey, have only to lift your little finger and you will get a civil pension. But if you are the widow of a worthless scoundrel you will get nothing.' That did the trick. Lady Irving withdrew her opposition and shortly after got her pension. I see no reason why the facts should not now be made known, though I would rather it was in a book than a newspaper article. You can also use my letter, which I had quite forgotten, but which I think is rather a good letter."

The talk throughout the meal was all about Irving, whose Charles I, G. B. S. said, was a wonderful mosaic. He said the moment when Charles went down on one knee and begged the soldier not to desert was one of the most moving things in the theatre. He said I had done the right thing about Irving in my broadcast talk. This encouraged me to ask whether, on the whole, he didn't think that Irving, who had begun as an illiterate humbug, had ended up as a magnificent actor. " I suppose you might say so," said G. B. S., " but he wasn't magnificent in the way Macready was." I asked how magnificent that had been. G. B. S. said, " I never saw Macready. But my father did, in *Coriolanus*, and when I asked him what he was like he said, ' Like a mad bull.' "

Feb. 16 *Wednesday.*	P.C. from Brother Edward saying his ladnlady has just told him a long story about meeting Mrs Patrick Campbell in a *hydrant* at Scarborough.

March 3 *Thursday.*	Took Mrs Shaw a basket of spring flowers, prim as one of Mrs Kendal's bonnets. We talked a little about *The Three Sisters*, which they had just

seen, and I recommended F. L. Lucas's *Land's End*. G. B. S. said, " But he's an old man ! " I said, " Oldish men have written goodish plays." And except for a short, musical bark answer came there none. We were standing in the middle of the room, Shaw with his back to the window and intercepting a shaft of brilliant March sunshine. He has become so insubstantial that even in ordinary light he looks like a figure in stained-glass. As he stood against the window I saw the outline of head and chin. William Archer once said mischievously that if you could see Shaw's face without the beard it would be hatchet-shaped and mean. Archer was wrong. To-day I clearly saw the chin, and it juts nobly. The point about the shaft of sun is that it stressed the unreality of one who is rapidly turning into a saint. Which I expect will make it very uncomfortable for some other saints. The sun streaming through the white hair made a halo of it, and I thought of Coleridge's " a man all light."

March 6   Lunched with Hamish Hamilton. Duck, cheese
Sunday.   soufflé, Perrier-Jouet 1928. As a protest against the performance of the Schumann Violin Concerto, which we regard as indefensible, we listen instead to a very good record of Mozart's Quintet in G minor. Then late to the Albert Hall to hear Menuhin play the Mendelssohn and Brahms Concertos. I doubt whether he is physically big enough for the latter, which he plays insinuatingly, whereas Kreisler in it is commanding. The Mendelssohn is of an agonising sweetness. I suppose in the Hallé Concert days I heard Norman Neruda play this a dozen times and Sarasate nearly as often. But never has it sounded so melting as to-day. Perhaps it isn't only the music or the playing. I keep thinking of the summer we spent as children at Appletreewick, and how, as I lay reading in the croft, the sound of Edward practising the first movement used to come through the open window. He was eleven, and next year, again at Appletreewick, played the whole Concerto very well. Later, at Giggleswick, I remember standing by the beck purling in the street beneath the windows of the music rooms and listening to little Lenny Watkins, the music-master, practising this same Concerto, which he played at the school concert.

He was a charming little man, an innocent who, having to go from Scarborough to Blackpool, solved the problem by going *via* London.

Altogether a day of reminiscences. Attended the annual dinner of the Gallery First Nighters, and talked to an exquisite old lady with white hair. It was Mabel Love.

March 22 The last six days are a jumble. These are the things
Tuesday. I remember. Going to a *Sunday Times* dinner at which I hold forth on the political situation, *nolens volens*, and because Lord Winterton overhears something I say casually to Sidebotham; am not too much abashed by my audience, which includes Sir George Clerk, formerly our Ambassador to France, Ernest Newman, Herbert Morgan, Beverley Baxter, Dick Shanks, Denison Ross, E. V. Lucas, and Lord Hewart. Wondering whether the English language has a clumsier sentence than one of St John Ervine's in Sunday's *Observer* : " The flight from the cinema justifies the hope that the fear that imbecility is increasing is unfounded." Attending with 700 other people the jubilee luncheon to Julia Neilson, listening to Sir John Simon talk a lot about his profession and a little about hers, and hearing Julia reply in a carefully prepared speech which she over-acts. Sitting through *The King of Nowhere*, yet another exasperating play by Bridie ; Pope's " Means not, but blunders round about a meaning," might have been written about this. Also Noel Coward's *Opérette*, which is *Bitter Sweet* all over again, and very much watered down.

And last, getting ideas for a volume of short stories to be entitled *Contes Scabreux*. The source of my inspiration is some-body's remark about meeting Villiers de l'Isle-Adam, and being shocked by the terrible irony and " coquetterie narquoise " of the old man's extraordinary tales.

A Cabinet Minister, visiting Paris, is accosted outside the Café de la Paix, and persuaded to buy a packet of improper postcards. Falling in love with the enterprising subject of one of them, he exhausts Paris and then ransacks Berlin, Brussels, Rome, Naples, Budapest, Cairo, etc., etc. The search—for he resigns his portfolio—lasts fourteen years, until he finally runs his ideal to earth at Lisbon, in a brothel of which she is the blowsy, raddled proprietress. He discovers that the photograph was already twenty years old when it came into his possession. This story is called *Feelthy Peecture*.

The second story is about the usual well-dressed man of fifty who pleads guilty to one of those curious happenings which park bye-laws describe as misdemeanours. He asks the magistrate to take into account 3744 similar eccentricities! Title : *In the Gloaming*.

The third is about a farm-hand who falls in love with an acrobat at a travelling circus. Next year the farm-hand again goes to the circus. But acrobats, alas, are come-and-go birds, and this one has flown. The farm-hand commits suicide, and everybody's sex is left nicely undetermined in a mush of Housman and Gide. To be called *An Essex Tragedy*.

March 25   I must be getting old. A year or so ago I should
Friday.   to-day have started to break lances with Jack De
           Leon and the Director of the Tate Gallery. With
Jack because he threatens to broadcast something about his new production at the Savoy between the acts of plays at other theatres. On the lines of the trailer in the cinema. It's no good Jack pleading that he proposes to do this only when the plays so be-sandwiched are farces. Other managers will be less conscientious, and presently we shall be having musical-comedy excerpts between the acts of *The Three Sisters*. It is the thin end of a monstrous wedge, and the proper thing to do with thin ends is to nip them in the bud! The case of the Director of the Tate—it sounds like a Sherlock Holmes title!—is even more heinous. It appears that, under the new Customs regulations, works by Brancusi and several other distinguished sculptors have been refused admission to this country as works of art because the Director does not like them : " When I am told that an ostrich egg in marble represents the birth of the world something must be wrong." The reason I am not taking up arms is that my sea of troubles is already big enough. At the

moment I am in the thick of three rows : (1) With *Truth*, which has a weekly attack on me because I dislike *French without Tears* and hold its success to be largely responsible for the inane comedies now flooding the English stage. (2) With Macmillans, the publishers, for advertising the bad things I said about Osbert Sitwell's *Those were the Days*, suppressing the good, and calling the whole " James Agate's Opinion." (3) I've forgotten what this is, but I know it's on.

March 26   Here are Four, Five, and Six in my *Contes Scabreux*.
Saturday.   In Number Four a purse-proud father of two
                sons adores the elder, who is a successful crook and
swindler, and hates the younger, who is an unsuccessful painter.
But the real reason for his hate is that he does not believe the
second child is his. On his death-bed he learns from his wife
that it is the first-born who is her lover's. I shall call this *Jean
et Pierre*. I hope I do not need to point out that Maupassant's
story is called *Pierre et Jean*.

The Statue is about a night-watchman at an art-gallery who
becomes enamoured of Antinous. As the statue persists in
remaining cold, he smashes it. Delivering sentence, the judge
says, " Had your victim been a female bust, the court, partially
understanding your infatuation, would have been satisfied with
sending you for six months to a mental institute at Harrogate.
But since you deliberately chose a male figure you will go to
penal servitude for forty years."

Six is about a black slave who commits suicide because of
the impossibility of becoming a white slave. A title for this
will doubtless occur to me later on.

March 29 *L'appétit vient en mangeant*. My *Contes* are coming
Tuesday. thick and fast.
                Seven is about a small boy who spends his summer
holidays delighting his soul with the combined aroma of sea-
breeze, cigar, and braided matches, for which purpose he follows
old gentlemen along the piers and promenades of Brighton,
Blackpool, Yarmouth, etc. The braided match goes out of

fashion, but the complex persists. Whereby, as the result of highly understandable misunderstandings, the poor fellow spends the greater part of his grown-up life in gaol.

Eight is called *The Sermon*. It is about the Dean of St Hugh's, who finds that he has a talent for pornography. But, alas, he cannot get the stories right, and the artist in him is in despair. One day Mrs Dean, coming across one in her husband's study, supplies the missing touch. Thereafter he leaves his stories about, and always they are put right, although not even in the most connubial moments is this other partnership alluded to. One Sunday the Dean ascends to his pulpit, and, opening his sermon-case, finds not his sermon, but his latest yarn.

Nine is about a gentlewoman and a pedomancer who

```
*     *     *     *     *     *     *     *
*     *     *     *     *     *     *     *
*     *     *     *     *     *     *     *
*     *     *     *     *     *     *     *
*     *     *     *     *     *     *     *
*     *     *     *     *     *     *     *
*     *     *     *     *     *     *     *
*     *     *     *     *     *     *     *
*     *     *     *     *     *     *     *
*     *     *     *     *     *     *     *
*     *     *     *     *     *     *     *
*     *     *     *     *     *     *     *
*     *     *     *     *     *     *     *
*     *     *     *     *     *     *     *
```

The Tenth *Conte, Chez Topinambour*, is my masterpiece to date. Topinambour is a restaurateur and, despite ferocious moustaches, essentially a kind and decent man and a good, though, alas, inadequate, husband! Wherefore Madame, a stout woman of exorbitant passions, must take a lover. She chooses the head waiter, a Greek of mean mind but noble muscle. Monsieur suspects, and the pair agree to put him out of the way.

Later, the wedding takes place. But it is *the wedding of Mademoiselle*, the pretty daughter whom the Greek has all along secretly preferred to her mother. The business continues. The Greek is now the smiling *patron*, his little wife bustles bird-like about the gay little room. The cash-desk is presided over by the Veuve Topinambour, a famished dragon whose gaze never leaves the young couple. One day the dragon asks the Greek whether he has noticed those sheep's eyes which *the new Cypriot* head waiter has begun to make at Madame. . . . I end the story here, since to pursue it to its conclusion would turn it into a full-length novel.

March 31   Annual Meeting of the Critics' Circle, of which
Thursday.   I am now President. This reduces my three
               unfulfilled ambitions to two. I still want to be
President of the Hackney Society, and to sit at the top table
at Mills's Olympia Circus.

April 20   Too many people are dying. First Edgar Jepson,
Wednesday.   who was a dear, though rather an acid dear, and
               now Filson Young. Filson could be what school-
boys call a " terror," and if he didn't like you, or wasn't liking
you at the moment, he would look down, or rather over, his
nose at you in a way a Roman Emperor would have envied.
But he had an absolutely first-class mind, was a perfect host,
and when the fit took him was capable of unexpected kindness.
A great editor and a beautiful writer. I have never forgotten his
saying in an article on the Escorial that the air was " strict with
frost." He would never, in any circumstances, tolerate anything
one jot or tittle below the first-rate, and his taste was impeccable.
He pretended, towards the end, to have outlived music, which,
he said categorically, had ceased to give him pleasure. But
Filson was always outliving things in the sense that he was a
pioneer, and the essence of pioneering is discarding the known
for the unknown. He took an immense interest in broadcasting
from its inception, and at the age of sixty taught himself to fly.
A man easy to misjudge : a man with something of the eagle
about him.

April 21   Two more *Contes*, which completes the dozen.
Thursday.   *One Good Turn* . . . is about the English mania
               for cleaning up London on the occasion of
Coronations and suchlike.   Comes news of another Paris Exhibition, and a daft Home Secretary invites his French colleague
to return the compliment.   The request is agreed to, the police
make a descent on a sumptuous apartment in the Avenue de la
Grande Armée, and everybody in it—proprietor, attendants,
clientèle—turns out to be English.

Story without Moral is about a brothel-keeper who after thirty
years acquires moral scruples and retires with 300,000 francs,
which he puts into a restaurant.   Dabbling in a business he
knows nothing about, he loses money and scruples, and has to
start his old job all over again.

Do these stories offend English taste ?   They have not been
invented to please it.   They are offered to the taste of another
people, in a day more amusing than this.   If ever I make a
book of them I shall preface it with the dedication :

À L'ESPRIT GOUAILLEUR

DE

VILLIERS DE L'ISLE-ADAM

ILLUSTRE ÉCRIVAIN

ET

VRAI CABOT

AUX GRANDS CHEVEUX ET AUX YEUX ÉTRANGES

À LUI QUI CONNAISSAIT

LA VIE MYSTÉRIEUSE

ET

L'INDIGENCE NAVRANTE

May 10   It is now more than twenty years since I first and
Tuesday.   last heard *Elektra*, and I remember thinking that
               if I were now to die no place would please me more
than the opera-house among the choice and master noises of
the age.   I thought so again last night.   How Charles, Ivor,
and the quietest bunch would hate this orgy of intensive theatre !
How they would despise Rose Pauly, who at the end of the
opera, instead of moping in a corner Bergner-wise, pranced

about the stage with her knee exactly where the horse Spotlight puts his when he is pulling out his best. At the culminating point she added her arms, and Jock said, " Rachel," and I said, " Siddons." There wasn't a cough throughout the two hours' length of the opera, coughing—as theatre managers ought to know, but don't—coming from the fact that the audience can't hear. There was no suggestion that you couldn't hear *Elektra*. As we came out I heard somebody say, " If that hasn't split the atom nothing will ! "

June 4   With great generosity and on the principle that
Saturday.   every crown should possess at least one diamond,
              Jock makes me a present for *Ego* 3 of this superb
letter from Edward. I know hundreds of people who have more talent than my brother, but nobody through whose mind genius whistles more nakedly. Carpers will say, " Genius for what ? " And I answer, " In his case, perhaps nothing. And I don't think it matters." Here's the letter :

> 12 *Lynette Avenue*
> *Clapham Common, S.W.*4
> *June 3rd*, 1938

MY DEAR JOCK,
   Carlyle tells us that parts of the Koran were written on shoulder-blades of mutton ; so I am not going to apologise for my writing-paper. My landlady thanks Mr Agate for his cheque, and, risking the rebuke that she should mind her own business, wonders what becomes of his old clothes ; as her dustman would be ashamed to go about like Mr Edward. And I believe it. I have one shirt ; it is on my back, and has been for three weeks. I daren't remove it or it would fall to pieces in the process. When finally it shuffles off me I shall go to bed and stop there till the undertaker brings me another. It can't be so very long now—ten or fifteen years in the nature of things—which will be gone in a flash. *Sur ces entrefaites* I will make one final grand effort. Some years ago James said to me, " If I were in your position I would never be off publishers' doorsteps. I should march into their offices, tell 'em what I can do, say I'm starving, and add, ' What about it ? ' " So on Monday I shall walk down to the West End, or any

other end infested by these people, and start the quest. I
shall avoid Gollancz, Hamilton, Barker, Cape, Chapman
and Hall, Heinemann, Constable, Howe, and other publishers who I know have had dealings with James. I shall
not say I am starving, for that would not be true ; and, if
asked, I shall admit being gratefully in receipt of a monthly
pittance. I shall begin with the Porcupine Press, as being
most suitable to my state of mind. If I am at a loss for words
I shall let my shirt speak for me. Pray God it doesn't rain !

I have just finished one-quarter of the stupendous Gibbon.
At which point I shall make what Italian musicians call " una
lunga pausa," before proceeding with the other three-quarters.
Ultimately, I propose to pass some strictures on the work
from the point of view of style—" proper words in proper
places," as (I think) Dryden called it. You will remember
Landor's *Imaginary Conversations*, in which he and Southey
criticise *Paradise Lost* much to the disgust of De Quincey. I
propose to take a similar line.

Some day, when you have made your money and retired,
I have a book for you to write : *The History of Comic Literature
since* 1800. The standard work on the subject, quoted by
every one, is *Geschichte der Komischen Literatur*, by C. F. Floegel,
but he died round about 1790, and the theme has never been
pursued further. I have read here and there in his book in
the Museum. It is an old torn and tattered copy bound with
string. I like to think it is the copy Carlyle and Hallam handled.

I have been reading Thiers's monument of patience, *Histoire
du Consulat et de l'Empire*, in English, or I should say, one
volume of it. It is the worst translation I ever saw. " *Always
knowing how to occupy himself, and to occupy others, he captivated
to the highest pitch, and dissipated around him those irksome sensa-
tions, or prevented their having birth, to which he himself was utterly
foreign.*" " *He imagined that it would be the full measure of success
and goodness, to terminate the matter in this way.*" Translate back
again " word to word," and you get excellent French. O tush !
And so it goes on through ten thick volumes—an absolute
waste of time and money. Publisher, Chatto and Windus, 1875.
And reprinted 1893 ! If Florio or Smollett, Urquhart or
Melmoth, ever look at it in the reference library of heaven,
they will stare ! Nonobstanting, the book is most interesting.

A short time ago I picked up, for a few pence, two well-
bound and mossy volumes of Bishop Burnet's *History of*

the Reformation of the Church of England. Unreadable? Oh, no! Listen! "I liked her before not well, but now I like her much worse. She has ill smells about her. I have felt her belly and her breasts, and, as I can judge, she should be no maid" (Henry VIII to the Lord Cromwell, the morning after the marriage with Anne of Cleves).

From the defence of Catherine Howard at her trial: "As for carnal knowledge, I confess that divers times he [Dereham] hath lain with me, sometimes in his doublet and hose, and two or three times naked: but not so naked that he had nothing upon him; for he had always at the least his doublet, and as I do think, his hose also; but I mean naked, when his hose were put down." Delicious equivocation of woman! If Mr Bax had incorporated *that* into his *Rose without a Thorn,* his play would have been still more sprightly.

During the years 1936, 1937, and 1938 there have fallen the anniversaries of the birth or death of Erasmus, Ben Jonson, James Mill, Pushkin, Boileau, Frobisher, Gibbon, Lady Jane Gray, J. R. Green, Pergolesi, Swinburne, Malebranche, Cuvier, Talleyrand, Gambetta, and Herschel. I do not remember the B.B.C. to have risen to the occasion once. And perhaps they are right. The Englishman does not want to hear a ten minutes' talk on Jonson or Gibbon. He prefers to accord a two minutes' silence to a football trainer who died recently in the North.

     .   .   .   .

Neander, in his *Life of Christ,* supposes that Pilate asked the question "What is truth?" in a depreciatory sense and with a shrug of the shoulders; for, if it had been meant as a direct question, we may be sure that Christ would have improved the occasion, whereas He answered not at all.

Hallam is daring enough to point out that the much-belauded English Bible, in its present form, may or may not be the perfection of our English language; but it is certainly not the language of the reign of James I. "It is not the English of Raleigh or Bacon. Further, it abounds with obsolete phraseology and with single words long since abandoned or retained only in provincial use." And I, myself, have found "they have hedged me about, that I cannot get out." How this bit of jingle was passed by 47 bishops beats me!

Yours ever,

EDWARD

June 5   With a great deal of dovetailing and contrivance,
Sunday.   which means bribing Jock to do some of my work,
            I managed to get the last half of the week clear for
the National Show, held this year at Bournemouth. Started
off with Julian Phillipson about tea-time on Wednesday. (His
father is well-to-do, and the idea is to get him interested in
Hackneys.) Just the other side of the New Forest, in which
the trees had been motionless, we ran into a gale worse than
one of Leo Pavia's tempers. The Royal Counties Show, of
which the Hackney Show is now a part, is most unlucky in
respect of weather. At Weymouth in 1935 the show was flooded
out, the horses in their boxes being over the fetlocks in water.
When we got to the showground on Wednesday the roofs of
the tents were sailing about the sky and great timbers cracking
like match-sticks. Fortunately the stabling turned out to be
solid, and to make assurance doubly sure the stud grooms
barricaded front and rear with their motor horse-boxes. As
the evening wore on the storm increased. Albert told me next
day that nobody in the yard slept a wink.

Once more Ego must measure himself against his old enemy
Nanette. His battles with this grand mare began two years
ago, and she must have beaten him on some dozen occasions,
though on four of them the decision was, to say the least of it,
doubtful. Last year I thought we had the horse a little too fat,
and Albert spent the winter fining him down to make him look
as he did on his first appearance at Olympia—a piece of Greek
sculpture. On Friday the omens were favourable. None of the
judges was on my Black List—every Hackney exhibitor knows
what that means—and I knew we should not come up against
one of those Hogarthian fellows, nine-tenths suavity and the
rest insolence, with squiny eyes—Lear's word—set in a face of
deceit bland and unwinking as an eight-day clock. Lean over the
rails and you can hear the tick of their nasty thoughts.

On Friday the tussle did not last long. Ego came in looking
superb. His lack of inches—for he is barely 14.1—means that
he can never have the majesty of Viking or Spotlight. But
the general consensus of opinion is that he has more elegance

and more charm than any other animal in the show-ring. Nanette
followed him in, and for the first time I thought that she showed
signs of becoming an old lady. She is thirteen, having done
as many years of hard showing as Ego, who is seven, has years
in all. This is the place to pay a tribute to this great mare,
perhaps the greatest at her height the breed has ever known.
Her liberty and range have always been extraordinary, and the
fights between her and Ego have always resolved themselves into
the age-long dispute between dash and force of action in one
animal and purity of action combined with poise and balance
in the other. On Friday there was an air of the departing
champion meeting the new, and in the show-ring as in the boxing
it is always something of a tragedy when a champion's colours
are lowered. This does not mean that I think Nanette is finished ;
Ego will doubtless find that there are plenty of kicks left in the
old mare, whose courage is still boundless. When it has been
touch-and-go between them, to see Nanette come up the grandstand with George Lancaster getting every ounce out of her
has always given me the thrill which belongs to any hateful and
glorious spectacle. On Friday the judges sent them round the
ring twice and then once up and down. All was over, and Ego
had won.

Much depended on this victory, including the dedication to
Ego 3. An old Saturday Reviewer once laid it down that
whenever a work of art concerns itself with buried treasure,
that treasure must be found. If Ego hadn't found his treasure,
then, as a former Saturday Reviewer, I must have been con-
strained to cut him out of this diary, which would still have
been dedicated to him. But to you who read, that dedication
would have been invisible. I am conscious that you are probably
saying, " What a fuss to make about a horse ! " If the reader
who says a horse is only a horse happens to be a poet, I shall
reply that to a horseman a poet is only a poet. Looking up
what I wrote on this theme in another book, I find that I quoted :
" He who has done a single thing that others never forget, and
feel ennobled whenever they think of, need not regret his having
been, and may throw aside this fleshly coil, like any other worn-

out part, grateful and contented." Whatever eminence I might have risen to as a dramatic critic, it would have been all the same in a hundred years. Nay, in ten years, a month, on Monday morning—for dramatic criticism perishes before the ink is dry. But this can never be taken from me, that on a day in March I saw an unbroken pony shivering under a hedge, and that I had the eye to sense his quality and the wit to buy him. If ever I could conceive myself throwing aside this fleshly coil with anything approaching content, it would be because I had the ingenuity, in the high Roman sense, to bring to victory a little horse which, in his own lifetime, became legend.